G. E. Mingay was educated at the University of Nottingham, and taught economic and social history at the London School of Economics. He is at present Professor of Agrarian History at the University of Kent. He has been a visiting professor at a number of American, Canadian and Australasian universities. His many books include: *English Landed Society in the Eighteenth Century* (Routledge, 1963), *The Agricultural Revolution 1750–1880* (1966), with J. D. Chambers, *Britain and America: a study of economic change, 1850–1939* (Routledge, 1970), with Philip Bagwell, and *The Victorian Countryside*, which he edited (Routledge, 1981: 2 volumes).

The Making of Britain
1066–1939

General Editor: Andrew Wheatcroft

The Norman Heritage Trevor Rowley
The High Middle Ages Trevor Rowley
The Age of Exuberance Michael Reed
The Georgian Triumph Michael Reed
The Transformation of Britain Gordon Mingay

G. E. MINGAY

The Transformation of Britain 1830–1939

PALADIN
GRAFTON BOOKS
A Division of the Collins Publishing Group

LONDON GLASGOW
TORONTO SYDNEY AUCKLAND

Paladin
Grafton Books
A Division of the Collins Publishing Group
8 Grafton Street, London W1X 3LA

Published in Paladin Books 1987

First published in Great Britain by
Routledge & Kegan Paul 1986

ISBN 0–586–08405–3

Printed in Great Britain by
St Edmundsbury Press, Bury St Edmunds, Suffolk

Set in Palatino

Contents

Illustrations

Photographs

Figures

Acknowledgments

The author gratefully acknowledges permission to reprint the following plans and maps: Hutchinson Publications Group, Limited, for 'The growth of Middlesbrough', which appeared in E. Smailes, *The Geography of Towns* (1953); Methuen & Company for 'The growth of the railways', which appeared in Wilfred Smith, *The Economic Geography of Great Britain* (1949); the Joseph Rowntree Charitable Trust for 'Plans of working-class houses' and 'A comparison of the causes of poverty in York', which appeared in B. Seebohm Rowntree, *Poverty: A Study of Town Life* (1941); and Routledge & Kegan Paul, PLC, for 'Designs in country workers' cottages', from John Woodforde, *The Truth about Cottages* (1969) and 'Elevations and section of Walsingham workhouse' from Anne Digby, *Pauper Palaces* (1978).

General Editor's Preface

To the archaeologist, the notion of material culture, of a society exemplified by its artefacts, is commonplace. To historians it has traditionally had less appeal, although Professor Fernand Braudel's *Civilisation matérielle et capitalisme* marks a foray into unknown terrain. The intention of this series, which follows chronologically from another of more directly archaeological approach,* is to see the history of Britain from the Norman Conquest to the Second World War, partly in human terms – of changing cultural, social, political and economic patterns – but more specifically in terms of what that society produced, and what remains of it today.

Few themes run with consistency through the history of the British Isles, save the land itself. This series seeks to show the way in which man has shaped and occupied the country, and how society has been moulded by the opportunities and constraints imposed by the landscape. The broad theme is of man's interaction with his environment, which is carried through the series.

As editor, I have tried to allow each author to write his approach to the subject without undue interference. Ideally, such a study would have appeared as a large single volume, but we have sought to make the divisions less arbitrary by allowing authors to cover a broad body of material in more than one book. Thus the volumes dealing with the medieval period come from the same hand, as do those spanning the sixteenth to the nineteenth century.

**Britain before the Conquest*, 5 vols, Routledge & Kegan Paul, 1979–81.

In little over a century, between 1830 and 1939 both the landscape and society of Britain were transformed; a rural world became an urban (and suburban) world. The pace and scale of change accelerated: a surge in population was housed in cities and towns, while the countryside became steadily emptier. Industry and trade demanded communication and transport on an unparalleled scale; a network of railways and roads spread into almost every corner of the British Isles. Technology was applied not on a local and limited scale, as in earlier centuries, but in every facet of life. Motor cars, radio, television, new and better means of waging war, were all part of this technological take-over of what had been a predominantly traditional society.

The dominant image of this era of hectic change is the Great Exhibition of 1851, an event which encapsulated the progressive transformation of British society. Those who flocked to it came from distant regions of the British Isles (and from abroad) taking advantage of the availability of new and reliable communications at relatively cheap prices. At the exhibition they saw the fertile intrusion of science and technology into the most traditional areas of life. Mechanical reapers, seeding machines, improved cultivation had all been under development for decades. But at the Great Exhibition they were exposed not merely to the few enthusiasts, but to the wonder and amazement of the many. The visitors left clutching their souvenirs, and fired with a sense of the boundless limits of technological innovation. This was the spirit which infused most industrial and commercial enterprise during the century or so of Gordon Mingay's book.

In those years Britain passed through the whole cycle, of a rise to dominance of the international economy, past a plateau of sustained success, into a long slope downwards of relative decline. In those same years, Britain acquired a world-wide empire, and then (with the creation of self-governing dominions) began the process which eventually led to the dissolution of imperial power. All these many changes left their impact on the British landscape. Industries like the cotton industry of Lancashire were closely bound up with the growth and decay of empire. Shipbuilding grew with the to-and-fro of imperial trade, while iron and steel depended on a substantial export market for their profitability. The factories to supply the new mass market, and the new urban expansion to house the workforce, imposed a new shape and structure on British society and politics.

The transformation has two faces. Over the century, the human consequences of change were apparently benign. To those who lived through it, the benefits often seemed elusive, and the complacent assertion of 'Progress' was an insult. The gains were tangible, in housing, health care, lower mortality, and a small move towards pensions and state financial support in times of need. The losses were more intangible, and in themselves the product of the transformation and the break-up of traditional society.

Andrew Wheatcroft

Chapter One

The Urban Explosion

Already by the middle of the last century the typical Englishman had ceased to be a country-dweller. By 1911 nearly 4 out of every 5 of the population were residents of towns. Urban growth was the result of many causes. At first it was not simply that there were fewer jobs in the countryside, for down to the 1850s employment in farming was expanding; while many other country occupations, such as mining and quarrying, brickmaking and woodworking, rural crafts like the blacksmith's and the wheelwright's, and domestic trades like metalworking, nails, boots and gloves continued to expand for years to come. Nevertheless, in many country towns and villages the numbers born and reared there were simply growing too fast for all of them to find full-time work, and in winter, especially, there were idle hands who had to subsist on casual jobs, on what the wife and children could earn, on what could be borrowed from neighbours and relations and on what little help was offered by private charity and that final bleak resort, the Poor Law.

Sometime in the 1850s the numbers of jobs on the farms began to fall, slowly for men, more rapidly for women. The fall continued right down to the present, though from near the end of the nineteenth century there was a tendency for large numbers of part-time female workers to be recruited for the busy seasons. A gradual mechanization of farm operations, with farmers using horse-drawn cultivators, drills, hoes and reapers, and steam-powered threshers and barn machines, was probably only a minor factor in the change. More influential were the limited employment opportunities on the land, the lack of prospects, the heavy hand of some squires and farmers, the lowness of the wages and the scarcity and badness of rural housing. These were the circumstances which made young people think of deserting their native heaths. And the towns had a certain attractiveness to country people as they became more aware of the greater variety of urban jobs, the better wages, the chance even of finding a house or at least a couple of rooms. The news travelled by word of mouth, spread by itinerant tinkers and hawkers, by the members of harvesting gangs who toured large areas of the country, while direct encouragement might derive from a daughter come home on a visit from her housemaid's post in the town or from the letter of a friend or relation who had already crossed the water to America or Australia. Newspapers, increasingly read in the countryside from about mid-century, carried notices about the cheap land and well-paid work waiting for the emigrant, and there were even journals which specialized in bringing to their readers the experience and advice of people who had recently travelled to the new countries, and which answered the questions of those who wished to know, for example, whether land was freely available in New Zealand, the rival merits of Canada and the United States, and whether governesses were much in demand in Australia.

Many migrants who entertained thoughts of distant places were likely to be put off by the cost, the length and the hazards of the voyage; the move to an expanding town at home was much easier and quicker to achieve, and more easily reversible. Already by the 1840s the railways had brought the major towns to within a few hours' journey. The ready availability of work was undoubtedly a prime attraction, for few migrants had the funds to support a lengthy search for employment. Thus it was that the numbers moving to the growing towns increased greatly when urban industries were booming, and fell away when times were bad. A severe industrial slump even saw a backward flow of migrants returning to their native villages in search of work.

The attraction was by no means solely the chance of finding a job in one of the new expanding industries like cotton, steel or engineering, or in the developing chemical works or railway workshops. The countryman usually preferred one of the smaller-scale industries, building and contracting, brewing, gas works and water works. He had a liking, too, for jobs which afforded regularity and certainty of employment, and even a modest pension at the end, and which might carry with them a free house and the glamour of a uniform – jobs as soldiers, policemen, railway guards and porters, postmen and borough workers. These jobs were not well paid, indeed the wages were little above those on the farms, but they had the great merit of stability. The same could hardly be said of other town jobs or the large field of domestic service – in 1841 the sixth largest source of employment for men. But many a country lad who could handle horses could find a niche as a carter, brewer, drayman, or van or omnibus driver, and failing these there were many openings as a gentleman's coach-driver or groom, or for training as a gardener, footman or valet in a private family.

For women domestic service was overwhelmingly the major occupation, employing nearly three times as many as textiles, the next biggest source of female employment. Not a few country girls left home at twelve or thirteen to go into service, for there were plenty of mistresses willing to train young girls, and domestic service was marked by a high turnover of staff. As the century wore on there were also more jobs, equally low paid and with perhaps even longer hours, in shops, as well as in hotels, boarding houses, schools, laundries and hospitals. Certain trades carried on in small factories, workshops or the home also employed large numbers of women and girls: dressmaking and shirt-making, corsetry and millinery, pickle and jam manufacturing, biscuit- and soap-making, even the manufacture of nails and the smaller size of chains, as well as fur-pulling, box-making and the manufacture of matches.

While many of the newcomers in these various urban occupations were fresh from the country, in fact most of the growth of the town population came from the increase in the towns' own native born. Down to the middle 1880s the birth rate was at a high level, and then slowly declined. In the 1860s and 1870s it was running at between 34 and 36 per 1,000, meaning that each year 16 out of every 100 women of child-bearing age had a new baby. For the time being a high death rate, especially among infants, kept the increase in check since 15 or 16 babies out of every 100 never survived to reach the age of one. From the 1880s, however, the infantile death rate gradually subsided and the general death rate was also falling, to be accompanied by a fall in the birth rate, especially among the better-off. The overall effect of the trends in births and deaths was that the total population, rising rapidly at the beginning of our period, entered a period of slower growth in the later nineteenth century, and one which became very slow indeed in the years between World Wars I and II. In 1830 England and Wales had nearly 14m. people and by 1900 over 32m., so that more than 18m. were added to the total in the course of seventy years, an increase of almost 134 per cent. But from 1900 it took as long as thirty-two years to bring the 32m. of that date up to the 40m. mark, and in 1939 the population stood at 41,460,000. Had the rise continued at its nineteenth-century rate it would have been well over 56m.

In actual fact some 27.7m. were added to the population between 1830 and 1939. The great bulk of this increase consisted of town dwellers, and the majority of these were people born in the town itself or in the district immediately surrounding it. Except for the substantial bodies of Irish established in London and Liverpool, and Scots and Welsh, most townspeople were native to the town and its environs.

Most towns tended to grow, unless they were small country places whose source of livelihood had declined.

Some places that had risen to importance in the previous century had a period of stagnation or grew only slowly. The Norfolk port of King's Lynn, for instance, expanded up until the mid-nineteenth century when it reached 19,000, fell away in the 1860s and 1870s, and recovered to 20,000 only in 1901. Bath, the great spa of a former age, had 51,000 in 1831, was up to 54,000 at the 1851 census, but by 1901 had fallen back to 50,000 – only to grow again in the present century. The larger country towns having major markets and some growth of industry, and possessing also importance as centres of law courts and country administration, tended to grow more steadily: Norwich from 61,000 in 1831 to 112,000 in 1901; York from 26,000 to 78,000; Chester from 21,000 to 38,000. New and popular seaside resorts like Brighton saw much more rapid expansion, with its 41,000 in 1831 nearly trebled to 123,000 in 1901, while Blackpool, a mere village in 1831, had reached 47,000 at the end of the century. Both of these resorts continued to grow apace as the forces supporting them waxed stronger – cheap rail transport, wakes weeks, paid holidays and day trippers; by 1931 Brighton had grown to 147,000 and Blackpool 106,000.

But it was London and the great ports and industrial cities that grew to be the monstrous wens so detested by William Cobbett. London was already over 1.75m. in 1831 and had reached 4.5m. seventy years later; Birmingham rose from 144,000 to over half a million; Manchester from 182,000 to 544,000, and Liverpool from 202,000 to 685,000. Most spectacular was the growth of the brand new industrial towns that hardly existed at all in 1831. Middlesbrough, entirely a creation of railways and iron and steel, rose from next to nothing, a mere 154 in 1831, to a substantial 91,000 in 1901, increasing in size nearly six hundredfold in only seventy years. Cardiff, similarly, a petty town of only 6,000 in 1831, was turned into a huge 164,000 by the development of its docks and the industrialization of its hinterland. Barrow-in-Furness was a North Lancashire fishing village suddenly swollen by the building of a

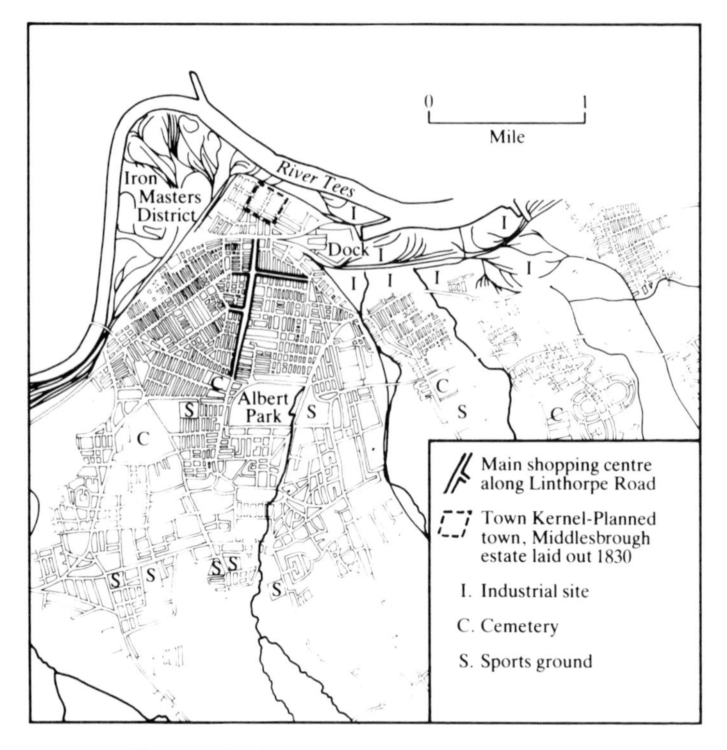

Figure 1 The growth of Middlesbrough

railway which brought in coal to smelt the local iron ore and led to the development of engineering and shipyards. In 1871 a half of its 6,170 adult males were employed in only four enterprises – very much a company town. In the seven years between 1868 and 1875 its number of houses doubled, and in 1891 its total population stood at 58,000.

The older industrial centres had already possessed some local industries before the nineteenth century, perhaps small workshop versions of what later developed into great works and factories. They might be dominated by one trade, or even by only one branch of a trade, as Lancashire cotton towns specialized, some in spinning, some in weaving. Like the new towns such as Barrow or Middlesbrough they were very liable to feel the effects of a depression in their trade and lacked the insulation that was provided by a more varied structure of employment (as in London), or by a more stable type of business such as brewing (Burton upon Trent), boots and shoes (Northampton), or railways (Swindon).

* * * * * *

Town growth meant streets, houses, factories, warehouses, railway stations, hotels, public houses, schools and town halls: all spelt work for the building industry. Throughout the Victorian era and after it was one of the largest employers, giving work to over 1m. men and boys in 1901, or over a tenth of the male labour force. And there were many thousands more employed in the making of the bricks, cement, glass and timber components. In the burgeoning industrial towns speed was the essence of the operation, the buying up of land, the throwing up of rows of cheap workmen's houses, the immediate creation of an urban wasteland without thought for anything beyond speed and cost. As Lady Bell, wife of a local ironmaster wrote in 1907, Middlesbrough saw day by day a fresh inrush of workmen and little houses springing hurriedly into existence. The town, she said, was designed for the working hours of the people, and not for their leisure: 'there is no building in the town more than seventy years old; most of them, indeed, are barely half that age. There is no picture-gallery: indeed, there is not a picture anywhere that the ordinary public can go to see'. The workmen's homes were bound to be crowded together and have no open spaces since they 'all struggle to be as near as possible to their work, to waste no time or money in transit'.

The houses themselves were minimal, consisting of four rooms:

> two rooms on the ground floor, one of them a kitchen and living-room, which in many of them opens straight from the

street, and in some has a tiny lobby with another door beside it, and another room behind, sometimes used as a bedroom, sometimes shut up as a parlour. A little steep dark staircase goes up from the kitchen to the next floor, where there are two more rooms. Sometimes there is a little scullery besides, sometimes a place hardly big enough to contain a bed, off the kitchen. Such abodes can house comfortably a couple and two or three children, but not the families of ten, twelve, and more, that are sometimes found in them.

The type of Middlesbrough workman's home described by Lady Bell was to be found with its minor variations all over the country. Commonly the two bedrooms were directly over and precisely the same size as the two ground floor rooms, though in the larger type of house there was a third smaller bedroom over the rear projection formed

1 and **2** The courts of working-class London in the early decades of the twentieth century: Providence Place, Spitalfields about 1909 and Crossett Place, Southwark in 1923. Shut in, mean, and overcrowded, little seems to have changed in the years between. Many remained until the slum clearances of the 1930s or Hitler's bombs finally disposed of them. (Greater London Council)

by the scullery. The sizes of the four main rooms might be as little as 11 × 6 ft., and go up to about 14 × 12 ft., although a parlour and front bedroom as big as the latter measurements would be offset by a more modest kitchen and second bedroom. Many of the houses were occupied by more than one family. Lodgers were frequently taken in, and often one room – probably the ground floor front – was let for 2*s*. or 3*s*. a week to a separate family. A six-roomed house might have two rooms let, perhaps the whole of the upper floor, and the 6*s*. or 7*s*. this brought in went a long way to meeting the rent of the whole house. When there was a basement and area with separate access from the street this was commonly let. The extent of a family's accommodation improved with the wage-earner's income and stability of employment. London policemen, for example, almost all occupied at least two rooms, while half the dock labourers had only a single room. From a survey carried out in London in 1887 Professor John Burnett also tells us that in the very poor district of St George's-in-the-East half of all the families existed in single rooms, while in the more affluent Battersea two-thirds of all families earned more than 25*s*. a week and rented three rooms or more.

The subletting of rooms, together with the large size of many working families, meant a good deal of over-crowding. Although national figures indicate that the building of new houses slightly more than kept pace with population growth, this does not mean that housing steadily got easier everywhere. There were wide variations in the pace of building, with marked peaks and troughs in activity, while building went on much more rapidly and more steadily in some places than in others. Moreover, the standard of housing that could be afforded depended greatly on the size and regularity of the family income. Before 1914, rent, which ranged from about a tenth to a third of income, was the second major item in a family budget after food, and its burden was relatively greater among the lowest paid than among those better-off working-class people with incomes substantially over a pound a week.

Overcrowding, as first defined in 1891, was taken as occurring when a room was occupied by more than two adults, with children under ten reckoned as a half, and infants under one year not reckoned at all. Even on this basis, which would allow a four-room house to hold four adults and as many as eight children and any number of babies, it was found at this date that over 11 per cent of the population – 3.5m. people – were living in officially overcrowded conditions. Twenty years later the figure was still nearly 8 per cent. As might be expected it was in the rapidly expanded industrial towns that the worst local figures were to be found – 35.5 per cent in Gateshead in 1901, 35.2 per cent in Finsbury in London, 30.5 per cent in Newcastle. By contrast Leicester had only 1.0 per cent, Bournemouth an almost negligible 0.6 per cent. Overcrowding was increased when old slum areas were cleared away for the building of new thoroughfares, docks, railway lines, depots, hotels and stations. In the fifty years after 1850 railway development in London displaced some 80,000 people, who perforce intensified the shortages of homes in neighbouring districts. And although legislation from 1866 allowed medical officers of health to deal with overcrowding and insanitary houses, there was the powerful restraint that this action might result in even worse conditions for the inhabitants: there were enough people sleeping in the streets without adding to them.

The consequences of urban improvements for overcrowding were felt in all the major cities where old slum quarters were pulled down for street widening, railway stations, omnibus and tram depots, schools and hotels, town halls and public libraries. London, however, with its dense rookeries concentrated in central areas, as round the Strand, Covent Garden and the Inns of Court, especially felt the impact of the new railway termini, new bridges, and new thoroughfares such as the Embankment and Kingsway. Certain extraneous factors might rapidly change the character of the district, as did the heavy Irish immigration after the Great Famine of 1845–6 and the influx in the later years of the century of poor Jews from the continent into eastern areas like Whitechapel and Aldgate. An investigation carried out in 1847 found that Irish newcomers had greatly added to the overcrowding in some poor areas. In one perhaps extreme case, Church Lane, the population had increased by 440, or two-thirds, since the census of 1841. One four-roomed house was occupied by as many as eight families, totalling fifty persons, all but seven of them Irish. The cellar of this house, in addition, had beds in it (for the use of which an adult paid *3d.* a night), and a further eleven people slept there.

The overcrowding in central districts and current developments in public transport encouraged the growth of suburbs. In provincial towns suburbs were typically only a few miles distant from the centre, and were fostered especially by the appearance of the electric trams in the 1880s and 1890s. Round London the new suburbs lay much further out, along the lines of railways fanning out in all directions. Cheap or even free season tickets encouraged middle-class families to buy new houses in Harrow, Finchley or Wimbledon, while working-class suburbs grew mainly in the north and east, especially after the introduction of cheap workmen's fares. After the mid-nineteenth century small and originally distant towns like Willesden and Leyton grew by some thousands of people a year, and indeed were amongst the most rapidly growing places in the whole country. By the beginning of this century the number of workmen commuting a considerable distance to work was already well on its way towards a million.

The move to the suburbs meant that more lower-income families occupied new homes and were better housed than ever before. For the existing residents of the places converted into instant suburbs, however, the change was less welcome. Their surroundings changed dramatically. In Camberwell, for example, estates were bought up, the mansions demolished, and the land laid out for hundreds of villas, squeezed in so tightly that back gardens barely existed. Some former mansions were converted into private schools, their grounds turned into a confusion of railway viaducts, alleys and courts, and the whole made obnoxious by the odours of newly-established cowsheds, piggeries and slaughterhouses, glue and linoleum factories, breweries, and haddock-smoking and tallow-melting yards. Public houses abounded – one for every 845 inhabitants in 1903 – and the old-established hostelries were stripped of the grounds that were formerly used for cricket, horse racing, quoits, and pigeon shooting. Churches, chapels and missions multiplied to 156, accompanied by numerous scholastic establishments and young ladies' seminaries. The streets were now thronged by milkmen and their cows, purveying milk direct from the udder into the customers' jugs, perambulating potmen from the public houses, sellers of watercress, lavender, flowers, and cat's meat, to say nothing of gypsies, knife-grinders, chair-menders, newspaper boys, tinkers and costermongers. Shops appeared in dozens: grocers, butchers, fishmongers, bakers, drapers, shoe firms and fancy bazaars. A branch of Lipton's Ltd opened in 1891, and next door two years later came Salmon & Gluckstein Ltd, tobacconists. There followed Dunn & Co., hatters, the Singer Sewing Machine Company, and in the opening years of the new century, Freeman, Hardy & Willis, sellers of shoes, the Maypole Dairy, Boots Cash Chemists, and the refreshment room of J. Lyons & Co.

* * * * * *

Such rapid expansion was often at the expense of amenity. Open spaces, private pleasure grounds and commons alike disappeared under bricks and mortar, and even Hampstead Heath was only just saved from the developer's grasp. The new cities lacked the means of breathing, and as they expanded so it became more of a discouraging trek for the inhabitants of the congested centre to reach the open countryside. Even there the common lands had shrunk and nearly all of those worth the cultivating were by now under the plough or fenced off for pasture, the woodlands carefully protected for the sake of the timber or the game. To ramble through country woods or fish in a country stream almost always meant a risk of being taken up for poaching or trespassing. The solution was to create parks in the towns themselves, but these were slow in coming. In 1845 the Health of Towns Commission could comment that 'the great towns of Liverpool, Manchester, Birmingham and Leeds, and very many others, have at present no public walks'. Among the earliest of the 'public walks' was Victoria Park in London's East End, and it was also in the 1850s that Manchester opened its Peel Park, a tribute to the lost statesman of free trade. Even when the parks appeared they were often shut on a Sunday, the only day the working classes could make much use of them. Experimental Sunday openings caused some surprise when it was found how little damage visitors from the poor parts of the town had done.

Recognition of working people's needs gradually extended to include public slipper-baths, wash houses, and public libraries. As late as the 1860s and 1870s even substantial eight-roomed houses intended for middle-class occupation were being built without bathrooms, on the assumption that a hip-bath, placed before the fire by a servant and filled by hand, would be used when required. Public libraries – a belated recognition of the spread not merely of literacy but of the reading habit, and also of the need for an educated electorate – owed much to charitable as well as municipal enterprise. The wealthy American steelmaker, Andrew Carnegie, was born at Dunfermline and presented the town with a free library; he and a retired London newspaper proprietor, J. Passmore Edwards, endowed many more in other towns. And legislation in the 1890s extended earlier powers for the public provision of libraries. For light entertainment there were the cheap theatres, music halls, workmen's clubs, and, above all, the pubs. The better-educated artisan belonged to his friendly society and perhaps a temperance club which offered newspapers, books, cards and dominoes. In the Midlands and North he was also quite likely to belong to a Mechanics' Institute, which had a more direct educational purpose, with evening classes for the young and a meeting hall featuring popular lectures by well-known speakers. There were further the seasonal attractions of fairs and circuses and, increasingly, cheap excursions by train to the seaside or inland beauty spots and places of historical interest. After the mid-nineteenth century wakes weeks were well established, and in Lancashire and Yorkshire especially, became the occasion for an annual holiday in Blackpool or Fleetwood. Race meetings and football matches drew large crowds, and racing tips became an established feature of the popular press. Many working men, particularly in the mining communities, had other absorbing pastimes, centring on the keeping of whippets and racing pigeons; elsewhere perhaps on an allotment and a few carpentry tools. The mean, monotonous streets which daily encompassed the womenfolk were enlivened by the constant intrusion of bread and milk roundsmen, coal merchants, costermongers and fishmongers crying their wares, and a wide variety of hawkers, itinerant knife-grinders and pot-menders, gypsies selling pegs and firewood – and Italian organ grinders. Italian firms set up shop in London to manufacture the organs and let them out to their compatriots at between *7s. 6d.* and *10s.* a week; about every six months they were brought in to be changed for others having the latest popular tunes. Some of the organ grinders prospered, lived frugally, and eventually saved enough to send money home or return there with a modest fortune.

With a high birth rate among the townspeople and a large inward migration of young folk, the rapidly-growing towns exhibited a marked deficiency in schools. A rash of private establishments supplemented the limited number of grant-supported voluntary schools, but even so there might be sufficient full-time places for only about a third of the children. In the Coventry of 1838 about two-thirds of children aged between two and fourteen attended some kind of school, though for many of them this meant only a few hours once a week at a Sunday school. To provide for the children of the town's working people there were at this time fifteen public day schools and seventy-eight private and dame schools, having together a total of 2,747 pupils; in addition, there were eighteen Sunday schools giving a minimal education to a further 1,346. Probably the least effective of these institutions was the dame school, which usually fulfilled little more than a child-minding role for the very young. Here an elderly lady charged a small fee for keeping a room full of children under her not very watchful eye, with perhaps incidental efforts to teach a little reading, writing, arithmetic and knitting. No requirements were laid down for private schools and there was no inspection. Anyone who was so minded could set aside a spare room and call it a school. The fees, at between *3d*. and *8d*. per child per week, according to age and subjects taught, were quite inadequate for attracting teachers of any ability. Hence those who taught in them, when they were not elderly ladies raising a little additional income without much trouble, were largely those who had failed at other occupations and had not the means of trying anything more lucrative. Sometimes, indeed, the teachers themselves were barely literate, and this applied also to the unpaid instructors in the Sunday schools.

Many of the children not in school, especially the older boys, were already out at work, but on any day large numbers of children could be found playing in the streets. The existence or lack of parental concern was a major factor in the length and quality of the schooling, and it is interesting that in Coventry in the early 1840s all the young watchmakers in the town could read and write, and had been at school until their early 'teens before taking up an apprenticeship. On the other hand, none of the children engaged in the poorly paid silk-winding trade could even sign their names, and only one of them could read, despite attendance at Sunday schools.

School provision improved slowly in due course as more public money went to support the voluntary schools, the training of teachers was improved, and legislation from 1870 onwards gradually raised the school-leaving age and eventually abolished the fees in publicly-supported institutions. Another area to benefit from public intervention and private desire for better standards was housing. By-laws were introduced before the end of the century to ensure such basic matters in new houses as sound foundations, external walls more than one brick thick, adequate drainage, and eventually a damp-course and a supply of water piped right into the house. Homes got a little larger, the typical four-room terrace house growing from a total of about 450 sq. ft. upwards to a minimum of about 570 sq. ft. Main-drainage sewerage systems were installed, and regular street sweeping, cleansing and lighting instituted. Towns became more sanitary if not less ugly. As street markets, omnibuses, trams, drays, wagons, carts, cabs and private carriages combined to swamp the main thoroughfares and block up junctions so the penalty of failing to plan the growth of the past was felt. The wider, straighter streets of the new part of the town poured in their traffic to a centre basically unchanged since medieval times. Often the largest space was still the ancient market place, from which the lines of the original streets and alleys ran crookedly. And though by-law housing was coming in, there was the legacy of neglected older structures surrounded by the substandard jerry-building of the Industrial Revolution. And so there was still a great public health problem, and still the occasional epidemic. Even in a substantial town like Lincoln, for example, water supplies were still dangerous in the 1890s, and in 1904–5 an outbreak of typhoid claimed over a hundred lives.

* * * * * *

Earlier, nearer the beginning of our period, matters had been much worse. Most large towns had extensive areas of insanitary slums where the essential basics for living a healthy existence – pure water, efficient disposal of sewage and of household waste and street refuse, removal of the more obvious encouragements to epidemic disease, and adequate space for life and leisure – simply did not exist. A reading of the public health records of the time conveys so overwhelming a scene of filth and infection as to make one wonder how working folk managed to survive at all, and why the town populations were not severely decimated by the sheer destructiveness of the environment. Here it is important to notice that not all towns were equally bad: much depended on the local circumstances, the rate of growth and availability of land for expansion, and the vigour and imagination of the town authorities. A progressive city like Birmingham, for instance, where there was a radical mayor like Joseph Chamberlain, fared much better than a reactionary one like Newcastle, where the vested interests of the night-soil contractors exercised a baneful influence on the authorities.

It was an uphill struggle, partly because so much needed to be done and the nature of the problems and the remedies were but imperfectly understood. The profession of sanitary engineer had to be created, and the reformer, Edwin Chadwick, was laughed at for his advocacy of glazed and egg-shaped earthenware drains. There was vast public apathy, which Chadwick, Shaftesbury and Dickens only dispelled, ironically, with the aid of the cholera epidemics; and there was influential opposition to interference with the rights of private property – even when that property consisted of insanitary slum dwellings, with water companies supplying polluted water.

But progress there was, first by bodies of improvement commissioners, then the local boards of health established under the shortlived Public Health Act of 1848, and later the new Medical Officers of Health and the more progressive municipalities. Together they provided paving, street cleaning, lighting and drains, and numbered the houses – but the more adequate improvements were made only in the better districts; some went as far as establishing fire engines, gas works and water works, electricity and trams. There was eventually the support of legislation, such as the 1851 Act governing common lodging houses, widely suspected of harbouring criminals and fostering disease. In 1883 there appeared the pamphlet by the Revd Andrew Mearns, *The Bitter Cry of Outcast*

London. Its revelations made their impact, and the very next year saw a high-powered Royal Commission on Housing, which included such eminent figures as the Prince of Wales, Cardinal Manning, Lord Salisbury, Goschen, the later Chancellor of the Exchequer, the housing reformers Cross and Torrens, the labour leaders Jesse Collings and Henry Broadhurst – under the chairmanship of a prominent political figure, Sir Charles Dilke. Public attention was complemented by private enterprise. Philanthropic societies and individuals, notably the English lady Octavia Hill, and the American millionaire merchant, George Foster Peabody, produced funds to erect blocks of sanitary tenements for the labouring poor – numbers of which are still lived in. Peabody gave half a million to housing the poor and the first of his Peabody Dwellings was opened at Spitalfields in 1864.

One difficulty was that money could be made out of sewage and refuse. Night-soil contractors cleared out privies and cesspools and carted the contents to their yards, where it was heaped up and allowed to decompose, a fruitful source of flies in summer and of unpleasant smells the year round. The resulting 'town muck' found a ready market among the farmers wherever it could be shipped to them cheaply by water. The Newcastle colliers on discharging their coal in London loaded up with the muck for the return voyage, and the Northumberland farmers set great store by it. Some contractors opened public lavatories by their yards to supplement the supply, and there was a firm which dried and packed the material in barrels and shipped it out to the colonies as 'horticultural manure'. It was discovered, too, that ashes, cinders and dust mixed well with clay for brickmaking, and after Napoleon's invasion of 1812 large quantities were sent to Russia for the rebuilding of Moscow. The trade was still of importance in mid-century when Mayhew described the way in which dustbins were empied into the carts, the men calling out 'Dust oy-eh!' to warn householders of their approach. In the yards gangs of women and old

THE LONDON DUSTMAN.
DUST HOI! DUST HOI!
[From a Daguerreotype by BEARD.]

3 An illustration from Mayhew's *London Labour and the London Poor* of 1851 (Museum of London). The collection of refuse was a thriving business, and one of Dickens's characters in *Our Mutual Friend* (1864) was Mr Boffin, the owner of several accumulated mounds of dust and who prided himself on being 'a pretty fair scholar in dust' if in nothing else.

men used iron sieves to separate the 'brieze' used in the brickmaking from the finer dust sold as manure. The rubbish heaps yielded other treasures: old bricks which could be sold for foundations and roadmaking; old tin kettles which went to form the fastenings for the corners of trunks; old shoes sold to London shoemakers for use as stuffing, but mainly for making the dye, Prussian blue; and the rags and bones that were disposed of in the marine-store shops.

As these trades eventually lost their markets, so the mounting problems of sewage and rubbish disposal confronted town authorities. Modern systems of treating sewage and dumping the residue out at sea, and of establishing rubbish tips on waste land outside the cities, had to be developed and introduced. But these were not the only problems of disposal. As towns grew in number urban cemeteries became inadequate for burying an increasing total of dead. As a result there were churchyards like those in St Bartholomew's in West London, described by a doctor in mid-century as 'impacted or stuffed, crammed with dead bodies', and lacking space for even 'a single body more'. Moreover, as the doctor went on to explain, adjoining the cemetery were the back rooms of houses which jutted out over a court where cesspools, ash-holes and privies overflowed; 'the persons living in this part of the metropolis are in the habit of emptying their chamber pots into the churchyard, and the smell is horrible'.

The shortage of burial grounds was eventually overcome, but a more enduring complaint was the lack of hygiene among the poor, a subject of particular interest since doctors believed that the source of disease lay in invisible miasmas supposed to originate from the bodies, clothes and bedding of infected persons and from wet or marshy land and rotting waste materials. 'It is well-known', said one physician, 'that the decomposition of animal and vegetable matter will produce typhus fever.' He went on: 'A great number of my patients reside on the

banks of old Fleet-ditch, that is a locality from which fever is never absent, and it is always of a malignant typhoid character; cholera showed itself there during its visit to London more particularly than in any other locality.'

Certainly the conditions of slum life were not conducive

4 and **5** Living conditions in the slums of London's East End. Damp disfigures the walls and a piece of old torn cloth serves as curtain; a mixture of resignation and resentment marks the faces of the women. (National Museum of Labour History)

to cleanliness. There was a lack of space, of water, of unpolluted air, even of privies – indeed, of everything that civilized life now takes for granted. In some working-class areas the water was not only impure, it was also deficient in quantity. Often it could be obtained only from a stand-pipe in the yard that was common to several houses, and as Rowntree noted in his survey of York at the end of the century, the grating below the tap might be choked with human ordure. Frugal water companies kept the supply turned off for long periods each day, and when it was turned on the women and children queued for it with their tubs and buckets. When people were doing their washing, wrote a medical officer of the Whitechapel Poor Law Union, 'the smell of the dirt mixed with the soap is the most offensive of all the smells I have to encounter. They merely pass dirty linen through very dirty water . . . The filth of their dwellings is excessive, so is their personal filth. When they attend my surgery I am always obliged to have the door open.' Water was not the only deficiency. A choked privy or a foul-smelling earth-closet might have to serve a half-dozen families. Cesspools overflowed for lack of regular emptying, their walls cracked and oozed out their contents to impregnate the walls of neighbouring cellars and contaminate the earth from which well water was drawn. Shelves and cupboards used for the storage of food, clothes and bedding reeked with damp and were overrun by mice and bugs.

The people themselves often made bad worse. They allowed refuse to accumulate in great heaps against the outside walls, so adding to the malodorous atmosphere and the dampness within. They littered the yards with broken bottles, old bones, dead dogs and cats, and rubbish of all kinds. They disliked fresh air, and windows were never opened, not even in a sick-room in the heat of summer. Fractured and blocked-up gutters poured water down the walls, broken windows were stuffed up with rags or boarded over to keep out wind and rain. As tenants they were careless and destructive – this was why Octavia Hill allowed no wooden fittings in her tenements which could be torn out and chopped up for firewood, nor exposed pipes which could be removed for the value of the lead. Common landings and staircases were rarely if ever cleaned: in one tenement building in York, Rowntree's investigator found accumulated dust between the banisters nine inches thick, and sixteen inches in one place. These were the people who rarely washed, whose feet were literally as black as their boots, who at the onset of each winter sewed up their children in their underclothes, not to be unsewn until next spring, who in a later period justified the old gibe about keeping coal in the bath.

Their ignorance, fecklessness and dirt were compounded by poverty, illness and drink – money that might have gone on more adequate food, a better home or new clothes went to the pub. Consider this from Mearns's *Bitter Cry of Outcast London*:

> Every room in these rotten and reeking tenements houses a family, often two. In one cellar a sanitary inspector reports finding a father, mother, three children, and four pigs! In another room a missionary found a man ill with small-pox, his wife just recovering from her eighth confinement, and the children running about half naked and covered with dirt. Here are seven people living in one underground kitchen, with a little dead child lying in the same room. Elsewhere a poor widow, her three children, and a child who had been dead thirteen days. Her husband, who was a cabman, had shortly before committed suicide.

In districts inhabited by costermongers or permeated by the surviving domestic occupations, homes were even more confined and cluttered by the tools, materials and odours of the trade:

> Here you are choked as you enter by the air laden with particles of the superfluous fur pulled from the skins of rabbits, rats, dogs and other animals in their preparation for the furrier. Here the smell of paste and of drying match-boxes mingling with the fragrance of stale fish or vegetables not sold in the previous day . . .

Indeed a good deal of the dirt, poor diet and neglect of children which characterized slum homes may be attributed as much to lack of time as to ignorance or fecklessness. Women who worked 13 to 15 hours a day – to earn some 12*s*. a week by making slippers, or a similar sum in sewing shirts, making cardboard boxes or the artificial flowers of silk or muslin that were used for decorating dresses – could have had little time or energy left for cooking, washing and the other household chores. Some home trades, especially the fur-pulling mentioned by Mearns, or the widely dispersed business of brush drawing – 'putting the tufts of bristles into the holes in the wooden back and drawing the tufts through with wire and fastening them at the back' – were dusty and unwholesome, and entirely unfitted for a home of any description. Fur-pulling, for which the worker got between 1*s*. and 2*s*. a 'turn' of sixty skins, involved pulling the unwanted long hairs from rabbit skins: 'these hairs float everywhere and fill the room, everything is grey with the hair . . . everything becomes covered with it, and the smell of the skins is most nauseating'.

Some of the descriptions by contemporaries, though couched in the most sober of language, defy the imagination. There were the courts in Manchester which the inhabitants had let off to 'porkers' for the keeping of their pigs; and Parliament Street in the same city where one solitary privy was all there was to meet the needs of 380 people. In Bury in 1842 there were '63 families where there were at least 5 persons to one bed; and there were some in which even 6 were pushed in one bed, lying at the top and bottom . . .'. In Bethnal Green Dr Southwood Smith reported habitations in Alfred and Beckwith Rows 'surrounded by a broad open drain, in filthy condition. Heaps of filth are accumulated in the spaces meant for gardens in front of the houses . . .'; in one of the rooms the 'window is not only kept permanently closed, but is carefully pasted all round, so that not the slightest breath of air can enter'. Nearby was North Street, where most of the houses were 'occupied by pig-dealers, and the filth produced by the pigs is seldom or never cleaned away'. And in Whitechapel nearly every labouring family had to live in only one room, with the consequence that when

6 Children in Manchester awaiting the arrival of the Duchess of Southampton, evidently a gala occasion. The year was 1900: some of the children are barefoot; all look dirty and dishevelled. (Manchester Polytechnic Archives of Family Photographs)

there was a death 'the corpse is therefore kept in that room where the inmates sleep and have their meals. Sometimes the corpse is stretched on the bed and bedclothes are taken off, and the wife and family lie on the floor. Sometimes a board is got on which the corpse is stretched . . . When children die they are frequently laid out on the table.'

* * * * * *

The slums, of course, did not comprise the whole of the working-class community. Above the slum-dwellers – nomadic, low-paid, irregularly employed, always living on the edge of bare subsistence – rose in infinite gradations the ranks of poor but better-off working people. The margin between the regularly employed skilled artisan and the hapless labourer or 'sweater' was not merely a two-fold or three-fold difference in earnings but a wholly different way of life. The artisan was himself relatively well educated and his children went regularly to school; he took part in a working man's club and benefited from the somewhat limited security offered by membership of a friendly society. He could enjoy his evening pint and his tobacco, read his newspaper, follow some sport and even indulge in a mild flutter on a horse without keeping his wife and family perennially short of food and clothing. He might well afford the 9*s*. which in the 1870s was the railway fare for a family of four to enjoy a day by the sea at Brighton. The diet of his family, by the end of the century, was considerably removed from the basic bread, cheese, potatoes and occasional bacon and liver, that was eaten by the really poor, and in Rowntree's York of 1898–9 extended to bacon for every day's breakfast and either beef, pork, mutton or sausages for every main meal.

His home, too, was in size and comfort miles away from the one-room tenements of the slums. True, it was only a simple five-room terrace house with scullery, in a wilderness of relatively new but drably uniform streets, its appearance hardly different from hundreds of its neighbours. But he paid a good rent – in York 6*s*. a week and 1*s*. 6*d*. rates – and the house was correspondingly 'respectable', moderately well built and in reasonable repair. Each house of this kind, reported Rowntree,

> has an entrance passage about 3 feet 6 inches wide, from which the stairs lead up. Out of it also open the sitting-room in front and the kitchen or living-room behind. From the latter a door leads into the scullery, which again has a pantry opening out of it. Outside the scullery is a small cemented yard, sometimes with a narrow border of earth, a sad apology for a garden.

This yard also contains the water-closet, with which most of these houses are provided, though some of them have midden privies [a combined closet and ashpit]. The sitting-room often contains a piano and an over-mantel in addition to the usual furniture, not to speak of ornamental mantelpieces of imitation marble and brightly-tiled hearths. It is chiefly used on Sundays, or as a receiving-room for visitors who are not on terms sufficiently intimate to be asked into the kitchen. Occasionally it is used by the husband when he has writing to do in connection with friendly or other societies, or by the children when practising music.

The real living room, as in the smaller houses, was the kitchen, kept warm and cheerful by a combination grate and oven. The floor was covered by linoleum, made more cosy by a home-made hearthrug, and there was a horse-hair sofa, an armchair, and china ornaments on the mantelpiece. The scullery had its sink and tap, and the convenience of a 'copper' for washing. Upstairs the two main bedrooms each boasted a small fireplace, the third small one usually not. There was seldom a bath.

Thus domestic comfort among the 12 per cent of the working class in York who could be described as better-off foremen and artisans: a very different world from the 'dirty and overcrowded' two or three rooms of the struggling poor who made up a quarter of the workers of the same city, paying their 2*s*. or 3*s*. rent (inclusive of rates); and even more remote from the true slums, 'often dark and damp and almost always dirty', with brick floors laid directly on the earth and a general state of dire neglect and fearful dilapidation: 'Deep holes in walls, where large pieces of plaster and bricks have fallen away. Frame-work of door partly torn away. Walls and ceiling extremely dirty . . . table and floor covered with crumbs, potato parings, scraps of meat on newspaper, dirty pots, etc.' Or another slum house of only two rooms, holding seven inmates:

Walls, ceiling, and furniture filthy. Dirty flock bedding in living-room placed on a box and two chairs. Smell of room from dirt and bad air unbearable, and windows and door closed. There is no through ventilation in this house. Children pale, starved-

7 An elderly couple in the parlour of their home at 22 Albury Street, Deptford, a photograph taken in 1911. The decorated mantelpiece, ornate coal scuttle, elaborately framed pictures, and display of ornaments and china indicate a home of adequate means, very considerably removed from the destitution and misery of the slums. (Greater London Council)

looking, and only half clothed. One boy with hip disease, another with sores over face.

Such was the legacy which the nineteenth century bequeathed to its urban dweller. The industrialization of Britain had made it possible for a population increased more than three-fold in the course of a century to subsist:

the majority at substantially improved living standards, a few in great wealth, a large minority in continuing and hopeless deprivation. It was this diverse inheritance which the twentieth century had to accommodate, modify, and reform as best it might – as much as the awareness of government and the depth of the national conscience would allow.

Chapter Two

The Industrial Age

England became an urbanized country; it became at the same time an industrial one. Though all kinds of towns were growing in the nineteenth century, it was the new factory towns and industrial conurbations, shipbuilding and commercial centres, that led the van. The cotton towns of Lancashire were the portent of things to come. In addition to Manchester – Cottonopolis itself – the lesser cotton centres sprang up round their mills at breakneck speed, Bolton expanding nearly ten-fold in the course of the century to reach 168,000, Oldham over twelve-fold to 137,000. Cotton was the first and archetypical factory industry, but the characteristic skyline of tall, belching chimneys was soon to be seen on the other side of the Pennines in the West Riding woollen district, and in iron and steel making centres like Middlesbrough, Sheffield, Dudley and Merthyr. Factory populations grew up round chemical plants at Widnes, glass manufacture at St Helens, soap at Bebington and beer at Burton, and of course in the engineering and metal-working complex of the Black Country and the five pottery towns of Stoke-on-Trent. By the end of the century the factory industries employed about one in every four men and women in the country.

The factory marked the triumph of large-scale production, of power-driven machines that turned out their products by the thousands or millions to meet the needs of the whole country, the whole world. When Victoria came to the throne the factory was yet in its infancy, still largely confined to the textile trades, still small in scale by comparison with what was to come. Even in cotton the standard size of mill of the 1830s employed no more than 150 or 200 workfolk, though there were some very large employers such as Horrocks, Miller & Co., who in 1816 employed as many as 700 spinners in four separate mills and some 6,000 handloom weavers as well. And in iron, the Staffordshire works of Samuel Walker and William Yates at Gospel Oak provided jobs for some 700 as early as 1824.

The factory grew up steadily so that what had been the giant plant of yesterday became the minnow in a pool dominated by new large works, the employers of thousands rather than hundreds. The factory went on to destroy one by one the great majority of the old hand trades. But the process was a slow one: even in 1851 the mechanized industries (even including the marginal one of coal) employed less than two millions, only about a third of those employed in the non-mechanized industries. Nonetheless, ancient industries which for centuries had formed the mainstay of an army of men and women plying their skills in their homes or small workshops, sooner or later succumbed to the superior economy of the powered machine – lace, hosiery and gloves, nails and chains, bricks and cement, paper and printing, cheap boots and shoes and ready-made clothing, furniture and carpets; the making of cheese, butter, bacon and jam, and the novel margarine and condensed milk. Even in 1849, there were as many as 12 steel-pen factories employing an average of 154 people each, while from the late 1890s the humble but ubiquitous trade of washerwoman was threatened by the rise of new steam laundries. The Census of 1871 listed 145 factories making boots and shoes, each employing an average of 125 workers. (Most of these factories, however, still employed numerous outworkers for some of the processes, though it is significant that even in the high-class London bespoke trade all but four of the masters were now getting their tops cut out and 'closed' (stitched together) by machinery.) In the cheap clothing trade there were at the same date 58 factories, employing an average of 136 workpeople apiece, though the sewing machines in use in them were still mainly driven by hand or treadle rather than by steam power.

The factories came in to take advantage of new machines which speeded up production and made possible a cheaper and more standardized product, suitable for the mass market. Both the boot and shoe and clothing factories used adaptations of the Singer sewing machine invented in 1851. (Ironically, the small hand- and treadle-operated versions of this machine went into the homes and helped sustain the livelihood of hand-workers, numbers of whom moved gradually from the cheaper clothing into the better-class end of the trade.) But the ultimate reason for the growth of the factory was the expansion of the market, both at home and overseas. At home there were more people to be fed, housed, clothed and generally supplied, and a larger and larger proportion of them came more effectively into the market as their real wages improved and consumer goods were cheapened by the application of new technology. Abroad, the opening up of distant countries for access to their supplies of foodstuffs and raw materials, together with the cheapening of sea journeys by steamships and of land transport by railways, provided new markets for exports of textiles, ships, railway equipment, steam engines, hardware and coal. The consequence was the rapid growth of the industrial workers of Britain, the factory workers, of course, featuring largely among them.

Thus employment in textiles rose from nearly 1.3m. in 1851 to over 1.5m. by 1911; clothing from 900,000 to over 1.25m.; engineering and metal working more spectacularly from over half a million to nearly 2m. . With the swelling demand for cheap books, newspapers and stationery, the employment in paper and printing increased five-fold to reach nearly 400,000; chemicals, oil and soap over four-fold to top 200,000.

The combination of new machinery and expanding markets enormously swelled employment, though as a partial offset there was of course the displacement of thousands of hands in the old domestic trades. The factory represented a new mode of production, often new in its location, and to a large extent new in its products. Its workforce, too, was set apart from the hand workers, requiring different skills, different habits of work, sometimes workers of a different sex. There were, it is true, some important links between the new industries and the old. In the early days of cotton, before weaving had followed spinning into the factory, the cotton masters themselves often employed a small army of men to weave on their handlooms the yarn spun in the factory. Factory-made lace was sent out to nearby homes where the women, often the lace-workers' wives, pored over it inch by inch to carefully mend the small holes and imperfections left by the machine. Again, the iron rods produced in a slitting mill provided the raw material of the hand workers who made from it their nails and chains. Subsequently, the leather for boots, shoes and gloves was cut out in the factory and then given out to home workers for finishing. Similarly, the pieces of cloth intended for mass-produced shirts and dresses were cut out and stitched together in a works but were finished, the buttonholes made and the buttons sewn on by hand workers in their kitchens and garrets.

Some of the early factory industries, such as cotton and wool, provided large openings for the employment of women and girls, and in textiles generally the proportion of women to men gradually rose so that by 1911 there were 3 women employed to every 2 men. Clothing, too, because of the large number of female outworkers, was an area of female predominance, with approximately two women to every man. (In the total labour force, women accounted for about 30 per cent.) In many factory industries, however, women were only in a small minority, as in the various branches of engineering and metal working, and in bricks and cement. In those early days of the factories children formed a substantial portion of the

8 From the later eighteenth century down to the first decades of the twentieth century, cotton mills were the great staple for female employment in Lancashire, as this picture of about 1910 shows. It was taken in Greensmiths Mill, West Houghton, near Bolton. (Manchester Polytechnic Archives of Family Photographs)

labour used, often employed by their own parents as assistants to fetch and carry, 'piece' or join the broken threads in cotton mills, and to clean the machines during rest periods. In a sample of some 7,000 workers in Lancashire cotton mills in the 1830s, 246 boys and 155 girls below the age of eleven were employed (a little under 6 per cent of the total), and another 1,169 and 1,123 respectively of the ages of eleven to sixteen (nearly 33 per cent). Cheapness was a major factor here, a boy or girl between eleven and sixteen being paid only a little over 4s. a week as compared with 17s. to 22s. for an adult male and 8s. to 9s. for a woman. Another consideration, especially important for factories in small towns and rural areas, was the availability of sufficient adult labour, since with the high birth rate at the time children formed a large proportion of the total population. (Employment of children continued in industry generally until well into the present century. Children under thirteen in cotton mills numbered as many as 67,000 in 1874, 14 per cent of the total workforce. In 1901, following the introduction of part-time schooling for older

9 The Factory Acts, beginning as far back as 1802, eventually became effective in limiting the employment of children in cotton mills. Nevertheless, there were still 67,000 children under thirteen employed in 1874, and even in 1901 21,000 children under fourteen were employed part-time. They were used mainly for 'piecing' the broken threads and cleaning the machinery. (Manchester Polytechnic Archives of Family Photographs)

children, there were 21,000 children under fourteen employed half-time, and a further 132,000 young persons under eighteen working full-time.)

The outcry over 'factory slavery' led by men like Richard Oastler and Lord Shaftesbury, forced the government to set official inquiries in process into the conditions in which the children were employed in textile mills. 'I have seen them fall asleep, and they have been performing their work with their hands while they were asleep, after the billy had stopped,' Joseph Badder, a spinner, told the 1833 Factory Commission. 'I have stopped and looked at them for two minutes going through the motions of piecening fast asleep . . .' The first Act effectively to regulate children's employment in factories, setting a minimum age for employment of nine, and a maximum working day of 9 hours for children aged nine to thirteen, was passed in 1833. ('Young persons' aged between thirteen and eighteen had a working day limited to 12 hours.) The inspectors appointed under the Act soon found that in order to operate it they needed reliable information about the children's ages: the consequence then was the institution of registration of births under an Act of 1837. More legislation followed as the inspectors revealed in their reports the weaknesses of the existing measures, and particularly, the need to deal with unfenced machinery, the source of many horrifying accidents. Inspectors reported rooms crowded with dangerous machinery 'so close that you can hardly pass; indeed, some operations have to be stopped in order that you may pass at all . . .'. In Wolverhampton the children working at the tip-punching machines were in constant danger of having their fingers punched off. 'They seldom lose the hand', said one of the proprietors to me, in explanation; 'it only takes off a finger at the first or second joint. Sheer carelessness – looking about them – sheer carelessness!'

Inquiries were extended to a wider range of occupations in which children were to be found, those living on the barges on the canals, and particularly, those working down the coal mines. There were not a few horrifying tales that found their way into the pages of the official reports. One concerned little Sarah Gooder, aged eight, employed as a 'trapper', responsible for opening and closing the ventilation doors in the underground passages when the loads of coal went through. 'It does not tire me,' she said, 'but I have to trap without a light, and I'm scared. Sometimes I sing when I have a light, but not in the dark; I dare not sing then.' In the Scots pits young girls were used for carrying the coal on their backs. An eleven-year-old, Ellison Jack, told how she carried baskets of coal down a series of ladders a total distance (as computed by the sub-commissioner) exceeding the height of St Paul's Cathedral. The basket hung on her back from straps placed over the forehead; the burden was such that fathers gave evidence of rupturing themselves from straining to lift the basket on to their children's backs. Perhaps, in the light of this evidence, it was not so remarkable that the Mines and Collieries Act of 1842 took the sweeping step of banning women and children from underground work completely.

The prohibition was not entirely to the liking of the mining workpeople. It was noted that 'families of boys are, amongst pit-people, valuable property, on account of their earnings in the pits. A widow with a family of boys is considered a *catch*'. The earnings of the women and children were important in family budgets, and in mining districts alternative occupations were not always easy to find. Some of the displaced females got work in brickfields or on farms; 'some have gone to service; one or two are married. Some are maintained by their relations; others earn a little by sewing'. The male miners were often better off when the women left the pits: ponies were introduced for haulage and the miners were paid the same rate for carriage as they got for hewing.

However, the concern with child employment in factories and mines did not arise solely from the extreme youth of some of the children, the long hours and the effect of excessive physical labour on young bodies; it arose also from the effects on young minds, the lack of education, ignorance of the Bible, and the implications for morality of working alongside coarse and possibly depraved adults. It was considered particularly bad that factory children saw adults change their clothes at work, that the female convenience was in a yard where to reach it the women had to pass a crowd of ribald, jeering men; that in the pits the children worked with miners who were often stark naked. Most deplorable was the children's ignorance: they had only the faintest idea of who the Queen was, or where Scotland was located; worse still, they were sometimes totally ignorant of the Holy Ghost and the blessed Trinity. Eight-year-old Sarah Gooder went to Sunday school and could read 'little words'. She was able to repeat the Lord's Prayer, 'not very perfectly', but although she had heard tell of Jesus 'many a time, I don't know why he came to earth, I'm sure, and I don't know why he died, but he had stones for his head to rest on'.

So the Factory Act of 1833 brought in part-time factory schools; though it was discovered subsequently that the 'teacher' might be the illiterate man employed to tend the boilers. The National (Church of England) and British (Nonconformist) Societies built and staffed schools, aided from 1833 by a government grant, set at first at the somewhat modest figure of £20,000 but much increased thereafter. However, it took nearly forty years after 1833 to supplement voluntary schools with publicly provided ones, even longer for compulsory school attendance to be established, and longer still for fees to be abolished in publicly maintained schools. The education of children employed in industry was only one consideration in the growth of state intervention: also relevant were the shortage of voluntary schools in rural areas, and the extension of the franchise after 1867. The beginnings of democracy made it essential to 'educate our masters'.

With Factory Acts affecting women and young persons, and later the influence of trade unions and further legislation, the hours of adults in industry gradually declined.

10 By the end of World War I, the period of this photograph, some progressive cotton mill owners provided continuation schools for their younger employees. Here girls employed by Tootal, Broadhurst and Lee Ltd attend a domestic science class; they went to the continuation school two days a week, without pay. (Manchester Polytechnic Archives of Family Photographs)

The 72-hour week common in the best textile mills in the 1830s was reduced to 60 hours after 1850, and to 56 in 1874. In the larger Birmingham establishments of the 1830s and 1840s the normal day was 12 hours, with 2 hours off for meals, and an earlier finish on Saturdays. Progress in reducing hours was slow until after World War I: the working week fell to 54 hours in the 1880s and 52 hours

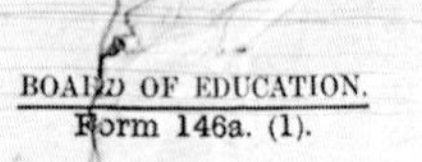

BOARD OF EDUCATION.
Form 146a. (1).

SCHEDULE III.

Local Education Authority BOLTON

LABOUR CERTIFICATE, No. 1 (a) (for total exemption after 13 years of age).

AGE AND EMPLOYMENT.

I certify that Hilda Snape, residing at 9 Keighley St. was on the 22nd day of June 1914, not less than thirteen years of age, having been born on the 20th day of June 1901, as appears by the Registrar's Certificate ~~[or the Statutory Declaration]~~ now produced to me, and has been shown to the satisfaction of the local education authority for this district to be beneficially employed.

(Signed) Fred. Wilkinson

(¹) Clerk ~~to the Local Education Authority~~ W.T.

PREVIOUS ATTENDANCE.

I certify that Hilda Snape, residing at 9 Keighley St. has made 350 attendances in not more than two schools during each year for five preceding years, whether consecutive or not, as shown by the (²) certificate furnished by the Principal Teacher of the (³) Brownlow Fold School.

(Signed) Fred. Wilkinson W.T.

(¹) Clerk ~~to the Local Education Authority.~~

Dated the 22nd day of June 1914

(²) For this certificate see Schedule VI.
(³) Here name of Schools in which attendances have been made.
(¹) or other officer.

N.B.—In districts where the bye-laws extend to the age of fourteen, this Certificate can only be granted if the bye-laws permit full time exemption on an attendance qualification.

(83,479). Wt.20,677—C4555. 40,000. 9/13. A.&E.W.
(86,855). „ 29,225—C4721. 60,000. 11/13. „

11 Before 1918 the Education Acts allowed children with satisfactory school records to work part-time from the age of eleven, and full-time from the age of thirteen. This certificate of 1914 shows a Bolton girl, Hilda Snape, had lost little time in obtaining employment. (Manchester Polytechnic Archives of Family Photographs)

was still the norm for skilled workers in 1914. In the cotton mills half an hour was allowed for breakfast and an hour for dinner, but part of the dinner hour had to be set aside for cleaning the machinery. When considering these long hours of work it has to be remembered that there were often stoppages caused by breakdowns of machines or boilers, or by other factors, and that in periods of poor trade a works might be put on short hours very often or closed down altogether. Slumps tended to occur every so many years, influenced by the trade cycle, or by some special factor such as the Civil War in America, which starved Lancashire of its raw material in the early 1860s. The 'cotton famine' saw imports of raw cotton from America, the main source of supply, reduced from 1,116m. lbs. in 1860 to an average of only 11m. lbs. a year in 1862–4, and great distress was caused in the cotton towns.

The workpeople, too, were not always very regular in their attendance, even when conditions were normal. Absenteeism was an industrial problem then as it is now. Workers liked to keep the traditional 'St Monday' as a holiday, a practice which sprang from the old domestic trades where Monday was the day for taking finished work back to the master's warehouse and collecting new orders and supplies of raw materials. As late as the 1860s numbers of works found most of their hands absent on a Monday, and it might be midday on Tuesday before full work was resumed. Other traditional holidays, such as Shrove Tuesday, also saw large numbers staying away from work. A fair coming to town, hot summer weather, or an attractive sporting fixture all claimed priority over work. Employers found it advantageous to accept the inevitable and make holidays less damaging to their interests. Regular breaks were therefore introduced when the works was shut down completely. Works closed completely for a week or ten days at Christmas or in summer for annual stocktaking; there were other holidays at Easter and Whitsun, and often annual works outings. Thus St Monday fell gradually into decline, most notably in Lancashire where the regular works holiday lengthened into a full 'wakes week' in the early years of the new century.

Workers were often irregular in other ways. They arrived late in the mornings (hence the employment of 'knockers-up' in factory and railway towns), brought strong drink into the works, swore, spat, and got into fights with other workers. They broke regulations by opening windows, by coming in dirty, and washing without permission. A system of fines was operated to try and check these frailties, and the fines were very heavy in relation to the men's wages, sometimes equivalent to a whole day's earnings, perhaps even two days' money. A worker heard whistling might be fined 1*s*. and as much as 2*s*. for being five minutes after the last bell or for 'spinning with gas light too long in the morning'; the tremendous sum of 6*s*. was deducted for steam wasted when the worker was sick and unable to 'find another spinner to give satisfaction'.

In many respects the heaviest burden of industrial employment fell on the married women who made up a considerable part of the workforce. The comforts of the homes, such as they were, might depend on her earnings, and far too often the husband was out of work or incapacitated, or had met an early death, making her the sole breadwinner of the family. In the Scots pits women went on working when they were far advanced in pregnancy: one woman told an 1842 commissioner that she had a child actually born underground – 'I brought it up the pit-shaft in my skirt'. Women with young babies left them with so-called 'nurses' while they went out to work, but if they could not afford a nurse they took the baby with them to the workplace, and resorted to one of the many readily available preparations of opium to keep him in a drugged state while they carried on with their work. Perhaps the best known of these was Godfrey's cordial, a cheap 'infant's preservative', made from treacle and laudanum. Mary Colton, a lace embroiderer of twenty, told how she gradually increased the dose of Godfrey's until it reached a teaspoonful, and when the infant was four months old it was so 'wankle' and thin that friends persuaded her to give it laudanum 'to bring it on'. 'She now buys a halfpenny worth of laudanum and a halfpenny worth of Godfrey's mixed, which lasts her three days.' Laudanum, of course, was the name given to an alcoholic tincture of opium; it was cheap and until 1868 widely available in thousands of small shops, and in the absence of other drugs was much used to relieve pain; it was often rubbed on the gums for toothache, as opium pills were taken for rheumatism and dropped in one's beer to induce a sense of well-being.

There were other consequences of female employment. Wives neglected their children and home, and cleanliness, diet, health and comfort all suffered. The earnings of unmarried girls made them independent of parents, self-willed and reckless, deficient in 'all refinements and delicacies' of their sex. Employment of girls was associated with large numbers of illegitimate children. At Darlaston, a Black Country town, the girls were reported to have three or four illegitimate children each. 'They often enter the beershop, call for their pints, and smoke their pipes, like men. . .' Families disintegrated under the pressures of the times. True, there were many instances where the whole family – husband, wife and older children – all worked in one mill. But there were many others where the husband was in a declining hand trade, under-employed and receiving a pittance; the wife had more regular employment in a textile mill or other kind of works; the boys went from home as apprentices, and the girls left at thirteen to enter domestic service. Disease, the old destroyer of family well-being, was supplemented by the ill consequences of bad trade, unemployment, crippling accidents and desperate poverty. Husbands left home or soaked in drink, and the wife was left to fend for herself and the children. None of these evils was new, but the strains of the transition to a different kind of urban, industrialized society magnified and intensified them.

* * * * * *

As the machine age advanced, numbers of old hand trades declined. The term 'spinster', though persisting to the present, was already an anachronism in its industrial connotation as early as 1830. Craftsmen, once well paid and respected, like the skilled handloom weaver, followed the spinster into oblivion, along with the framework knitter. But their disappearance was often protracted, painfully so: indeed, it has been remarked that the quick kill effected by the more strikingly efficient factory processes was preferable to the slow, gradual death agony of the struggle against powered machinery which took decades to prove its economic and technical superiority. The last stages of handloom weaving and of framework knitting, for example, were marked by a prolonged deterioration of employment, wages, status and living standards that was worse than anything the rigours of the new industries could offer.

The 'Industrial Revolution', in fact, saw not merely a rise of large-scale industry; in its early stages it also stimulated the expansion of certain of the hand trades. For example, the transfer of spinning to the factory created more work for handloom weavers in the years before efficient powered looms were established. To that extent the eventual collapse of such trades was the more far-reaching. And even in the middle of the nineteenth century there were still a number of large hand trades that were as yet little affected by machinery. At the time of the 1851 Census milliners, dressmakers and seamstresses together totalled 340,000 women and 500 men, making them the fourth biggest industrial occupation after cotton, building, and general labourers. There were over a quarter of a million shoemakers, over 150,000 tailors, and the straw-plait workers, glovers, and nailers amounted each to about 30,000. The ubiquitous horse, indispensable for farms, canals, short-distance road transport and private carriages, gave employment to no fewer than 113,000 blacksmiths – many more than were employed in the iron industry or on the railways; while as many as 30,000 wheelwrights made and repaired wagons, carts, carriages and traps. Rather more millers, nearly 38,000 of them, ground the corn in their wind-driven mills – steam engines were still supplementary to wind power, and purpose-built steam flour mills were not common till after 1850. Some technological advances, such as the sewing machine of 1851, actually helped prolong the life of a number of hand trades, especially in the clothing industry, while the growth of retailing created others, such as cardboard box making.

The clothing trades (not including boots and shoes) employed 130,000 women in 1891, the largest part of them in London but with significant numbers in garrison and naval towns like Colchester, Portsmouth and Plymouth, and in some rural areas where there was female labour to spare. As the sewing machine came within the ambit of working women – it fell to about £10 or less and could be bought by instalments – some women set up their own little workshops and acted as sub-contractors: in one instance a little group of relations and neighbours turned out 12 pairs of trousers a day at 10*d*. a pair, producing a gross income of 10*s*. to be divided among four workers. Such miserable rates of pay attracted only those who really needed the money or felt a compulsion to occupy their time to some little profit. The Black Country nailmakers, said to be 50,000 strong in 1830, worked in a declining market, one increasingly invaded by imported foreign nails and machine-made ones produced in factories at home. As the trade shrank and became less remunerative so it fell more under the control of 'foggers' or middlemen; the men nailers gradually dropped out and the surviving hand trade became more dependent on women. An enquiry of 1871 found that some two-thirds of the nailers were paid wholly or partly in kind – in nails – and dependence on the foggers for work forced the hands to buy from his shop and pay his price for groceries, fuel, carriage and tools. Women hammering out the common nails earned only between 4*s*. and 6*s*. a week, from which fuel and other expenses had to be deducted, while the men making the more valuable horse-nails earned between 14*s*. and 16*s*.

In chain making – another Black Country trade, which

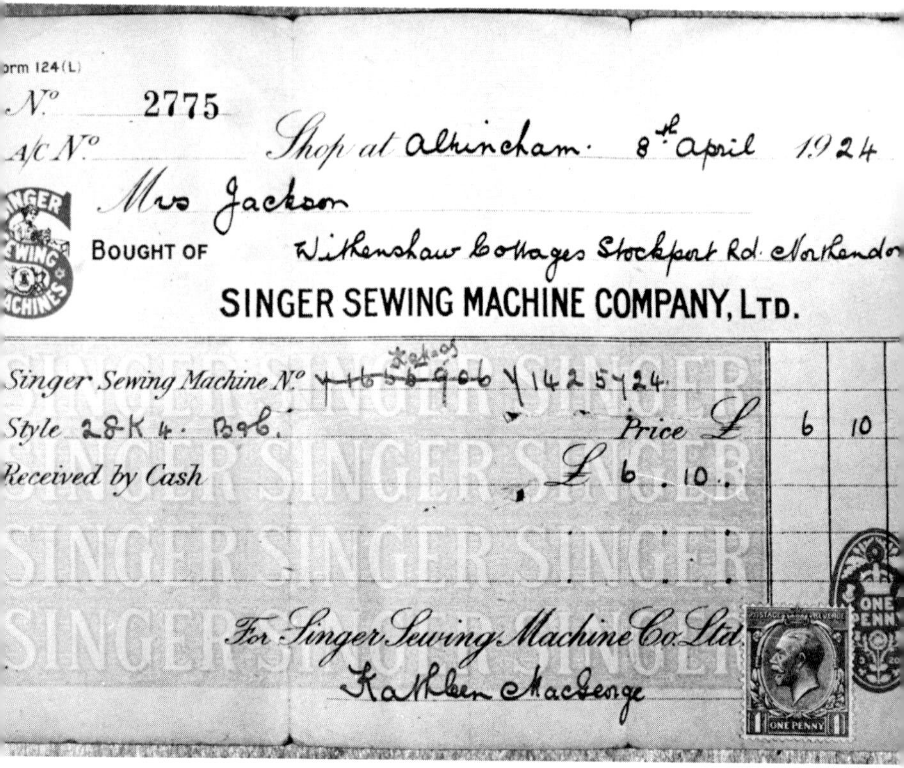

orm 124(L)

No. 2775

A/c No. Shop at Altrincham. 8th April 1924

Mrs Jackson

BOUGHT OF Withenshaw Cottages Stockport Rd. Northendon

SINGER SEWING MACHINE COMPANY, LTD.

Singer Sewing Machine No. ~~Y1656906~~ Y1425724

Style 28K4. B96. Price £ 6 10

Received by Cash £6.10.

For Singer Sewing Machine Co. Ltd.

Kathleen MacGeorge

ONE PENNY

12 The first practical domestic sewing machine was produced by Isaac M. Singer in Boston, Massachusetts, in 1851. The machine was quickly adapted to large-scale production in both the United States and in Germany, and as it was cheap and could be bought by instalments was rapidly acquired by women not merely for home use but as the basis for commercial dressmaking and the widespread clothing trades. (Manchester Polytechnic Archives of Family Photographs)

was concentrated round the village of Cradley to the south of Dudley – there was also a marked division between the types of work carried out by men and women. The men worked in the factories producing the heavy chains, while the women made up a large proportion of those employed in the hundreds of domestic shops which produced light chains made with hand tools. A woman working full-time on very small chain might make a hundredweight in a week. In 1889 an adult man in a factory averaged earnings of 26*s*. 11*d*. a week, while women could get only some 8*s*. to 9*s*. from which 1*s*. was deducted for workshop expenses. It is remarkable that even in 1910 the new trade board appointed to regulate the industry required that, as a minimum, women should be paid the magnificent sum of 2½*d*. an hour if the shop, tools and fuel were supplied, or 3½*d*. if not. At this rate a woman would have to work at least 40 hours a week to earn the 1889 average!

As in the clothing trades, the advent of the sewing machine in the making of boots and shoes resulted at first in the bolstering up of outwork. It was the sudden export demand from Australia during the gold rush, and from the British army bogged down in the trenches round Sebastopol, which precipitated the first stage of change. The factories of the 1850s introduced the machine sewing of uppers, though making little use of steam power. The other processes were still largely the province of outworkers, both men and women, and this remained much the state of affairs until the 1890s, by which time there were American machines available for speeding up 'clicking' (cutting out the separate leather pieces) and 'lasting' (attaching the inside and sole and heel to the upper). In 1895 a major lock-out frustrated the attempt of the shoeworkers' unions to control the introduction of new machines, and the triumph of the employers was followed by a rapid shift of the industry into factories. However, outwork persisted in some centres of the trade, like Norwich, where in the early years of this century men averaged year-round earnings of 12*s*. a week, and women 3*s*. Much higher earnings could be obtained in busy seasons, but the surviving outwork trade was marked as ever by irregularity of work and sharp fluctuations in earnings.

There were other trades, however, in which outwork

did not merely represent additional capacity, to be utilized fully only when demand was brisk, but was the permanent mode of production. The mass-production of chairs in High Wycombe was one such trade – the chairs made in workshops or small 'factories', the cane or rush bottoms put on by women and children in their homes. The expansion of the retail trade in the later nineteenth century created a big demand for cardboard boxes and paper bags, and though the simple processes became increasingly mechanized, the production of fancy boxes, such as those used for chocolates, was still the province of outworkers. Outworkers could survive, too, by meeting sudden rush orders, like the widow in South London who in 1897 worked long hours, together with her four children, to supply paper bags to a large bakery making hot-cross buns. The rate was ¾*d*. a gross, and when there was pressure of work the family could earn 2*s*. 4*d*. a day.

The small boxes for matches, involving not only the making of the box but the pasting on it of a printed wrapper and a strip of sandpaper, were paid for at the rate of 2¼*d*. for a gross (144). The sewing on to cards of machine-made buttons, hooks-and-eyes, safety pins and hair grips, was a speciality of the Birmingham district. Many of the women who worked at this were in reality petty subcontractors who took the work to their neighbours 'in a perambulator or wheelbarrow or anything they can get to carry it in'. Some 15,000 or 20,000 casual hands were so employed in the later nineteenth century before machines took over. Rates of pay varied with the extent to which machinery provided competition: in button carding, a depressed part of the business, the rate was down to 2*s*. 6*d*. or 3*s*. for carding no fewer than a hundred gross – 14,400 buttons!

Some of the petty outwork trades were not merely miserably paid but positively dangerous to health. The hand-making of matches entailed the handling of phosphorus and resulted in the disfiguring condition known as 'phossy jaw', gangrene of the jawbone, arising from

13 While a combination of factory and outwork production cheapened the making of boots and shoes and drove the bespoke craftsman out of business, the repair trade flourished. The low-paid working man repaired his own and his family's boots at home, but there was plenty of custom from the better-off classes. This photograph was taken in Lancashire, as the notice concerning 'cloggers' reminds us, the wooden clogs being widely worn by working women of the north down to the time of the Second World War. (Manchester Polytechnic Archives of Family Photographs)

exposure to phosphorus fumes. Fur-pulling meant working all day, and perhaps much of the night too, in an atmosphere floating with 'millions of almost impalpable hairs'. It took 12 hours to pull out the long coarse hairs from 'a turn and a half' – 90 rabbit skins – at the rate of 11*d*. a turn. 'Yes, it stuffs your chest up', one puller said, 'but you get used to it when you've been at it all your life.'

The long survival of outwork is to be explained on a variety of grounds. To some extent, hand workers made good the deficiencies of the early machinery and plugged the gap between the mechanization of one process and the later introduction of efficient machines for dealing with the other processes in the production of a good. Outwork made it possible to combine low costs of production with wide variation of the product in respect to quality, design and style, important in such trades as clothing, hosiery and boots and shoes where there was both a high-class and a cheap end of the business. Outwork thrived where there was a large supply of suitable labour, perhaps that left over from the decline of an older hand trade, as when the making of boots and shoes filled a void left by the waning of the woollen industry in districts round Norwich and Leicester. Outwork labour was cheap, consisting as it did of men unwilling to submit themselves to the discipline of factory conditions, unmarried girls, women with husbands away in the army or navy, widows, children. Such labour made for extremely low costs of production, low prices and a large market, and reduced the advantage of introducing machinery. Outworkers, too, were unorganized, their wages and conditions at the mercy of the market, and competition for the available work ensured that rates of pay were kept down to the minimum. Then there was the flexibility which outwork offered to the larger employers: they need employ directly only those hands whom they could be sure of keeping in full work, leaving any seasonal or sudden demand to be met by putting more of the work out.

In some respects it is curious that the public concern with workers' conditions began with the factories and mines, and came so late to the outwork trades. The Factory Acts go back to the beginning of the nineteenth century, legislation on the mines to 1842, while concern over the 'sweated trades' surfaced only in the late 1880s. By then, of course, factory wages and conditions were generally much superior to those found in the small workshop. One reason, perhaps, was that many of the hand trades were clearly moving to extinction; another was that the workers, though concentrated in a geographical sense, were scattered among hundreds of small workshops and were employed by a multiplicity of masters and middlemen. Yet another was the casual nature of the trades and the rapid turnover of the workers engaged in them.

'Sweating' became a vague, if widely-used, term, meaning inadequate wages, excessive hours, and insanitary working conditions. An Anti-Sweating League was in being from 1905, with some eminent public figures in its ranks, and in the following year the *Daily News* organized an exhibition of sweated industries and their products in the Queen's Hall in London. In the next two years Private Bills on the subject were introduced into Parliament, and soon after, in 1909, came the Trade Boards Act brought in by the President of the Board of Trade, Winston Churchill. The main purpose of the Act was to fix minimum wages, originally in men's clothing, cardboard box manufacture, lace finishing and chain making. (Sugar confectionery and food preserving, shirt-making, wrought hollow-ware and tin-box making, and hand embroidery were added in 1913. Some 400,000 workers were covered by the Act, the great majority of them women.) It is a tribute to the publicity which the cause had received, and to the changed attitudes of government and public, that there was little opposition to so deep a breach in the principles of *laissez-faire*. Factory Acts, after all, had regulated the age of employment, hours of work, and dangerous machinery, with women and children principally in mind; now the public regulation of wages themselves, for both men and women, was added to the scope of industrial legislation, a clear sign that a new age was dawning.

* * * * * *

The great inventions of the Victorian era are familiar, if not to every schoolboy, then at least to many: the new sources of power and light – coal-gas, the dynamo for producing electricity and Sir Joseph Swan's carbon filament lamp, the steam locomotive for railways, and compound engines and iron screws for ships – in iron and steel the hot-blast, steam-hammer and the Bessemer and Gilchrist-Thomas processes; in engineering Whitworth's machine tools and gauges, accurate to the ten-thousandth of an inch, and Armstrong's hydraulic cranes, lifts, capstans, swing-bridges; in textiles and clothing the self-acting mule, ring spinning and Singer's sewing machine; in chemicals the Solvay process and artificial dyes such as Sir William Perkin's Tyrian purple (vulgarly mauve), and turkey red.

There were in the field of transport, besides railways and steamships, the portentous invention of the motor vehicle – Karl Benz's three-wheeler was constructed in 1885 – and the humbler 'safety bicycle' of the same year; and for greater comfort on badly constructed roads Dunlop's pneumatic tyre of 1888. A new era of rapid communications dawned with the electric telegraph, first mainly adopted on the railways, subsequently by the Post Office: the 6*d*. telegram appeared in 1885. In 1870 a sea-bed cable connected England with Bombay and the Indian Empire; four years earlier, as soon as the ending of the Civil War had allowed, the Atlantic too had been spanned. Bell's telephone was invented in 1876, but it was 1884 before London got its first trunk line, one connecting the metropolis with Brighton. By American standards the telephone was slow to spread, partly because of inadequate equipment and the cost, and partly, it was said, because of the cheapness of the telegram. Wireless telegraphy came in later still, though by 1900 it was being tried out in manoeuvres of the British fleet. Four years later *The Times* had a vessel equipped with wireless to send immediate news of the Russo-Japanese conflict at sea, the conflict which ended in the triumph of the new Japanese navy in one of the most conclusive of all sea battles, Tsushima. In 1913 it was wireless that brought *Carpathia* tearing through iceberg-ridden seas in a vain attempt to reach the stricken *Titanic*; and in World War I incautious use of the new invention was to bring disaster to many ships, both men-of-war and merchant vessels.

There were many inventions which had a less immediate impact but proved valuable as they were developed for a widening range of applications. Such was the case of rubber, eventually used in railways, engineering, surgery and a variety of miscellaneous fields. A combination of rubber and fabric was in use for garters at the beginning of the nineteenth century, and subsequently Thomas Hancock devised a method of making blocks of rubber to serve as springs and buffers. Another pioneer was Charles Macintosh, and the first factory to produce 'mackintoshes', waterproof sheets and clothing, opened in Manchester in 1824 – a not unimportant event in an age when travellers were much exposed to the elements. The mackintosh was widely adopted, and a Swiss industrialist visiting the Great Exhibition of 1851 noted that the policemen carried 'rolled up india-rubber coats under their arms'. In due course Hancock and an American, Charles Goodyear, took the first steps towards creating an effective process of vulcanization, which eventually opened the way for making rubber valves, conveyor-belting, hoses, shoes and tyres. There were other new materials which came into their own mainly after World War I: the first man-made plastic, celluloid, invented in 1869 and first used in photography; artificial silk (1884); and in 1907 bakelite, the first plastic which could be moulded, named after its American inventor, Lee Baekeland – in the 1930s Woolworth's stores were full of cheap bakelite articles.

Effective preservation of foodstuffs greatly reduced the problems of transporting meat, soups, and eventually a wide range of foods across the oceans, helped in overcoming gluts and shortages, and provided short-cuts for the family cook. The use of tinplate for canning was pioneered in England, and soups and preserved meats were supplied to the Royal Navy from a Bermondsey cannery during the American War of 1812. Another and far greater conflict, the American Civil War, provided a new stimulus to the industry, and soon after Armour, Swift and others began to develop the great meat-packing plants for which Chicago became famous. Refrigeration owed much to two Australians, James Harrison and T. S. Mort, who in 1861 established the first meat-freezing works at Sydney. In 1877 frozen mutton was successfully shipped from the Argentine to Le Havre in a ship equipped with a refrigeration plant: owing to a collision the voyage took six months, but the meat eventually reached its destination still in excellent condition. In February 1880 a British ship brought forty tons of frozen Australian beef and mutton to London, and in the same year a sailing ship carried the first frozen mutton all the 13,000 miles from New Zealand.

There were new devices to improve the kitchen and lighten the labour of the housewife and servant. The first practical carpet sweeper came in 1865, gas cookers, replacing the solid fuel range, were popular by 1880, though the electric cooker was widely adopted only after 1914; a successful vacuum cleaner was patented in 1901. The use in the home of electric light, electric cookers and other electrical appliances had of course to await the installation of an electricity supply; many older houses were wired for electricity only in the 1930s or later. Home life was enriched, too, by devices for filling leisure hours. Pianofortes began to become popular in the later eighteenth century, and by 1900 were to be found in working-class homes. Quite a good instrument could be bought in instalments towards the end of the century for as little as £30 or less, and in 1900, in addition to large German imports, there were eight British manufacturers which each produced a thousand or more pianos a year, as well as many smaller producers. By 1910, estimates Cyril Ehrlich, the modern historian of the piano, there was a total of between two million and four million pianos in the country. The gramophone, invented by Edison in 1876, was for a long time a mere curiosity, but by the 1920s had become commonplace. Photography began with the daguerrotype process in 1839, but was brought to the masses in a cheap and simplified form by George Eastman with his Kodak box camera in 1888. And a series of advances in printing, beginning with the steam press first adopted by *The Times* in 1814, led the way to an eventual flood of popular magazines, such as George Newnes's penny vehicle of 1881 for the conveying of potted information and advertising, *Titbits*, and in 1896 the first important morning newspaper catering specifically for those who wanted 'a penny newspaper for one halfpenny', *The Daily Mail*.

Many of the inventions were British, but many were not. Unlike the preceding era of 'Industrial Revolution' the Britain of the later nineteenth century could not claim a near-monopoly of the new advances in industrial technology. The authorities hold, indeed, that much of Britain's industry, even such formerly advanced sectors as textiles, iron and steel and railways, became characterized by conservatism, outdated techniques and a low growth of productivity rate. This was particularly marked in the years between 1880 and 1913, and indeed over the whole forty-three year period 1870–1913 the average annual rate of improvement in total industrial productivity has been estimated at 0.6 per cent. Other industrial countries, it is agreed, were comfortably exceeding our rate of progress, both in total output and in output per man-hour, notably the United States, Germany and Belgium. The British economy of the later nineteenth century entered a period of slower growth which some economic historians have described as 'retardation'.

A number of reasons have been found for this slowing down, some of them connected with the nature of our foreign trade and overseas financial relations; this will be considered in another chapter. Here it is a relevant point that British industry reached a kind of plateau, showing no strong tendency to rapid change in either its structure or its technology. A few key staple trades dominated industry throughout the period 1870–1913: coal, textiles, iron and steel, and engineering. Together these accounted for about a half of total industrial output in 1907, employed a quarter of the working population, and provided nearly three-quarters of British exports. There were, of course, some significant shifts in the structure of the economy: agriculture's share of the occupied labour force fell substantially, while the shares of both mining and transport grew somewhat. But manufacturing industry remained stable as a proportion of the labour force, occupying a third of the total or slightly under, for the whole of the forty years between 1871 and 1911; and the building and trade sectors of the economy also saw little change in their shares. On the other hand, the proportion engaged in public and professional services rose by as much as two-fifths, while domestic and personal services retained some 15 per cent of the labour force – more than was involved in trade, or as large as mining and building put together, and not far from a half of those engaged in manufacturing. Thus, as some economic historians have pointed out, the shifts which occurred in the nation's resources tended to be ones between sectors of low productivity and did not make for rapid growth of the economy.

* * * * * *

The breakdown of the figures of the employed population show a remarkable growth in 'public and professional services' and a near-stability in those categorized as 'domestic and personal services'. The professions rose

Table 1 *Distribution of occupied labour force in Great Britain (as percentage of total)*

	Agri-culture	Mining	Manu-factures	Building	Trade	Transport
1871	15.0	5.0	32.5	6.7	13.3	5.8
1911	8.6	6.4	33.3	6.4	13.4	8.1

	Public and Pro-fessional services	Domestic and personal services
1871	5.8	15.0
1911	8.1	14.0

(Source: Derek H. Aldcroft and Harry W. Richardson, *The British Economy 1870–1939*, Macmillan, 1969)

rapidly in late Victorian Britain in both status and numbers as professional bodies were established, entry qualifications were imposed and standards of conduct laid down. To the old professions of the church, the law and medicine were added such relative newcomers as surveying, architecture, accountancy, nursing and teaching. Stockbrokers flourished with the growth of the London stock exchange and the appearance of specialized provincial exchanges, such as that for cotton in Liverpool. Bankers became increasingly recognized as pillars of the respectable community, the insurance companies and their agents perhaps somewhat less so.

The Civil Service, together with local government officials, grew in numbers and in respect as the functions of government were expanded and as educational and professional requirements were imposed on new recruits. The increase in numbers might even be described as spectacular, as a mere 43,000 in 1841 increased more than seven-fold in six decades, to reach as many as 321,000 in 1911. True, for long enough there was hostility in high places to the very idea of competitive entry by examination, and for some time the examinations were rigged in favour of preferred candidates. But the general trend was towards the establishment of a corps of well-educated and devoted, if still amateur and untrained, public administrators.

Industry, commerce, banking, insurance, the Civil Service, local government and the professions all required office staff – clerks, book-keepers and messengers – essential but lowly figures who provided Dickens with some of his most memorable characters. There was even a major technological development here as the typewriter eventually made obsolete the old first-grade and second-grade letter copiers who laboriously transcribed correspondence in their copperplate into letter books. Clerks and typists, too, rose in status after Dickens's day, as employers came to demand recognized evidence of competence in the three R's and more general education (thus giving a stimulus to the revival of grammar schools), as well as the relevant qualifications of minimum speeds in shorthand and typewriting. (Sir Isaac Pitman had developed and published his improved system of phonetic shorthand as long before as 1837.) Already by 1921 there were nearly 600,000 males and almost 500,000 females listed as engaged in clerical occupations. Ten years later their numbers had grown to 778,000 and 648,000 respectively – one of the few large occupations to expand in the depressed years of the 1920s and 1930s.

A striking change in the later Victorian period was the growth of a distribution network able to cope with the expanding urban populations and the huge flow of consumer goods that factory machines and railways were making possible. The goods had to be got to the consumer as efficiently as possible, at the least possible cost, and in the case of perishables like imported meat and dairy produce, fish, milk and margarine, as rapidly as possible. There was an enormous expansion of retail outlets – not merely a duplication of existing markets, street stalls and shops, but a revolution which produced many thousands of specialized multiple shops. As Charles Wilson has written, 'the 1,500 odd multiple stores of 1880 became the

14 Book-keepers at work in the offices of Armstrong Whitworth, the big armaments manufacturers. The expansion of industry, commerce and the civil service saw an increased requirement of office staff, and by 1921 there were over a million men and women engaged in clerical occupations. (Manchester Polytechnic Archives of Family Photographs)

11,645 such stores of 1900'. Large-scale manufacturing of boots and shoes required thousands of shoe shops, among them those of Freeman, Hardy and Willis; a manufacturing chemist like Jesse Boot, beginning with his father's store in Nottingham, opened his chain of 150 chemist's shops in 1900, while the spate of cheap books, newspapers and magazines filled the shops and station bookstalls of W. H. Smith. Many other familiar names appeared: multiple grocers like Lipton's, and Home and Colonial, bakers like Joseph Lyons, dairies like Express Dairies, tailors like

Hepworths, and tobacconists like Salmon and Gluckstein.

The branded products found in such stores were made household names by the advertising columns of *Titbits*, *Answers*, *The Daily Mail*, *Evening News* and their like – Singer's sewing machines, Broadwood's pianos, Sunlight soap, Brasso metal polish, Hovis bread, Chivers's jams, Bird's custard, Beecham's Pills, Dr J. Collis Browne's Chlorodyne, and Eno's Fruit Salts. Player's and Wills competed for the custom of smokers, Rowntree, Fry and Cadbury

15 A scene outside Cadby Hall, the headquarters of J. Lyons and Co. Ltd. Lyons was among the many new multiple retailers which increasingly changed the appearance of high streets from the 1880s onwards, creating new sources of employment not only in shops but also in manufacture and distribution. (Museum of London)

for the drinkers of cocoa – Cadbury's factory trebled in size in twenty years after its removal to Bourneville in 1879, and its labour force rose more than ten-fold.

The new batteries of shops impinged relentlessly on the activities of the hawkers and street stalls, more particularly as customers required better quality and wider choice, and as the delivery boy with his bicycle and basket became a familiar sight in residential districts. Markets selling meat, fish, greengrocery items, household necessities and cheap clothes managed to survive, removed now to yards and permanent market halls situated off the main street to avoid the old congestion and nuisance to traffic. And there were still the Italian organ grinders, German brass bands, Highland bagpipe players, rag-and-bone men and itinerant knife-grinders. Surviving, too, were the permanent tea and coffee stands, newspaper stalls, whelk stalls and fruit and flower sellers. But many others disappeared. Fried fish shops replaced the vendors who cried 'fish and bread, a penny' in the streets and public houses, and confectionery stores made obsolete the man with his tray of halfpenny lollipops, bulls-eyes and almond toffee. Professional photographers' establishments put paid to the sixpenny street photographer and penny profile-cutters, though pavement artists still chalked the flagstones in a few favoured locations. Rat poison, available from a store, killed off not only the rodents but the former rat-catchers who had walked the streets with a cage of ferrets and an oilskin belt painted with the figures of huge rats. Respectable grocers and branded tea put an end to the not inconsiderable street trade in dried and re-dyed used leaves posing as new tea. And vanished, too, were Mayhew's 'river finders' who dredged the bottom for miscellaneous things thrown overboard, the 'mud-larks' who scoured the Thames banks, and the 'toshers' or 'sewer-hunters' who defied armies of ferocious rats to search for coins, rings and other treasures lost in the mud and slime of the subterranean depths.

At length the shop girls became so numerous and

familiar a sight as to arouse the compassion of the upper classes. Even in the better-class shops the regular hours ran from 8.00 a.m. to 10.00 p.m. – 14 hours on the feet. The girls sat down for 20 minutes for dinner and 15 minutes for tea – breaks which might be interrupted by the needs of customers – and on occasion a girl's boots had to be cut from her swollen feet at the end of a long Saturday. Those girls who lived in at the shop were expected to help dust and prepare the displays before the opening hour, and were expected, too, to subsist on a meagre diet, working all morning on a breakfast of bread and butter and tea. The Shops Act of 1886 extended factory-type protection to

16 Although children were widely employed for long hours in factories, workshops and retail stores, and at street stalls, there were still some pleasures. In this street scene outside the Exchange Station in Manchester some young boys sample the ice-cream man's wares (Manchester Polytechnic Archives of Family Photographs)

shops, but only to the children and young persons employed in them who had a prescribed maximum week of 74 hours, including meal-breaks. But the Act was held to be 'generally unenforced and even to a great extent unknown', and it took a new Act in 1912 to bring all shop assistants within the scope of regulation – hours, meal-breaks, the half-days and early closing.

There were still many unprotected youngsters working, part-time, in the wholesale and retail trades: the butcher's boy who went to market every day at four in the morning and shouted, 'buy, buy' outside a stall till late at night, in the interval going to school 'voiceless and stupid'; another who minded carts at Covent Garden from 4.00 a.m. to 8.30 in the evening; an eleven-year-old who delivered milk for 3 hours beginning at 5.30 a.m. and for 4 hours after 5 p.m.; a nine-year-old who sold papers from 6.30 to 9.00 a.m., and from 5.00 to 8.00 p.m., and for 16 hours on a Saturday. This was in 1897, and the earnings of these children were pitiful. A greengrocer's boy made 3*s*. from some 34 hours of spare-time work in a week, a boy of nine in a newspaper shop a halfpenny for 2 hours of evening work each day, a barber's boy 2*s*. 6*d*. a week and food for 5 hours every evening from 5.00 p.m., all Saturday and part of Sunday. 'General work' in a private household – cleaning shoes, polishing knives, running errands – averaged less than a halfpenny an hour.

And so finally to domestic servants. Victorian and Edwardian Britain depended for its leisure and comfort, even its efficiency, on an army of well over a million domestic servants – in 1851 the largest occupational group after agriculture. If we may sometimes wonder how Victorian businessmen and professional men got through the amount of work they did we should not forget the servants who freed them from most ordinary chores of home and office. The army of domestics continued to increase through the later decades of the century, if less slowly than did the population at large. Their vast numbers are largely explained by their cheapness. One

17 In 1886, when this photograph of a housekeeper and her brood of young domestic servants was taken, there were not far from two million women and girls employed in the category of 'domestic offices and personal services', accounting for nearly a half of all female employment and constituting by far the largest single female occupation group. (The textiles and clothing trades employed less than 800,000 each.) (National Museum of Labour History)

did not have to be wealthy to keep servants: indeed, the servant-keeping class went far down the social scale, as is clear from Dickens. In the 1850s the family with £1,000 a year could run to a cook, parlourmaid, housemaid, nursemaid and kitchenmaid, a butler and a coachman. Subsequently, a higher income would be required to employ domestics on this scale, but even in 1907 an income of as little as £200 a year made it possible to afford a young girl for rough work. At £300 she could be replaced by a general servant, and above £500 one could contemplate both a cook and a housemaid. At £1,000 a manservant – a true sign of wealth – could be added.

Already by this time many young girls were avoiding going into service with its long hours, restricted freedom and sometimes domineering employers. Wages had always been low in cash terms, but there was board and lodging as well, livery or uniform, and in a large household the duties were often light, while there was greater security of employment than in many alternative occupations. In 1907 advertisements in *The Times* specified £25 a year for a cook and about £20 for a housemaid or general maid, rather more for a nursemaid or parlourmaid. Improvements in the wages reflected the greater scarcity of servants as the number of alternative occupations increased, but the status of the occupation remained low and even sank as it was increasingly recruited from the poor, the unskilled and badly educated.

Servants, shop girls, clerks and many others made up the base of cheap labour whose services oiled the wheels of Victorian Britain. In their own spheres they were as vital to the country's progress as were the coalminers, ironworkers, shipwrights, railwaymen and textile hands. Indeed, in some ways the shop girl and clerk were more indicative of the future path of the economy than were the workers in the staple trades for which Britain was renowned. In this, as in so many other respects, World War I was a dividing line, marking the end of the old industrial Britain, opening the way to the predominance of the new.

Chapter Three

The Railway Age

The railway, wrote Sir John Clapham, 'having conquered Britain by the early 'fifties . . . consolidated and extended its conquest during the next generation'. A framework of lines already covered much of the country by the mid-nineteenth century, and although the network subsequently spread over new areas the technology employed changed little for many years. The first expresses of the London and North-Western averaged 37 m.p.h. in 1845; in 1871, 250 express trains running nationally averaged the same figure; twelve years later there was a little more speed, but only very little, for the figure was still less than 42 m.p.h. The locomotive of the 1880s, indeed, was closely related to that which had inaugurated the era of 'railway speed' forty years earlier.

The steam locomotive was the truly novel element of the railways. The track itself was very much older, having originated in the wagon-ways used from the later sixteenth century to ease the movement of coal from pithead to wharf. In the eighteenth century wooden rails were replaced by ones made of iron, and flanged wheels on the wagons were also an early improvement. It was in fact the traditional width between the wheels of the Tyneside coal wagon – 4ft. 8½ ins. – which was adopted by the Stockton and Darlington line in 1824, and which eventually became the standard gauge, adopted all over Britain and most of the world, ousting Brunel's more comfortable, but also more expensive, broad gauge of 7ft. 0¼ ins.

Experiments with steam engines for road carriages go back to 1769, but four years of the nineteenth century had elapsed before Richard Trevithick, a Cornish mine engineer, designed a locomotive to pull a 10-tons load on a 10-mile track between Penydaren ironworks at Merthyr Tydfil and the Glamorganshire canal. So novel was the idea that a rival ironmaster bet 500 guineas with Samuel Homfray, the owner of the Penydaren works, that Trevithick's invention would not work. More decisive was the 1829 triumph of George Stephenson and his son Robert in producing the famous *Rocket*, whose tubular boiler and direct drive between piston and driving-wheels formed the prototype of later locomotives. The lead established by British engineers enabled them to take their designs to many countries of the Empire and the continent of Europe, laying the foundation of an important export business in steel rails and railway equipment. The *Rocket* was the victor of the celebrated Rainhill trials, held prior to the opening of the Liverpool and Manchester railway, at which rival engines competed over a length of level track on the Manchester side of Rainhill bridge. Each engine was not to exceed 6 tons in weight, have a working steam pressure of not more than 50 lbs. per square inch, and was not to cost more than £550 to build. The test was ten return journeys with a set load at full speed over 1½ miles of track, making 30 miles in all, representing the journey from Manchester to Liverpool and back. The *Rocket* was the only one of four engines entered to complete the trial, which it did in two trips at an average speed of 13.4 and 14.2 m.p.h. respectively.

Rolling stock was developed from the single horse-drawn coach, designed by George Stephenson, which appeared in the opening procession of the pioneer Stockton and Darlington railway. The early first-class coaches much resembled the carriages to be seen on the roads, from which indeed they took their name and design; the provision for third-class passengers, similarly, was an open wagon, much the same as the carriers' wagons they might normally use – at a walking pace – for journeys between the villages. America led the way to more elaborate coaches with such amenities as sleeping cars, dining cars and lavatory facilities, and the first imported Pullman car came to Britain in 1874. Immediately afterwards the Midland Railway set a new standard of comfort with upholstered seats for all three classes of passengers. The standard British side-corridor coach, with small compartments and lavatories at either end, came in 1882, electric lighting not until the 1890s. Though innovators in the early days, British railway companies later showed much conservatism, not least in the highly important matter of braking systems. There was great reluctance to go over to the automatic compressed air brake (which operated independently on the engine and every carriage) invented by the young George Westinghouse of Schenectady – due in some cases to sheer prejudice against American ideas. Trials carried out in 1875 on a section of the Nottingham-Lincoln line of the Midland Railway showed that from a speed of 50 m.p.h. a train fitted with the Westinghouse brake was stopped in 777 ft., 124 ft. less than one fitted with a hydraulic brake, and 700 ft. less than another having only a simple vacuum brake. It took repeated accidents with the old types of brakes, and much loss of life, before some companies made the change: the climax came with the ghastly tragedy in 1889 when a runaway excursion train, having the simple vacuum brake, crashed into another train near Armagh: 78 of the more than 600 passengers (mostly children) packed into ten coaches were killed, 250 injured. A Bill was rushed through Parliament making automatic continuous brakes compulsory for all passenger trains.

Total British railway mileage was 4,646 in 1848, 16,700 in 1886. The impact was immediate and enormous. Sir George Head made a journey in 1835 on the railway between Leeds and Selby soon after the line had been opened. The train consisted of a dozen carriages and the whole distance of almost 20 miles was covered in 1 hour and 4 minutes, including four intermediate stops. The passage of the train gave rise to great excitement:

men at work in the fields and quarries stood like statues, their pickaxes in their hands, in attitudes of fixed attention, and immoveable as if turned by the wand of a magician into blocks of stone; and women in troops, in their best gowns and bonnets, fled from the villages, and congregated at the corner of every intersecting lane . . . every horse was on the alert, viewing the huge moving body as it approached with a mixture of fear and surprise, stamping, pointing forwards his ears, snorting, and evincing a degree of curiosity so intense, that it appeared as if to the instinctive faculty was added reason and the desire of knowledge – even the cows, as they cocked and twisted their tails, spit out mouthfuls of unchewed grass, and tried to gallop.

But it was the 1860s or later before many country towns and villages could share in the excitement of having their own railway service. The coming of the train was a huge dramatic event, to be marked by a public holiday, banners, feasts, toasts and speeches. The main street of Williton, when the West Somerset Railway reached it on 31 March 1862, boasted a banner bearing 'Hail, Steam the Civiliser!'. The first train to arrive at Llanidloes in central Wales in the September of 1859 carried 3,000 people and was ushered in by booming cannons and peals of bells, and the first arrival at Askrigg in Wensleydale on 1 February 1877 'was besieged by delighted crowds at every station' along the way.

The railway was synonymous with progress, and more concretely, with cheaper coal, a more varied supply of consumer goods, wider markets for producers and more job opportunities for workers. Farmers, fruit-growers and market-gardeners, got their produce to market from a greater distance and more expeditiously, fishermen could tap the latent demand of remote conurbations, and country manufacturers disposed more readily of their cloths, shoes, gloves, building materials, barrels, tubs and poles. There were annual outings, excursions and sports fixtures, and shopping trips on Saturday afternoons to nearby market towns. There was the cheap post, the London newspaper, and for emergencies the telegraph.

Rural isolation was vastly reduced and country people felt that for the first time they were really part of the national life.

Such far-reaching consequences could not but make an impact on the rival means of transport. Canal and river traffic, coach and carriers' services, the coastal cargo vessel and passenger steam packet all felt the effects of railway competition. The 4,000 route miles of canals open to traffic at the beginning of Victoria's reign had already brought some of the benefits later offered more plentifully by the railways – cheaper goods, especially coal, wider markets, more employment, even some cheap passenger services. But the canals suffered from their age and their diversity – their varying depths, widths and size of locks – and from the country's topography. Coal was the basis of their success, and consequently there were few prosperous canals in southern England. Numerous locks, and the occasional need for trans-shipment of cargoes, made for long delays. To go by canal from Yorkshire to Lancashire meant the negotiation of 45 locks going up and 54 going down, and those not all of a size: the same journey by railway took two hours. There were obstacles like the Huddersfield tunnel, 3¼ miles long, costing £300,000 but still only made large enough for single working, so that boats had to wait their turn in one of the alternate four-hour periods when the tunnel was open in their direction. Then the horses had to be sent over the hill by road while 'leggers' were hired to 'walk' the boat through the tunnel:

> two 'leggers' in each boat lying on their sides back to back, derive a purchase from shoulder to shoulder, and use their feet against the opposite walls. It is a hard service, performed in total darkness, and not altogether void of danger, as the roof is composed of loose material, in some parts continually breaking in. Two hours is the time occupied in legging a boat through, and a legger earns a shilling for a light boat; after twelve tons he receives one shilling and sixpence; and so on.

When the railways came a great many canals gave in rather than fought: they were outdated and unimproved and could not compete. Some, however, had little difficulty in surviving. They were the well-situated ones with a profitable short-haul traffic, like the antiquated Bridgewater canals; the Weaver Navigation with its coal, salt and chemicals; and the Aire and Calder with coal to go down the canal and timber and other bulky cargoes to come up it.

Coaches, too, could survive in areas where the railways were slow in penetrating, and in some country districts they were still in business until late in the century. But the main routes were a different story. As early as 1839 the opening of the London and Birmingham line had meant the demise of fifteen coaches which once left the Bull and Mouth inn for the Great North Road every day, including the famous 'Tally-ho'. The last coach set out for Bristol in 1843, for Plymouth in 1847. One weakness of the surviving coach traffic was the limited progress made in replacing road surfaces of gravel with macadamized ones of broken granite. New kinds of surface, granite 'sets', asphalt and wood blocks used in towns, came in late, and side roads remained muddy, mended only with an occasional load of cinders. But in the countryside, carrier services continued to expand throughout the century, for even at the peak of their mileage the railways touched no more than one village in every six. At least 20,000 carriers were operating in the 1880s, and for the local carriers, as distinct from the long-distance ones, the railways meant additional business. As late as 1881 the small Sussex town of Horsham was served by nine carriers who provided a means of sending or collecting goods from eighteen nearby villages. Many carriers combined their business with dealing in coal or farm produce or with some other occupation, and they still provided a cheap if slow means for country folk to get about – though Shanks's pony was the usual resort of people used to walking several miles a day. For remote hamlets and farmsteads the carriers were supplemented by pedlars with donkeys or little carts. Only the coming of the motorized delivery van, as Professor Philip S. Bagwell has remarked, put an end to carriers' wagons and pedlars' donkeys alike.

18 Until late in the nineteenth century local coach services continued to thrive where the railways had failed to penetrate, and to act as feeders to distant railway stations. Here is the coach, evidently much used for luggage and parcels, which connected Tenterden and Cranbrook, country towns of south-eastern Kent, with the railway town of Ashford. (Professor Philip S. Bagwell)

Before the railways reached ports and isolated coastal places it was the steam packet which gave their inhabitants the same kind of service as was provided elsewhere by the carrier. Villagers of the Furness peninsula had quick and inexpensive access by sea to Liverpool, and little harbours round the coast of Wales and the south-west of England were connected with major ports like Bristol, Swansea and Cardiff. Regular steam packet sailings made it possible to get from Watchett on the north Somerset coast to Cardiff for as little as 2*s*., and a steamship service connected the Isle of Wight with the mainland from as early as 1820. The coasting trade in coal, building materials, farm produce, provisions and miscellaneous goods was of vast importance – indeed, was greater in total cargo tonnage than the whole of our overseas trade. The small tramps, sailing sloops and schooners, Thames and Medway barges plied a multitude of small harbours and were especially important in Scotland, lingering on long after the railway era itself was on the wane.

* * * * * *

Railways affected employment in at least four separate ways. First, railways had a stimulating effect on large areas of the economy, widening markets, cheapening commodities, especially such basic ones as coal, foodstuffs, building materials, iron and steel products, and fertilizers; and railways reduced the cost of travel, encouraged greater mobility and speeded up the pace of business life. Land values rose and new railway towns erupted on to the scene. The economy moved into a higher gear, with new levels of investment and expanded general activity. The weight of goods moved by rail increased enormously, from 90m. tons in 1860 to 425m. tons in 1900. More impressive still was the new mobility given to people. From the outset passenger traffic was far larger than the railways expected, and indeed provided almost two-thirds of the earnings in the middle 1840s. But for a long time, provision for working-class passengers was neglected. Parliament found it necessary to include in the Railways Act of 1844 the famous clause obliging companies to run the daily 'parliamentary train' – to cover the line in both directions at the rate of at least 12 m.p.h., to stop at every station, to have carriages with seats protected from the weather, at a fare of not more than a penny a mile, children under three free, children from three to twelve half-price – though this, like the powers of compulsory purchase included in the Act, was to apply only to new lines or lines seeking new powers. After mid-century the numbers of working-class passengers rose dramatically as the railways realised the enormous size of this untapped market and provided more facilities; the Midland announced in 1872 that in future third-class passengers would be carried on all its trains. The total number of passengers carried (exclusive of season ticket holders) increased in the second half of the century from 73m. to 1,142m.

Secondly, the railways themselves created a new demand for the products of a variety of industries. Engineering developed new techniques and new materials to build the locomotives, rolling stock, coupling gear, signalling equipment and buffers, while the iron industry, and later steel, met the demand for vast numbers of rails and the chairs in which they were keyed. Coal was needed to fuel the engines: a loaded express train of the 1860s using the latest economical design of fire-box consumed 23 lbs. of coal to the mile – more than a ton to every hundred miles. The building of scores of bridges, viaducts, tunnels and hundreds of stations, depots and workshops meant a huge demand for bricks, stone, iron, timber and other materials of construction. That the linkages – as economists call these new demands – were of importance there is little doubt, but it is rather easy to be so impressed by the rapid spread of railways as to exaggerate their effects. Professor G. R. Hawke has pointed out that in England and Wales in 1865 the savings to the national income represented by the more efficient carriage of coal and other minerals was only 1.4 per cent of the total; and that railways were not significant in the development of steel before 1870, nor were they responsible for technical advance and external economies in the finishing process and rolling mills. The total saving to the national income represented by the advent of railways, including both passenger and goods traffic, was of the order of 10 per cent: about two-fifths of this figure was the consequence of the new, superior comfort of personal travel.

Thirdly, there was the new employment created by the

building of the lines. The work was a prodigious feat of earth-moving: levelling, cutting, embanking, tunnelling – all done by pickaxe, spade and wheelbarrow, horses, windlasses and carts. Much of the labour required for this arduous but largely unskilled work was recruited from the towns and villages along the route, together with itinerant gangs of Irish, Scots and Welshmen. A number of expert excavators and embankers came from the fenland districts of Lincoln and Cambridge where they had much experience of this kind of work. Men from Northumberland and Durham, used to the construction and operation of mine tramways and steam engines, were to be found laying the track and working the locomotives. Rates of pay varied between 2*s*. 6*d*. and 5*s*. a day, the top figure being paid for expert tunnellers or when men were working against time. The highly skilled men, the surveyors and engineers who set out the levels and determined the exact place for building the tunnels, bridges and viaducts, and those who carried out the dangerous work of blasting out the tunnels, were on more permanent terms and went on from contract to contract. At the peak of railway construction, in the years 1846–8, nearly 200,000 men were involved in cutting out the path for the rising juggernaut.

The big railway contractors like Brassey, Jackson and Peto sublet the straightforward work to subcontractors, who in turn let out sections of brickwork to master bricklayers, and of earthwork to excavation gangs. The railway 'navvy' acquired a reputation for hard working, hard drinking, and licentiousness. They left behind them a trail of petty thefts, brawls, and illegitimate children. 'Do you believe that many of them are Socialists?' a clerical witness before a Parliamentary enquiry was asked. 'Most of them in practice', he replied, 'though they appear to have wives, very few . . . are married.' In a different sense, the navvies accorded more with the modern view of a socialist, for the subcontracting gangs shared their pay, and often helped support the men who were injured and the widows of those who were killed.

The work was indeed very hard, especially the making of cuttings. Sometimes the earth from the cutting was needed for an embankment a short way along the line and was loaded into trains of horse-drawn wagons. But when there was no use for the soil the barrows had to be run up the sides of the cutting and dumped on the top. Planks were laid up the side of the cutting, and a rope, attached to the barrow and to the man's belt, ran over a pulley fixed to a post at the top and then to a horse. When the barrow was loaded the driver of the horse was signalled and the man and barrow were pulled up the run to tip the load at the top of the cutting; coming down the man went first, the weight of the barrow again eased by the

19 An early photograph of navvies engaged for railway construction in Cornwall about 1850. This was the peak period for railway building, when some quarter of a million navvies were employed throughout the country. (Manchester Polytechnic Archives of Family Photographs)

horse. So long as the horse was steady, the barrow was kept balanced and the man did not slip on the muddy planks all went well. Tunnelling caused the worst accidents. The notorious Woodhead tunnel, more than three miles long, on the line between Sheffield and Manchester, had to be blasted through millstone grit and treacherous shale and sandstone: the casualty list of one of the surgeons who attended the men included 32 killed, several maimed, nearly 100 fractures, 140 cases of burns from blasts; severe contusions, lacerations and dislocations, together with some 400 minor accidents, including trapped and broken fingers, and injuries to scalps, feet and shins. One man lost both his eyes, another half a foot. Such casualties, the reformer Edwin Chadwick pointed out, were almost as high in proportion to the numbers involved as Wellington's great battles: Talavera, Salamanca, Vitoria and Waterloo. Numbers of accidents were caused by haste: men undercut too far into the rock face and were buried by a sudden collapse; blasting was done with iron tools which caused sparks, and with inadequate fuses. There were illnesses caused by working in the cold and wet, by the drinking of contaminated water. Cholera broke out at the Woodhead tunnel, and when the navvies saw the supply of coffins brought up to meet the expected need they decamped in large numbers.

Although the best contractors tried to establish weekly pay-days, the inadequate capital possessed by the small subcontractors made for much longer intervals, two weeks, a month, or more. Often the 'long pay' was associated with 'tommy-shops' and advances made to the men in the form of tickets exchangeable for goods in the shop. At remote sites, like Woodhead, a contractor's shop was a necessity and might even benefit the men; but in many instances it was a means of selling them dear and inferior goods, or of discounting their tickets at a penny in the shilling. The housing varied, too. Often the men lodged out in nearby villages, or were accommodated in wooden barracks designed to hold twenty-five men each, sleeping in hammocks. At Bangor, Jackson ran up wooden cottages for his married men, but in Devon the huts were of mud and turf, for which a man paid 3s. a week. At Woodhead some of the huts were of stones or mud, with a roof of thatch or flags, put up by the men themselves. There were 'tally-women' or camp followers, wives were sold for a shilling or lent for a gallon of beer, and both men and women suffered severely from venereal disease.

The railways attracted large sums of capital from a public who were formerly limited to investments in property, government gilt-edged, and a few safe stocks such as that issued by the Bank of England. Railways, it has been said, acted like a huge sponge, soaking up savings from far and wide, not merely, as at first, from the district in which the line was to be constructed, but from the whole country. Large amounts of British capital also flowed abroad to finance the building of railways, and the movement of the capital was associated, in the early days at least, with a corresponding migration of the labour required to build the new lines, working under the great contractors like Thomas Brassey and Morton Peto.

Lastly, the railways themselves provided a new source of permanent employment: for engine-drivers, firemen and guards; for signalmen, station masters, booking clerks and porters; for carters and van men to move the goods from the depots, and for the gangs who laboured to maintain the permanent way. There were a mere 29,000 such men on the railways of 1851, but as many as 157,000 thirty years later, and a huge 370,000 (together with 3,000 women) at the peak of railway employment in 1911.

* * * * * *

The nation's diet was changed by the railways. Imported hard wheat, carried from over the seas by sailing vessels and increasingly by steamships, was milled into flour at the ports and distributed by rail to the centres of consumption, eventually displacing the local windmill with its wooden sails and its traditional grindstones. Steamships fitted with refrigeration plant later brought in frozen meat from Argentina and Australasia, as well as tropical fruit. The meat and fruit were stored in refrigerated warehouses at the docks and then again distributed by rail. Well before the advent of refrigeration the British consumer was enjoying Danish butter and bacon, American cheese and canned milk, Irish dairy produce, French butter and fruit, Dutch butter and margarine, and Mediterranean nuts, raisins and sultanas. Even the horses, growing more numerous every year, were eventually getting their ration of imported hay, as were the cattle their feeding stuffs and concentrates. The new roller-milled flour provided a new kind of bread, less nutritious in fact than that made from the soft wheat flour produced in the former way. And the cheapest of the canned milk, though more convenient for the housewife lacking cool storage, was deficient in essential vitamins, the children fed on it alarmingly marked by rickets.

Dairy farmers at home gradually abandoned the butter and cheese trades to the foreigners and concentrated more on producing liquid milk. The market for liquid milk was still a small one in terms of consumption per head, but was expanding with the growth of the population and the rising popularity of beverages in which milk was used, tea, coffee, cocoa and chocolate. Railways opened up the big urban markets to more distant suppliers, and the old unhygienic town dairies, greatly weakened by the arrival of the rinderpest in 1865, slowly succumbed to the competition of the new 'railway milk'. Soon London's milk was coming from up to as much as 150 miles away, from as far afield as the West Country and Derbyshire. By the early years of the new century milk had become one of the farmers' great standbys, accounting for a fifth of the value of all farm produce.

Fruit, vegetables and salad stuffs also came by rail to grace the tables of the better class of urban consumers. Special vans were attached to the trains coming from the favoured districts in Kent, the Vale of Evesham and the

20 Unloading meat in the London docks. The trade in imported meat grew more rapidly after 1879 when the first chilled beef was brought in from America using a compressed-air refrigerating machine, to be followed the next year by 40 tons of frozen beef and mutton from Australia. By the eve of World War I meat imports into Britain were valued at over £60m. a year. (Museum of London)

Sandy area of Bedfordshire. Apples, plums, pears and cherries, strawberries, raspberries and gooseberries, could be loaded at a Kentish railway station in the late afternoon, sold in Covent Garden at midnight, and displayed on the greengrocers' counters the following morning. The second quality of fruit went to the jam-makers, like Chivers,

Hartleys and Tiptree; cheap factory jams increasingly replaced the home-made product. Early potatoes, vegetables, and salad produce grown under glass in the Channel Islands or on the Continental mainland, reached London within a day or so of dispatch, and the tomato – once a rarity, like the banana – became commonplace. Again the markets, though growing, were not without their limits, for the consumption of these items was very much related to income, and little fruit, lettuce or water-cress was to be found on the tables of the poor.

The market for fish was also one much expanded by railway transport, which enabled the boxes to move from quayside to fishmonger's slab overnight. Formerly, fresh fish had to be sold and consumed within a few miles of the port where it was landed. Railways and ice – the latter imported from Norway or stored in icehouses from British winter supplies – were big factors in the growth of the deep-sea trawling trade. Hull's 21 small fishing smacks in 1844–5 had turned into 400 first-class boats of 65–90 tons each less than forty years later. The discovery of the 'Great Silver Pits' in the North Sea, 60 miles from the mouth of the Humber, brought in a rich source of cod, soles, turbots, brill and halibut, the fishermen throwing back as offal the plaice, haddock, whiting and ling. Consumption of fish increased greatly in London, and herrings, in particular, became standard fare among the metropolis's poor – so much so, said Mayhew, in his *London Labour and the London Poor* that he always associated 'the smell of herrings', with 'squalor and wretchedness'. It was the Manchester, Sheffield and Lincolnshire Railway that so successfully revived the ancient fishing port of Grimsby that by 1873 there were as many as 248 trawling smacks and 82 live cod-smacks fishing out of its harbour. The railway offered Grimsby fish merchants free tickets when they travelled on business, and Sheffield's new wholesale fish market became the centre from which supplies were sent to the brimming markets of the West Riding and Lancashire.

The fried-fish trade expanded with the increase in

supplies, and was well established in London in Mayhew's day. The fried product was a valuable outlet for the fishmongers' left-over supplies, disposed of in districts where a high consumption of gin had the effect of obscuring the inhabitants' olfactory sense. Professor W. H. Chaloner tells us that in the 1850s Madame Rachel, a notorious and fraudulent beautician, kept a fried-fish shop near the present site of the London School of Economics in Clare Market. The frying of chipped potatoes began as a separate business, and the combination of chips with fried fish is said to have originated in Lancashire as a quick meal for the women working all day in the mills. John Rouse, an Oldham cotton mill engineer, claimed to be responsible for popularizing the joint sale of fish and chips, using a mobile range with a long chimney resembling that of the *Rocket*. He gave away the chips with the fish he sold from this vehicle in Oldham's Tommyfield market.

* * * * * *

So far as the ordinary people of Britain were concerned, perhaps the most remarkable effect of the railways was on their personal mobility. People who had never strayed beyond the next town, had never seen London, had never seen the sea, were liberated from the thrall of distance. Former means of travel had been too expensive or too slow, while within twenty years of the Liverpool and Manchester the railways were covering distances at four times the speed of the fastest coaches and at a fraction of their rates. Moreover, it paid the railways to encourage passenger travel, especially at weekends and on holidays when normal traffic was lacking: this made sense in an industry with high overhead costs – the permanent way, stations, engines, rolling stock – and low marginal costs when an additional train or extra coaches were run.

Thomas Cook, the founder of the great travel business, has been credited with originating railway excursions when in 1841 he organized a visit to Loughborough by 510

Leicester temperance workers by the Midland Counties Railway. However, Professor Bagwell tells us that ten years earlier the Liverpool and Manchester had carried over 120 teachers of the Bennett Street Sunday School in Manchester to Liverpool and back for 3*s*. 4*d*. each return, instead of the normal second-class single fare of 3*s*. 6*d*.; and this, in fact, appears to have been the very first of railway excursions. But it was the Great Exhibition, held in Joseph Paxton's Crystal Palace in South London in the summer of 1851 which provided the great occasion for the railways to promote mass travel. The London and North Western alone brought over three-quarters of a million excursion travellers to London from the North of England for as little as 5*s*. return. Altogether it is estimated that over 5m. people used the railways to visit the Exhibition. Sixteen years later the railway companies were offering cheap package trips to Paris for people wishing to see the Exhibition there: organized parties could have the journey to Paris, their lodging, part board, and entry to the Exhibition for only 30*s*. – surely one of the great travel bargains of the age.

With a shorter working day on a Saturday, and cheap and easy travel, the age of fans journeying to distant sporting fixtures had arrived. Professional football clubs developed and with them, as John Arlott has said, the tall and gaunt fences and grandstands, 'harsh new features of the urban fringe'. The strong northern clubs met 'a huge, hungry demand for football as Saturday afternoon excitement', and in 1888 the Football League was formed. The first Cup Final, played at the Oval in 1872, attracted fewer than 2,000 spectators; but that of 1901, at the Crystal Palace, was watched by nearly 111,000 – the 'cloth-capped hordes' who descended on London 'in their northern-voiced, thick-suited, and heavy-booted thousands'. In the same year as the Crystal Palace Final the Football Association ruled that no player might receive more than £10 for signing on as a professional or be paid more than £208 a year: modest indeed by the standards of today, but even

21 The racing crowd flocking from the train for the 1913 Grand National at Aintree. (National Railway Museum)

then this represented about four times the wage of an unskilled worker. The beginning of later trends was seen in 1905 when as much as £1,000 – a great sum for the time – was paid by Middlesbrough for Alf Common, the Sunderland forward.

Cricket was virtually the only summer spectator sport, attracting crowds at forty grounds in sixteen counties. And there were great cricketers to watch: Dr W. G. Grace had his fiftieth birthday celebrated by a jubilee Gentlemen vs. Players match at Lord's in 1898, and played his last Test Match in the following year. At Hove one might see G. B. Fry and Ranjitsinhji, at Old Trafford A. C. MacLaren, J. T. Tyldesley and R. H. Spooner. The Oval had Jack Hobbs, the great master batsman; Somerset boasted Lionel

Palairet; Nottingham George and John Gunn; and Yorkshire the great all-rounders George Hirst and Wilfred Rhodes. Worcestershire had R. E. Foster, who scored 287 against Australia in 1903 – a score long unmatched – Kent the graceful Frank Woolley, while Gloucestershire, after the retirement of W. G. Grace, was led by that unique fast scorer, Gilbert Jessop. C. B. Fry was a great Captain of England, and his six consecutive innings of over a hundred in Test Matches, though equalled by Bradman, was never surpassed. He was a fine all-round sportsman

22 Saturday half-day excursions from Manchester, about 1910, aimed mainly perhaps at the football crowds. Notice the accompanying match posters and the permanent advertisements for Golden Shred marmalade, Stephens' Inks, and the Waverley Pen. (National Railway Museum)

and a scholar who wrote a novel, an autobiography, a history of the League of Nations and three technical studies of cricket: he was even offered the throne of Albania!

The strength of both sports lay in their local roots. Writing of cricket, John Arlott says:

> Not a town or village but had its club, while churches, institutes, schools, factories, collieries, and the most fortuitous groupings of young men had their teams. Never, before or since, were there so many active cricketers in England. There was, too, one uniquely Edwardian aspect of the game, the social phenomenon of country-house cricket. An entire eleven – and more, for reserves – often with their wives and fiancées would be invited to stay as guests at the mansion to play a week or more of cricket on their host's private cricket ground.

The railways' opening of the way to nation-wide sporting fixtures and train-loads of supporters also meant invasion of the Sabbath peace for excursions to country and seaside. There was much middle-class hostility to 'excursions of mere pleasure leading inevitably to most extensive desecration of the Lord's Day'. As late as 1895, James Walvin tells us, the Anti-Sunday-Travelling Union could count over 22,000 members, and some companies bowed to the pressure and closed their lines to Sunday traffic. Relaxation of this policy came about only near the turn of the century.

Despite the attempt to deny any real alternative to Sunday church attendance, a day at the seaside, later a whole week there, was made possible for many working families who earlier had never been able to venture far from home. The seaside excursion began before the railways, encouraged by the belief in the medical properties of sea-water, and by the facilities offered by the coaches, and especially by the steamboats in the decades after Waterloo. By 1829 there were ten steamboats on the London–Margate run, and in the 1830s and 1840s the average steamboat fare was down to 4*s*., and in certain years much lower still. The numbers arriving at Margate pier shot up from an average of under 24,000 a year before 1820 to reach over 85,000 in the 1830s. The journey itself was an attraction, with elegant cabins fitted with 'every possible attention to comfort'.

The company are provided with draughts, chess boards, etc., and an excellent band of music, and when the weather permits, they often join in the dance, for which the clean and spacious decks of these vessels are peculiarly adapted . . . the dinner, which consists of joints, boiled and roasted, of the very best quality, all vegetables that are in season, and pastry, wines, dessert, etc., is served up in a style both pleasing and surprising, when the limited size of the kitchen is considered . . . There is always a female attendant on board to wait upon the ladies.

Nevertheless, it was the railways which brought in the heyday of the English seaside resort. To older venues like Scarborough, Weymouth and Brighton were added a nineteenth-century generation of railway-created resorts: Blackpool and Fleetwood; Skegness, Clacton and Southend; Folkestone, Hastings, Eastbourne and Bournemouth. Frequently it was the landed proprietors who saw the possibilities of railway-based urban development. Thus Sir Lawrence Palk developed Torquay to such effect that its permanent population multiplied more than fivefold in under seventy years. The Earl of Scarbrough built a hotel and houses on his windswept Lincolnshire coast estate at Skegness, and soon railway stations displayed the famous poster of the bouncing fishermen announcing that 'Skegness is so bracing' – a well-justified claim! More aristocratic were the Folkestone of the Bouverie family, with its grand Victorian hotels high on the Leas, and Bournemouth, laid out by Sir George Tapps-Gervis's architect, with 'detached villas' admirably 'suited to the convenience of either large or small families'. The work was continued by Decimus Burton who used the natural surroundings to lay out walks, drives, gardens and pleasure grounds. Bournemouth as a result attracted 'a very superior class of visitor', and also a resident population which climbed from under 6,000 to 47,000 between 1870 and 1901. Different

23 A Blackpool postcard. The queen of the Lancashire resorts, Blackpool was a railway-created holiday town that catered primarily for the mill workers; its permanent population grew rapidly from the 1870s when its 6,000 inhabitants multiplied ten-fold in forty years. (Manchester Polytechnic Archives of Family Photographs)

again in character were Blackpool and Southend, the one catering for the mill workers of the Lancashire towns, the other for the cockle-eating throngs of London's East-Enders.

Old resorts that were off the railway line – such as Exmouth and Lyme Regis, Jane Austen's favourite resort – lost ground and stagnated, while those fortunate in rail connections continued to thrive. Brighton's population, already a substantial 47,000 in 1841 was up to 123,000 by the end of the century. The first excursion train arrived on Easter Monday 1844, so heavily loaded that it took 6 engines to haul the 57 carriages. The August Bank Holiday, inaugurated by an Act of 1871, was immediately popular. At London's Fenchurch Street Station hundreds struggled for tickets to Margate and Southend; and people arrived at Cannon Street and Charing Cross for Ramsgate

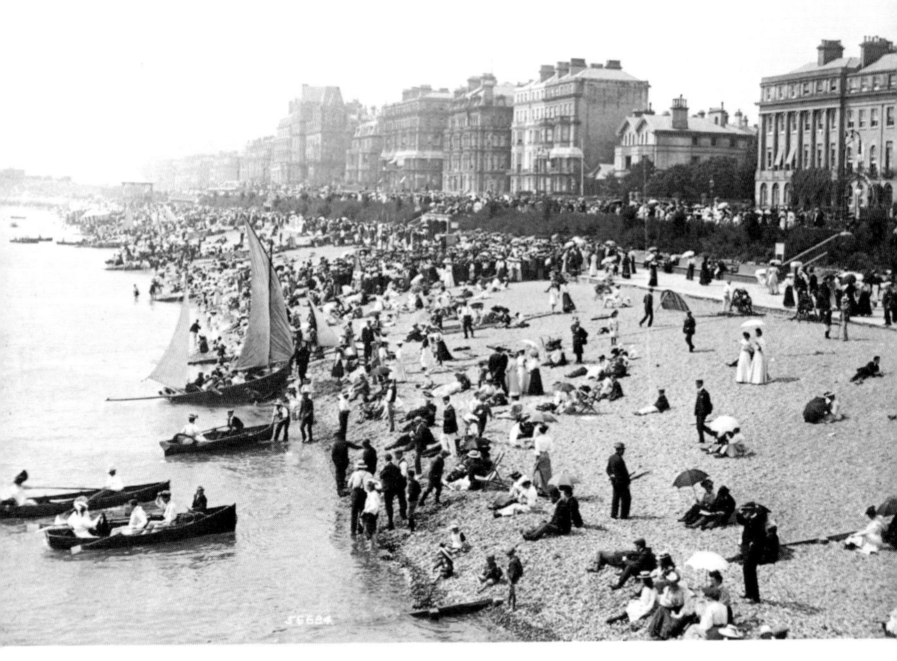

24 More middle class in its clientele was Eastbourne on the south coast, a resort which like Bournemouth was deliberately established on genteel lines to attract 'a very superior class of visitor' and to avoid the low rowdiness of the vulgar railway resorts such as Blackpool and Southend. Here is the Eastbourne front on a fine day in 1906. (National Maritime Museum)

at 8.00 a.m. 'Seven "specials" were sent from Cannon Street, and probably as many more from Highgate Hill,' reported the *News of the World*. 'It was simply impossible to get to the seaside.'

But people did in fact get there and continued to fill the summer specials. The resorts responded with many new or greatly expanded facilities for leisure and amusement. Piers were extended, and new ones built: as many as

25 Another type of summer outing that was popular in the decades before 1914; a pleasure cruise on the upper reaches of the Thames as pictured in 1911. Steamboat services on the river began as early as 1815, though the most favoured direction was downstream to Greenwich, Woolwich, Gravesend, Margate and Ramsgate. (Museum of London)

thirty-three in the forty years after 1870. There appeared promenades, theatres, music-halls, bandstands, zoos, boating lakes and penny-in-the-slot machines. Negro minstrels and pierrots became firmly established attractions, and there were German bands, brass bands, light orchestras, organists and sing-songs. Working people saved up through their factory, their pub or club to be able to splash out on minstrel shows, shooting galleries, oyster stands and whelk stalls when they went to the sea. The simple vulgar jokes of the seaside picture postcard were born, and thousands discovered what it was the butler saw. The poorer working class were not excluded. In the 1840s the fare from Manchester to Fleetwood on a Sunday excursion was 2*s*. for a male adult, 1*s*. for females and children: a family of five could reach the sea for 6*s*. – not an impossible sum to find.

The railways did much, too, through unexpected and gradual means, to unify the nation. Language and speech were standardized. In Wales the warning boards at stations and level crossings appeared in both English and Welsh. Travel made people more accent conscious. Standardized time, too, became essential if railway timetables were to make sense. The Great Western operated originally on the basis that London was 4 minutes ahead of Reading, 7½ before Cirencester time, and 14 minutes before Bridgwater. 'London time', or more strictly, Greenwich Mean Time, was brought in by the device (formerly used by the mail coaches) of sending an Admiralty mess-

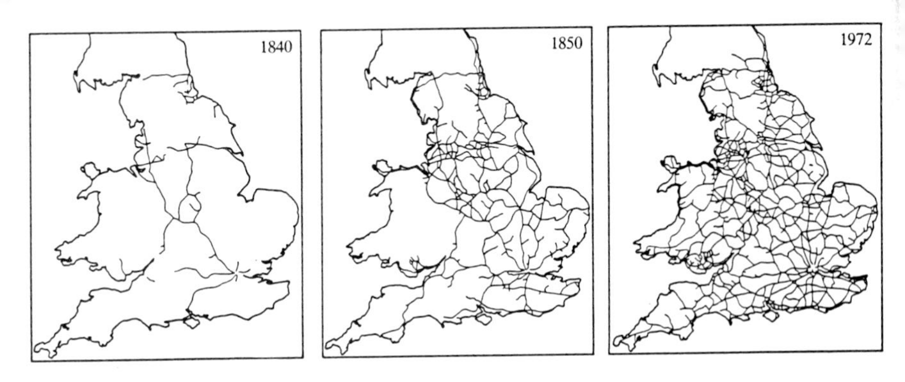

Figure 2 The growth of the railways (Source: *An Economic Geography of Great Britain*, Wilfred Smith, 1949, p. 160; Report on Railway Amalgamations, 1872)

enger with a watch on the Irish Mail: on arrival at Holyhead the correct London time was passed on to officials on the Kingstown boat who then took it over with them to Dublin.

Rowland Hill's penny post of 1840, and the later electric telegraph service operated by the Post Office, were both by-products of railways. Political news and business information could be sent across the country, soon round the world, in hours rather than days, weeks or months. Families and friends could keep in touch even when separated by hundreds or thousands of miles. People became better informed, more in touch with national and international events. The London press, aided by technical advances in printing, by the telegraph, and the reduction, then abolition, of the newspaper stamp duty, gradually became the national press, so reducing the former influence of the provincial papers. In 1830 less than 42,000 copies of daily newspapers were circulated, by post, outside London. Before two decades had passed W. H. Smith, the newsagents, were chartering six special trains to get the London papers to Glasgow within ten hours of publication.

The cheapening of newspapers added to the effects of the new means of distribution, and saw a great increase in the number of newspaper titles. In 1851 there were 563 newspapers of all kinds in the United Kingdom; by 1895 the total had quadrupled to reach 2,304. The year 1836 saw the birth of the mass-circulation Sunday press with three famous titles, the *News of the World*, *Lloyd's Weekly News*, and *Reynolds News*. By 1855 these three papers had a joint circulation of 0.25m. copies. In that same year, 1855, the newspaper stamp duty was abolished and the *Daily Telegraph* (its very name redolent of the new technology) became the first penny newspaper. The next great innovation in the British newspaper world came in 1896 when Alfred Harmsworth, later Lord Northcliffe, launched the *Daily Mail*, the first mass-circulation halfpenny newspaper. The Prime Minister, Lord Salisbury, might

26 Sir Rowland Hill, the inventor of the postage stamp, was responsible for the introduction of the penny post in 1840. Here is a Mulready envelope of that date complete with the famous Penny Black stamp. (Haringey Public Libraries)

THE ELECTRIC TELEGRAPH COMPANY,

INCORPORATED 1846.

REDUCTION IN CHARGES TO THE CONTINENT.

Opening of the New Telegraphic Route via the International Telegraph Company's Line.

On and after 15th AUGUST, 1853, the STATIONS of THE ELECTRIC TELEGRAPH COMPANY, established in all the principal Towns of Great Britain, will be placed in DIRECT COMMUNICATION with the whole of the LINES of TELEGRAPH on the CONTINENT. Great facilities will thereby be afforded for the transmission of dispatches to all parts of Europe at the following reduced rate:—

Charges for MESSAGES not exceeding TWENTY WORDS to

Place	£	s.	d.	Place	£	s.	d.
Amsterdam	£0	8	4	Hague	£0	7	6
Antwerp	0	11	6	Hamburg	0	15	6
Augsburg	0	17	6	Hanover	0	15	6
Berlin	0	17	6	Leghorn	1	10	2
Bremen	0	13	6	Lubeck	0	15	6
Breslau	0	19	6	Milan	0	19	6
Brussels	0	11	6	Presburg	1	1	6
Cologne	0	13	6	Rotterdam	0	8	4
Dantzig	0	19	6	Stettin	0	17	6
Dresden	0	17	6	Strasburg	0	19	6
Elberfeld	0	13	6	Trieste	0	19	6
Florence	1	12	2	Venice	0	19	6
Frankfort-on-Maine	0	15	6	Vienna	0	19	6

And to other places on the Continent at proportionately low charges.

The above rates will be uniform from all the Company's Stations in Great Britain, and thus—Messages delivered to the Telegraph offices at Brighton, Bristol, Holyhead, Hull, Leeds, Liverpool, Manchester, Newcastle, Edinburgh, Glasgow, Plymouth, &c., will pay precisely the same amount for the whole distance as messages forwarded from London.

For further particulars, apply at the Company's Stations.

By order, J. S. FOURDRINIER, *Secretary.*

Central Station, Lothbury, London, August, 1853.

REDUCTION IN CHARGES IN GREAT BRITAIN.

On and after 15th AUGUST, 1853, the CHARGES for MESSAGES not exceeding TWENTY WORDS will be—

Within a circuit of 50 Miles .... **1s. 0d.**

Beyond 50 Miles and within a circuit of 100 Miles **2s. 6d.**

Beyond a circuit of 100 Miles .... **5s. 0d.**

PRINCIPAL OFFICES:—

LONDON,
CENTRAL STATION, LOTHBURY,
448, WEST STRAND.

LIVERPOOL, 35, Castle Street.
MANCHESTER, Ducie Buildings, Exchange.
LEEDS, Park Row.
BIRMINGHAM, Temple Buildings, New Street.
GLASGOW, Exchange.
EDINBURGH, 68, Princes Street.
NEWCASTLE-ON-TYNE, Sandhill.
SUNDERLAND, William Street.
HULL, Lowgate.
YORK, Micklegate.
PLYMOUTH, Union Baths.
BRISTOL, 1 Broad Quay.
BATH, 16, Old Bond Street.
WINDSOR, 48, High Street.
BRIGHTON, York Hotel.
PORTSMOUTH, 12, The Hard, Portsea.

No charge will be made for the delivery of Messages within half a mile of the Company's Offices.

For further particulars apply at the Company's Stations.

By order, J. S. FOURDRINIER, *Secretary.*

Central Station, Lothbury, London, August, 1853.

WATERLOW & SONS, PRINTERS, CARPENTERS' HALL, LONDON WALL.

27 After many years of experiments in Britain and various parts of the continent, the electric telegraph was adopted for use on the Great Western Railway in 1838. This railway telegraph received enormous publicity in 1845 when a suspected murderer was seen to board a train at Slough and was arrested when he alighted at Paddington. So great was the demand for the new means of communication that the inventors of the British system formed in 1846 the Electric Telegraph Company, which by the time of this notice, 1853, had installed over 4,000 miles of telegraph in the country. (Haringey Public Libraries)

scoff at 'a journal produced by office-boys for office-boys', but such scorn did not prevent the *Mail* from reaching a circulation of over 0.5m. after three years. It was advertised as 'The Busy Man's Paper', smaller and easier to read than its more august rivals, and it came at the right time to catch the swelling market of commuters who needed something with which to pass their daily journey. It attracted women readers by borrowing from the French the idea of printing every day an instalment of a story. And it deliberately set out to attract the lower end of the reading public by providing light reading, interesting scraps, on the pattern already shown to work in *Titbits* and Harmsworth's own *Answers*. It said little about politics or money; wrote Harmsworth:

> The new sort of newspaper reader cares little about Government nor is he excited about investments; he has none. Most of the things that interest him are things which the pre-*Mail* newspapers never used to mention . . . You could search the Victorian newspapers in vain for any reference to changing fashions, for instance. You could not find in them anything that would help you to understand the personalities of public men . . . What we did was to extend its purview to life as a whole.

* * * * * *

The railways created new towns, substantial if unlovely, out of former market towns and villages – or, as in the case of Crewe, out of nothing. Crewe did not figure at all in the Census of 1841 for it did not exist. But by 1900, when the locomotive works there produced its 4,000th engine, there was a town which boasted 42,000 inhabitants. Crewe began its career as a railway centre because four routes converged there, making it a major junction; and it was geographically half-way between Manchester and Birmingham and therefore a good stopping point for refreshments and the changing of engines. The same reason, the changing of engines, in this case to take advantage of the long fast level stretches between Paddington and Didcot, originally determined the choice of Swindon as the workshop centre on the Great Western's line. The refreshments at Swindon are another story. The company unwisely let the refreshment facilities on a long-term contract and agreed that all regular trains should stop there for about ten minutes. The result was a disastrously low standard, Brunel, the company's engineer, writing: 'I have long ceased to make complaints at Swindon. I avoid taking anything there when I can help it.'

Just as Swindon was a town very much created by the railway company, so at Crewe the London and North-Western built the principal schools, the Mechanics' Institute, four churches, and over 800 houses. In a similar way

28 Workmen operating a mobile steam winch, mounted on a flat truck, used for moving the roof scaffold during the construction of St Pancras Station 1866–7. (National Railway Museum)

the obscure little towns of Wolverton in Buckinghamshire and Ashford in Kent were enlarged and revitalized by the establishment of railway workshops: in these instances by the London and Birmingham and the South-Eastern railways respectively. Other railway workshops sprang up at Stratford in East London and Gorton in Manchester. Numbers of other towns owed much of their growth to the arrival of railway communication, as did, for instance, Barrow-in-Furness, a former fishing village converted into an important steelmaking and shipbuilding centre after the Furness Railway brought in the coal needed for smelting the local haematite ores. Middlesbrough (steel), and Redhill (London commuters) are other examples.

The development of railways helped the great cities of the country to grow and draw their labour force from new suburbs and from dormitory areas even further afield. Nowhere was this function of railways more significant or more needed than in London. In the capital the railways supplemented existing means of getting to work, the private carriage, coach, horse-bus, river boat, and in due course electric tram and bicycle. More than this, the railways opened up completely new areas for residential building, a crossroads like Golders Green, a hamlet like Winchmore Hill, and by offering cheap fares induced people to go and live there while still working in the centre. On the eastern side of London the extension of branch lines to Walthamstow and Chingford in the early 1870s was followed by a building boom in these districts.

29 The construction of the roof of St Pancras Station, London, under way in 1867. Notice the massive scale of the supports for the girders, and the huge timber scaffold on which the roof was constructed. (National Railway Museum)

The Great Northern, similarly, brought suburban growth to the unspoiled area between Wood Green and Enfield. What 'used to be a very nice district indeed' – the area round Stamford Hill, Tottenham and Edmonton – 'occupied by good families, with houses of from £150 to £250 a year, with coach houses and stables, a garden and a few acres of land', was tranformed by speculative builders and workmen's trains, so that in consequence 'each good house was one after another pulled down, and the district is given up entirely . . . now to the working man'.

Middle-class inhabitants of the metropolis moved out to villas where they could enjoy country air and find room for tennis courts, croquet lawns and paddocks for ponies. Harrow became a popular middle-class residential district after the London and North-Western Company offered a free rail pass to anyone taking a house rented at not less than £50 a year, though the inducement was at first slow to work. The central underground lines extended long fingers into territory to the west and south-west of the metropolis. Richmond was reached by the District Railway in 1877, and Hounslow six years later; to the north-west the Metropolitan line probed beyond Swiss Cottage, Willesden and Harrow to touch Pinner in 1885 and Aylesbury seven years later. At this one of the last surviving mail coaches came to an end, running for the last time between the Old Bell Inn, Holborn and Wendover.

In the 1880s the four fastest growing places in all England and Wales were all London suburbs: Leyton, Willesden, Tottenham and West Ham; in the 1890s, too, eight London suburbs were among the fastest-growing places. The three decades after 1871 saw the resident population of the City fall by 48,000 – no less than 64 per cent – and that of Holborn by 34,000, Westminster by 65,000. Clerks, craftsmen and shop workers moved out to new homes in railway suburbs, encouraged by cheap workmen's fares. The same sort of process was advancing round other major cities. The opening of the line from Manchester to Chester in 1849 created a superior suburb of gardens and villas at Alderley fifteen miles from the city centre. Later lines had a powerful influence on such small places as Urmston, Flixton, Heaton Park, Cheadle Heath, Chorlton, Withington and Didsbury. Round Birmingham railway suburbs like Acock's Green and Olton followed on those developed nearer in by private carriages and omnibus, such as New Hall and Edgbaston, or the less select Small Heath, Sparkbrook, Aston and Ashstead.

In central London the stifling congestion and colossal traffic jams caused by the excess of horse-drawn traffic in narrow streets were somewhat eased as the railways extended their lines to new termini built closer to the commercial heart of the metropolis: Victoria, Charing Cross, Blackfriars and Cannon Street were all opened within a few years of 1860, Liverpool Street in 1875. Further help to commuters was given by underground railways: the first, the Metropolitan, was opened for business in 1863, running from Paddington to Farringdon Street. Four years later, when the line had been extended to Moorgate, some 15m. people over a six-month period braved the tunnel fumes – steam locomotives were used on the line – to take advantage of its fast route. The 'cut and cover' principle of construction, first digging a deep trench and then covering it over by cast iron girders or brick arches, was used for the next underground venture, the District Line, which opened its route along the recently established Victoria Embankment in the summer of 1871. The Inner Circle Line, linking together most of the main-line termini, was completed after long delays in 1884. Other underground lines crossed the Thames itself. The old Rotherhithe–Wapping tunnel – which after many years of enormous difficulties and a disastrous inundation by the Thames had been completed by the elder Brunel (Sir Marc) as long before as 1843 – was converted from foot-passenger use to railway use in 1869 and extended to Liverpool Street seven years later. Commuters arriving at Waterloo, and bound for the City could take the fast connecting line to the Bank, from 1890. By the early years of the new century the underground railways' function was changing: originally it had been to meet the needs of people travelling within the central area of the metropolis; now the new lines – the Piccadilly and Northern – were busy connecting new areas of dormitory suburbs. The inhabitants of the suburbs were not merely a commuter market: they used the lines to visit theatres and exhibitions, attend football and cricket matches, and to go shopping. The big London department stores began to assume their modern form in the 1860s when the Civil Service and the Army and Navy Stores appeared, to be followed by Harrods, Whiteleys and the rest.

The irruption of railways into the centre of cities was not all gain. For large numbers of poor people it was a disaster. When the companies decided to build their new great central termini, with their hotels, approaches, sidings, goods yards and warehouses, it was the poor who were displaced. Dozens of mean streets and thousands of little dwellings were pulled down so that the railway might come in. The displaced flocked into neighbouring areas where they added to the housing shortage and overcrowding, for these were the very poor, those who could not afford to go off to a suburb but had to live within a short walking distance of their work. The change in the face of the city was sweeping and abrupt, and caught the eye of Dickens, for one, who featured the transformation in his novel *Dombey and Son*. Great numbers – it is uncertain how many, but somewhere between 76,000 and 120,000 in London alone – were dispossessed, while similar upheavals occurred in other major cities. It is strange in this day and age to learn that the railway companies deliberately chose densely-packed working-class districts for the sites of their new stations; but they preferred them, especially when great numbers of little houses were owned by one landlord. This made it cheaper to redevelop, and simpler too, than if they had to tackle an area of factories and warehouses. This was the age of private property, and the property-less and unenfranchised poor could be disregarded. The railways were not alone in their callousness: the big urban road improvements and bridge building of the period had very similar effects.

* * * * * *

The railway age was studded with great achievements, symbolized most flamboyantly perhaps by the triumphal arch at Euston, the recumbent lions at Waterloo, the wrought iron and glass cathedral of Paddington – the last influenced by Paxton's Crystal Palace: 'no exterior', as its architect, Brunel, truly said, but 'all interior and all roofed in'. The vast sweep of lofty arches, now obscured by modern platform entrances and indicators, was intended to overawe the traveller who suddenly burst in upon it

30 Gothic splendour in the heyday of the railway age: the booking hall at St Pancras photographed about 1912. Half-past twelve on a Sunday, perhaps, since business seems slack. (National Railway Museum)

from the unhinting and very ordinary streets outside – was meant to impress upon him a sense of the significance, the magnificence, of railway enterprise.

There were, too, great personalities: the big entrepreneurs, like George Hudson, the 'Railway King', who attempted to build up a vast empire of railway companies, and Edward Watkin, a magnate second only in importance to Hudson. There were the big contractors, Peto and Brassey – Brassey who at length graduated from navvies' camps to install himself in a noble if antiquated residence, Lord Westmorland's Apthorpe. Then there were the great engineers, men of vision, enterprise, ingenuity and endurance: Trevithick; the Stephensons; Joseph Locke, the unlucky Vignoles, Daniel Gooch, the locomotive designer, and the great Isambard Kingdom Brunel, whose genius comprehended not only the broad-gauge Great Western Railway with its amazing Saltash Bridge over the Tamar, but also those enormous steamships, ships before their time, *Great Western*, *Great Britain*, *Great Eastern*. These men were the Victorian 'captains of industry', the entrepreneurial and technological giants of the age, whose monuments changed the very face of the country, changed the nature of the contemporary civilization, and have endured to the present.

Chapter Four

Workshop of the World

Britain's Industrial Revolution or economic 'take-off' (in the terminology of W. W. Rostow), was followed in the middle and later nineteenth century by a new phase of development, one which Rostow called the 'drive to maturity'. This was a refinement and broadening of previous technical changes, centred round steam power and textiles, together with new advances in railways, shipbuilding, steel and chemicals. This new phase brought about a great 'surge of production', an economic expansion, which Professor R. S. Sayers has suggested was at least as impressive as the more famous industrial revolution itself.

With their early lead in the production of textiles, coal and iron, and with the use of steam power by land and by sea, Britain's works and factories were enabled to pour out a mounting flood of cheap and useful commodities to meet the needs of people all over the world. Other countries, too, were expanding their populations, their markets and their production; railways opened up the untouched interior of the three new continents, and steamships broke down the distance barrier posed by the oceans. A latent demand for cheap textiles and hardware, for steam engines, locomotives and the rails to run them on, for ships and the coal to fuel them, was there for British merchants and industrialists to arouse, and supply. For a period the Indian's dhoti, the Arab's robe and the African's loin-cloth came from mills in prosaic Blackburn; the rails to be laid among the buffaloes of the Great Plains or across the scorching plains of India and Australia came from ironworks set among the green hills of Staffordshire, Durham, the West Riding and South Wales. When ships came to be built partly or entirely of iron, and later steel, an amazing proportion of the world's tonnage – nearly 82 per cent at the peak – was launched in British shipyards. Supremacy in shipbuilding went on into the opening years of the new century, and in 1907 nearly a third of the more than a million tons of vessels built in Britain was to the order of overseas customers; in 1913 the total of new and old ships sold abroad amounted to more than 700,000 tons.

In its industrial heyday Britain was truly the workshop of the world. British goods were to be found on all five continents, even in the newly penetrated markets of China and Japan. British entrepreneurs, merchants, contractors, agents and sea-captains were active everywhere. Cecil Rhodes established in southern Africa the great diamond business of De Beers; George Taubman Goldie created a commercial empire in the jungles of the Niger; W. D. Pearson, later Lord Cowdray, was 'indisputably the largest contractor in the world', responsible more than anyone for providing Mexico with public utilities, and also building tunnels under the River Hudson. The total value of our export trade rose from some £50m. a year about 1840 to £1,750m. about 1910. (The figures, despite fluctuations in prices, are roughly comparable.) The employment and living standards of Britain's people became extraordinarily dependent on the export trade. About 1880 it could be said that roughly one in every five of the working population made goods for export, and the livelihood of this large number rested on the success of British manufacturers and merchants in selling their products in some near or remote part of the globe.

In fact, the markets of Europe remained the most important outlet for British trade, though their relative significance fell slightly over the seventy years between 1840 and 1910. Asia, including Britain's Indian empire was, surprisingly perhaps, next in importance, taking in 1910 a fifth of British exports. Roughly equal, at about half the level of the Asia trade, were the West Indies, the United States, and Central and South America; though the United States market was declining relatively, falling to only some 7 per cent of the total British trade in 1910, while the newer markets of Africa had assumed a comparable position. The growth of our markets in Asia was mainly the achievement of Lancashire. Cheap calicoes, and better quality cottons, had come to supersede the 'unapproachable beauty' of the Dacca muslins, and were expelling from the market the traditional shawls of Kashmir. When in 1834 the East India Company's monopoly of the China trade was overthrown, further outlets were found for Manchester's merchants, while China tea made an acceptable return cargo for the British vessels that sailed into exotic Foochow.

Throughout the period cotton maintained pride of place as Britain's leading export, though gradually its share of British trade fell from a little under a half to less than a quarter. In 1913 coal and iron and steel were of almost equal value – each accounting for about a tenth of exports – followed by machinery and chemicals. Exports of coal had grown considerably over the preceding decades, but otherwise the composition of British export trade was indeed slow in changing, reflecting both the structure of British industry and the nature of much of world demand. As new parts of the world were opened up one after another by railways and steamships the same demand for cheap cloth, for hardware and steel, for machinery and fuel was repeated. Some changes were in train, however. In the process of economic development one of the first and easiest industries to establish was cotton. Increasingly the mills of Lancashire had to seek new outlets as old ones diminished because of rival local production. India, the first great market where the old hand technology collapsed before the onslaught of steam-powered machinery, herself became a large factory processor of cotton. In 1885 the mills of Bombay and the other Indian manufacturing centres consumed 585,000 bales of raw cotton – a figure nearly seven times as great as that of fifteen years previously and already approaching a fifth of the consumption of British mills. In iron and steel, similarly, powerful competition arose from the United States and Germany. This was an industry in which the economies of scale were of great significance. The export trade enabled British steelworks to produce and sell far more than could ever have been disposed of on the home market, but nevertheless the big American furnaces each produced eight times the amount of the average British one, and the American market consumed five times as much steel as could be sold at home in Britain; even the home market of Germany, a newly-industrialized country, was half as great again as that of Britain.

Fortunately, world trade continued to grow substantially, and by finding new expanding markets to replace old declining ones, British industry was still able to expand its export trade in the era of rising competition which sprang from the increasing industrial activity of the United States, Germany, Belgium and France. As competition and tariff protection made the European and American markets more difficult for British products, so improved or new outlets were established in South America, Africa, Canada, Australia, India and the Far East. But the ease with which British producers were able to continue selling their traditional goods abroad encouraged a degree of complacency and reinforced financial and technical reasons for not departing too radically or too quickly from existing products and the existing methods of making them. In Lancashire, especially, the long-held predominance of cotton in Britain's export trade gave rise to a sense of unreality, an unwillingness to look at unpalatable facts. Talk of foreign competition, exclaimed a Lancashire manufacturer when taxed with the growth of spindles in Japan and the decline in the British trade there, was 'just twaddle':

> In the first place, we've got the only climate in the world where cotton piece goods in any quantity can ever be produced. In the second place, no foreign Johnnies can ever be bred that can

spin and weave like Lancashire lasses and lads. In the third place, there are more spindles in Oldham than in all the rest of the world put together. And last of all, if they had the climate and the men and the spindles – which they never can have – foreigners could never find the brains Lancashire cotton men have for the job. We've been making all the world's cotton cloth that matters for more years than I can tell, and we always shall.

While the export trade continued to expand Britain was also becoming a large-scale importer of other people's goods. It was only to be expected that Britain would have to import many of the raw materials for its industry to process, like raw cotton, wool and undressed hides, timber, rubber, and various oils, gums and resins. Nor was it remarkable that the nation should import, as it had long done, the food products of the Mediterranean and the tropics – tea, coffee, sugar, wine, nuts, fruit and also tobacco. But it was also taking in large, and increasing quantities of foodstuffs that it was well capable of producing itself, if not so cheaply – grain and flour, beef and mutton, butter and margarine, bacon and cheese, apples, pears and vegetables – to the detriment of the British farmer. More significant still, Britain was importing many industrial commodities which it did not produce in sufficient quantities, or at a competitive price, or did not produce at all: such basic and vital goods as some special types of steel, various non-ferrous metals, electrical equipment, scientific instruments, dyestuffs and fine chemicals. And beside these were many of the ordinary goods to be found in the British home, including the children's toys, the newsprint for the morning paper, and even the materials of the uniforms worn by the servants. All these were made in Germany:

Roam the house over, and the fateful mark will greet you at every turn, from the piano in your drawing-room to the mug on your kitchen dresser, blazoned though it be with the legend, *A Present from Margate*. Descend to your domestic depths, and you shall find your very drainpipes German made. You pick out of the grate the paper wrappings from a book consignment, and they also are 'Made in Germany'. You stuff them into the fire, and reflect that the poker in your hand was forged in Germany. As you rise from your hearthrug you knock over an ornament on your mantelpiece; picking up the pieces you read, on the bit that formed the base, 'Manufactured in Germany'. And you jot your dismal reflections down with a pencil that was made in Germany. At midnight your wife comes home from an opera that was made in Germany, has been here enacted by singers and conductor and players made in Germany, with the aid of instruments and sheets of music made in Germany. You go to bed, and glare wrathfully at a text on the wall; it is illuminated with an English village church, and it was 'Printed in Germany'.

Britain did not lack inventiveness, witness the commanding figures of Bessemer, Brunel, Thomas and Gilchrist, Parsons, Swan and Whitworth, to mention but a few. There were still enterprising industrialists and commercial men of vision: Armstrong, Boot, Cunard, Lever, Lipton, Player and Wills. It has been argued that British entrepreneurship was effete, in decline, as politely educated, cautious and circumspect gentlemen replaced the thrusting, horny-handed and indefatigable adventurers of the past. There was certainly some conservatism and complacency. Old methods of working were retained because the equipment was still sound, and because management and men were accustomed to them. Many firms were family owned, where the main objectives were to keep the business happily ticking over and minimize risks, rather than take in new capital, branch out and attempt to maximize profits. Managers worked their way up through the shop floor; few were men of imagination or had any scientific or specialized training. Huge capital was locked up in obsolete plant, the pioneering spirit had flagged; and British labour was ill-educated, hostile to new ideas and low in productivity, and was already substantially unionized. Thus, although Britain claimed to be the workshop of the world, many of the industries of the future were developing elsewhere, especially in the United States and in Germany. Britain lagged behind in the new technology and production of electricity, oil, fine chemicals and motor vehicles. Partly, it is true, this was because the nation already had cheap coal and gas, and a comprehensive system of railways and urban transport; and partly because it could readily import what it had not. Partly it was because of a tradition of making things well, on a small scale, built to last: so Britain came late into the age of mass production. It was, for example, producing well-engineered, expensive cars by the handful, and neglected the potential mass market which Henry Ford exploited by his assembly-line methods in Detroit. On the eve of World War I Britain might still consider itself the workshop of the world, though increasingly it was the workshop of only the newly developing parts of the world, and one that was relying increasingly on old-fashioned goods produced in old-fashioned ways.

A number of contemporaries were acutely aware of the growing technological gap and, like Lyon Playfair, stumped the country to warn of the danger. A lot of emphasis was placed on defects in the British system of education. The excellence of Germany's technical institutes and schools was compared with the British emphasis on the classical training. Little attention was paid at Oxford and Cambridge to science, and provincial universities and technical colleges were late in developing in the United Kingdom, while the curricula of the public schools reflected the traditions of the two old universities. Many working children had little education beyond what passed for teaching in primitive dame-schools, overcrowded voluntary establishments, and Sunday schools. Primary education was not even made universal until after 1870, and for long after that few children had any full-time schooling beyond the age of eleven. It was the weakness of primary education that had limited the role of the once-flourishing Mechanics' Institutes, and this weakness continued to undermine the potential of technical colleges and adult evening classes long after they first appeared on the scene.

But the failings of Britain's educational structure were

only one element in the country's modest industrial performance. Some other factors have been mentioned above, and it is impossible to be sure which were the most significant. Some historians have argued that Britain was paying the price for its early start in the process of industrialization, that it lumbered the nation with a legacy of inconvenient buildings, outdated plant and congested sites, and influenced its receptiveness to new ideas and the ability to utilize them; while newer industrial powers like the United States and Germany could make their start with the best and most up-to-date technology and rapidly establish a competitive lead. Others have pointed to the limited size and conservative nature of the British market, the fragmentation of demand consequential on the class structure, and the country's relatively slow rate of economic growth. Others still have emphasised the flow abroad of British capital, attracted away by higher rates of return, leaving British enterprise short of the resources needed for expansion and the initiation of new industries.

None of these explanations is wholly convincing, though each may contain an element of the truth. Certain it is, however, that by the late nineteenth century Britain's early industrial lead had disappeared, and that new techniques were being adopted more slowly here than elsewhere – with eventual adverse consequences for employment and living standards in the decades after 1920.

Before 1914 the ability of the country to import freely its raw materials, foodstuffs and manufactures and at the same time improve its living standards owed much to the strength of our export trade. The earnings of exports, however, were not wholly sufficient. Throughout the nineteenth century there existed a gap between the income brought in by British exports and the country's spending abroad for imports: the balance of trade, as it is said, was adverse or negative. Fortunately, this income-expenditure gap was more than amply plugged by earnings abroad from services, the so-called 'invisible' earnings. For a time the principal source of such earnings came from shipping

– the carrying of other people's goods in British vessels. In 1865–74 the net invisible earnings of British shipping exceeded £46m. a year, and by 1900–8 the figure was up to £75.7m. The next largest source of invisible earnings at the earlier date consisted of the interest and profits on British capital invested abroad: in 1865–74 they amounted to £37m. However, over the years these earnings of capital overseas rose much more rapidly than did the foreign earnings of British shipping, and in the years 1900–8 had far surpassed the latter at nearly £122m.

Together with other sources of invisible income, mainly the profits of the external financial services of the City of London and British insurance companies, total invisible earnings more than doubled between 1865–74 and 1900–8. Standing at the latter date at almost £242m., the 'invisibles' comfortably covered the deficit on the balance of trade and produced an overall surplus in the balance of payments, thus allowing additions to the growing fund of capital invested abroad and strengthening the international status of sterling, at that time the world's leading trading currency. It was the strength of Britain's balance of payments – the consequence of the nation's predominance as a supplier of capital, shipping and financial services – which made it possible for Britain to finance its role of chief international lender, while maintaining a policy of free trade and buying year after year more goods from overseas than it sold there – a remarkable combination of circumstances. With free trade Britain was able to take advantage of new sources of food and raw materials, to benefit from other countries' growing productivity, with beneficial effects on the living standards of the nation. This happy situation was not to last very long into the twentieth century – World War I and its aftermath saw to that – but while it did British employment and consumption rose with the growth of the world economy. What followed after 1920 is another story.

* * * * * *

31 Shipbuilding and repairing were industries in which Britain led the world before 1914, creating major sources of employment on the Tyne, Tees, Clyde and elsewhere. Here the SS *Cherbourg* is seen in Langton graving dock at Liverpool, a photograph taken in April 1895. (National Maritime Museum)

In terms of its share of the world market Britain's most successful industry before 1914 was shipbuilding. A major reason for this was the lead achieved in developing the technology of ships, particularly of steamships. The basic advances were the changes in the material for the hull, from wood to iron, and later to steel; and in propulsion, from sail, to sail assisted by steam, to steamship proper. In the 1840s all but 10 per cent of the world's merchant shipping was built of wood, and given the cheapness of

American timber and the enormous size of the American and Canadian seaboard, lake and river traffic, British yards could not hope to compete with their American rivals.

A series of changes were soon to alter this situation. The first stage in the revolution in shipbuilding was the use of iron for the hull, a change which long pre-dated the widespread use of steam for propulsion. Iron barges could be seen on some canals at the beginning of the nineteenth century, following the first experiment in 1787 with a 70 ft. barge made of bolted cast-iron plates by John – 'iron-mad' – Wilkinson, the great pioneer ironmaster. Then came some experiments with steam power, and the first iron steamship to cross the Channel was assembled from the pre-fabricated parts made in a Staffordshire ironworks. Iron held some obvious advantages over wood, in its ability to survive accidental collisions and groundings, and especially in the rigidity which enabled much larger vessels to be built than the 300 ft. or so which was the maximum length for a wooden ship. Transverse frames constructed of single bars of iron provided great strength and formed the skeleton to which the iron plates were fastened, at first in clinker fashion, and then end-on, held in place by rivets. It was near the end of the century before the millions of rivets which went into the making of a large ship were driven in mechanically by hydraulic riveters. Before this they were all hammered in by hand: one man took the rivet from the boy who had just heated it in a portable hearth, forced it through its hole, and held it in place while two riveters flattened its point with alternative blows.

The first designer to see the possibilities for building much larger ships in iron was Isambard Kingdom Brunel, the great railway and bridge engineer. He produced the plans for three famed iron steamships, the *Great Western* and *Great Britain* intended for the transatlantic service, and the *Great Eastern*, launched in 1858 for the Australian run. The *Great Eastern*, in particular, was an incredible monster by the standards of the day, nearly 700 ft. long, over 80

32 Small vessels, both screw and paddle-steamers, were widely used for coastal journeys and for the summer holiday excursions to seaside resorts. The coastal trade, indeed, and the short ferry routes across the Channel, the North Sea and Irish Sea, were the first to use ships propelled solely by steam. Here the paddle steamer *Waverley* is seen taking on passengers at Burnham-on-Crouch, Essex on 26th June 1898. (National Maritime Museum)

ft. broad, with a gross tonnage approaching 19,000. The problems of merely launching a vessel of this size were huge and unexpected, requiring as many as eighteen hydraulic presses, many weeks of experiments and frustration, and a fatal accident before she was finally floated off sideways into the Thames at the fourth attempt. To get an idea of what such dimensions meant in contemporary terms they must be compared with those of the four wooden paddle steamers which the new Cunard Line used to launch its transatlantic mail service in 1840: these vessels had a length of only 207 ft., a breadth of 34 ft. and a gross tonnage of 1,154.

Brunel's ships, however, were not successes in a commercial sense. It is true that the *Great Western*, completed in 1838, made sixty-seven crossings of the Atlantic in eight years and was the first wearer of the Atlantic Blue Riband for the fastest crossing; but she never made her owners much money. The *Great Britain*, a larger and improved design, survived running aground on the coast of County Down to be used on the Australian route. She was, however, originally intended for the Atlantic, and so had to be refuelled at the Cape of Good Hope with coal specially brought out from Penarth; and it was, indeed, the problem of designing a ship big enough to carry enough coal to get to Australia and back that led Brunel on to his enormous *Great Eastern*.

The *Great Britain*, meanwhile, ended her chequered career as a hulk in the Falklands, where in the years between 1886 and 1937 she was used as a store ship in Stanley harbour, after which she was beached, a rusting hulk, at Sparrow Cove. There she remained forgotten for thirty years until in 1967 a letter to *The Times* led to the formation of a committee to raise funds for her rescue and restoration. It was a daunting project, not merely because of the distance of the Falklands but also because of doubts about the strength of the old ship's hull (which had an alarming crack and several holes) and the feasibility of floating her off and getting her back to Britain in one piece. However it was done: she was towed home in a floating dock and on 19 July, 1970, 127 years to the day that Prince Albert had launched her, she was returned to the same Bristol dock, and with HRH Prince Philip aboard. There she rests, a unique monument to the genius of her designer and to the new age of the screw-driven ocean-going steamship which she inaugurated.

The *Great Eastern* never fulfilled the hope that she could make the Australian run without refuelling, and she, too, could not be made to pay. She ruined her builder, Scott Russell of Millwall, and had to be sold in the year of her launching for little more than the launching itself had cost. The patriotic investors who subscribed the funds for her completion never recovered their money, but after eight unprofitable years and a number of accidents her enormous holds proved to be just what was required for laying cables across the Atlantic and in the East. Then she was tried and failed again as a passenger ship – her beam was too broad for the newly-opened Suez Canal – and she suffered the ultimate ignominy of being moored in the Mersey for use as a floating concert hall and gymnasium, complete with daring young men on the flying trapeze. *Great Eastern* was broken up in 1888, and such was her reputation for ill-luck that it was rumoured that the skeletons of a riveter and his boy had been discovered, sealed for thirty years in her double hull. This, however, proved only a rumour and has never been substantiated: the ship's career was sufficiently unfortunate without this embellishment.

The *Great Eastern* failed in her primary purpose because of the vast quantity of coal required to drive her combined paddle- and screw-engines – developing an enormous 6,600 hp – at her designed speed of 14 knots. Brunel was ahead of his time. The true way forward lay with more modest vessels, such as the iron screw steamer *City of Glasgow*, of 1,600 tons, launched in 1850, the prototype of many later steamships. Her disappearance at sea with the loss of nearly five hundred souls four years later did not prevent the production of a succession of similar, if somewhat larger, vessels for the Inman line: *City of Manchester* and other *Cities*, with clipper bows and bowsprit, and square-rigged fore and main masts.

The major problem remained that of propulsion: how to design a steamship that could carry a huge dead weight of engines, shafts and paddles or screws, together with vast bunkers of coal, and still prove a commercial proposition. It took forty years of experiment to achieve the first successful screw steamer, the little *Archimedes*, only 237 tons, in 1838. And it took another generation for the screw to óust the paddle-steamer from ocean routes, and much longer from short-distance ferries, river and pleasure boats. Twin screws came in with the Inman line's *City of New York* in 1888. Compound engines, in which steam was kept at different pressures in two or more cylinders, made little progress while boilers were built to withstand pressures of only about 20 or 25 lbs. per square inch. However, improved boilers were designed to withstand 45 or 65 lbs., and then followed the triple-expansion engine working at a steam pressure of 150 lbs. By 1900 quadruple expansion and pressures of 200 lbs. or more were deemed essential. These more powerful and more efficient engines eventually made possible a drastic fall in the consumption of fuel. Gone were the days when even the compound engines in big ships required vast bunker stocks: the Cunarders *Etruria* and *Umbria* of 1885 each consumed over 300 tons of coal a day and needed as many as 112 firemen and trimmers to keep the boilers fed. Gradually steamships got larger and were increasingly built of steel. The steel-built Cunarder *Servia*, with compound engines and incandescent electric lamps, was the wonder ship of the early 1880s.

The changes were slow: less than a twentieth of the total tonnage of the British merchant fleet of 1850 had steam power, and an even smaller proportion was iron built. Sailing ships continued to grow in number, and indeed reached their maximum total tonnage of 5m. as late as 1865, manned by 158,000 seamen. It was not until 1882 that, as Sir John Clapham remarks, 'the mounting curve of the steamer tonnage crossed the descending curve of the sailing ships'. The substitution of steel for iron in hulls and boilers was held back by the higher cost of the steel, but was virtually complete by 1895 when electric drilling and riveting were beginning to come into general use.

Iron, later steel, screw-driven ships dominated because of their evident advantages. They were stronger, more durable, more watertight, more consistent in speed, and they could be built to almost any size, an important consideration in the long-distance carriage of bulky cargoes like grain, coal and ores, and in the accommodation of the rising flood of European emigrants looking to reach the Americas, Australia or New Zealand. The more emigrants that could be carried the lower the fares that could be offered and the greater the market, and soon it was shown that for Atlantic shipping the screw-driven iron steamship could compete successfully against paddle steamships, even when operating without the financial prop of a mail subsidy.

Ships became more diversified: there were luxurious passenger ships, with palatial saloons, luxurious cabins and groaning dining tables; there were combined cargo and passenger ships on less-travelled routes, tankers, and refrigerated vessels for carrying the new cargoes of frozen meat or holds with controlled temperatures for a delicate cargo like bananas. The sailing ships, fighting a long rear-guard action, were increasingly confined to the less profitable trades and the more remote parts of the world where coaling stations were few and far between. Down to the 1880s, it is true, most passenger ships continued to be fitted with auxiliary sails, though their usefulness was passing. Increasingly sails were carried merely to keep the ship's head to the wind in case of engine failure – a not infrequent event in the early steamships. Even the newer and larger sailing ships were almost always built of iron – cheaper, stronger and less prone to fire, and giving much greater cargo capacity.

* * * * * *

The finest days of the sailing ship appeared just as the steamship era was in its infancy. The opening of the India and China trades following the cessation of the East India Company's monopoly, the physical expansion of Britain's

Indian empire, the sudden upsurge of emigration to Australia and the growth of the wool trade from the Antipodes all served to encourage enterprise on routes which steamships could not yet invade. Bombay became the telegraphic terminus of the European cable, Calcutta grew into a vast entrepôt linking Europe with China via Stamford Raffles's new port of Singapore. In China itself the Opium War of 1841 formed the prelude to the opening of treaty ports to Western commerce: Shanghai, Amoy, Foochow and Ningpo. Some of the finest of the fast clipper ships developed to trade with the newly-opened East and Australia were American built. Liverpool owners put their orders to shipyards in distant Massachusetts, and it was the all-wood *Donald McKay*, launched at Boston in 1855, which created the remarkable record of six consecutive voyages made from Liverpool to Melbourne in an average 83 days.

But from the later 1830s there was a revival in British designed and built sailing ships, a revival soon to be pushed on by the use of cheap iron in the hulls, giving British yards a competitive advantage. Before this development came the famous wooden Blackwall frigates, launched from 'Dicky' Green's Blackwall yard, led by the *Seringapatam* of 1837. They were not really clippers but smaller and much improved East Indiamen, ranging upwards from less than a thousand tons, and intended for first-class passenger and cargo traffic. The first British clippers, fast, sleek, pedigree sailing vessels, came from Hall's yard in Aberdeen; among them were the tea clippers for the China trade, *Stornoway* and *Chrysolite* of 1851. Many of the most famous British clippers were of composite construction – wooden planks on an iron frame. Experience taught that an iron-framed ship could be driven harder than one all of wood, and that a copper-sheathed wooden hull fouled less quickly than iron plates, an important factor when smoothness of movement through the water might determine which vessel should dock first with the new season's tea. The celebrated *Cutty Sark*, completed in 1859 of composite construction, and now preserved in a dry dock at Greenwich, is the sole surviving memorial to the great age of the fast sailing ship.

The Chinese tea, opium and silk trades were first exploited by American clippers, loading at Canton and racing back home to New York or Boston. The zenith of British tea-clipper racing was in the years between 1859 and 1872: in 1859 eleven ships sailed from the China ports, the first leaving Foochow on 10 June and arriving in London on 24 October, and the fastest passage one of 102 days. The most famous of the tea races, that of 1866, was the subject of many paintings, notably those by J. M. Spurling. Amazingly, three of the ships, *Ariel, Taeping* and *Serica,* arrived in the Thames on the same tide after a voyage of 99 days, while two other ships, *Fiery Cross* and *Taitsing,* arrived within another two days. These were vessels of some 700–900 tons, having a length of a little under 200 ft. and a breadth of some 31–34 ft., and their cargo of tea varied from a little under to something over 1m. lbs.

It was the *Cutty Sark,* a slightly larger vessel, that held the record for the best day's run, 363 knots – more than 15 knots per hour – achieved more than once in her career. For many years after steamships had taken over the China route she was in Portuguese hands, renamed *Ferreira,* engaged on a regular run between Lisbon, Rio and New Orleans. As late as 1890 after her spars and sail area had been cut down she was still extremely fast, once covering 3,737 miles in 13 consecutive days, an average of over 287 miles a day. Her most famous rival was *Thermopylae,* and in the great race between the two held in 1872 *Cutty Sark* had the misfortune of losing her rudder and having to spend some days in fitting a new sternpost and jury rudder – yet she still arrived home only six days after her opponent. In 1922 *Cutty Sark* was bought from her Portuguese owners by Captain Dowman, a retired windjammer skipper, who restored and re-rigged her; and in 1938, after his death, his widow presented the famous old ship to the Thames Nautical Training College.

The age of ocean racing between the beautiful clippers with their huge spread of canvas came in when steamships, gradually growing in size from their original few hundred tons, began to offer regular scheduled sailings, first across the Atlantic and then, after the opening of the Suez Canal, to India, Australia and the East. With the

33 The celebrated clipper ship, *Cutty Sark*, seen crossing the line in 1893. In her heyday she held the record for the best day's run: 363 knots, an average of over 15 knots an hour. She was in continuous use, first in the China tea trade, and then on the Lisbon, Rio and New Orleans run, for over fifty years. (National Maritime Museum)

shorter route created by the canal (obviating the overland journey by the Nile and the desert from Alexandria to Suez), and with the larger and faster ships, the vessels of the P. & O. line were making the journey from Bombay in 16½ days and from Melbourne in 35 days by 1887. One attraction of this line was that all the beer, wines and spirits served on board were free of charge, and such bounty no doubt helped to wash down the very substantial fare of the dining table. A typical menu offered seventeen choices of main course, which included roast turkey, suckling pig, mutton, beef, geese, ducks, sheep's head, pig's feet and curry. First-class passengers of 1850 were allowed 4 cwt. of personal baggage, a limit often exceeded. In early steamships the heat of the engine-room was so much in evidence in the passenger quarters that an Indian-style punkah, complete with punkah-wallah, were provided to create a welcome draught. With a following wind the smuts and cinders from the funnels floated over the decks and through the ports, and the ship so heated up that occasionally the captain would turn her about to get a good cooling breeze flowing through the vessel for a few minutes. On the outward passage the cabins on the port side got the early morning sun but had the whole day to cool off, while on the homeward voyage it was these cabins that got the worst roasting from the sun. This led to favoured passengers asking for 'P.O.S.H.' – port outward, starboard homeward – a suggested origin of the term 'posh'.

The superior carrying capacity of steamships, their greater speed as against the general run of sailing ships, their superior reliability for length of passage, and eventually their lower freight rates proved, in the long run, the key factors in the demise of the sailing ship. For example, the steamships employed by the Blue Funnel Line in the China tea trade in the later 1860s could carry three times the cargo of a clipper and lop a couple of weeks off the homeward passage, so arriving first with the tea which could be sold at a premium. The P. & O. Line, similarly, early opened up a fast mail route to Bombay, and then extended the service to Galle on the southernmost tip of Ceylon (Sri Lanka), and so on to Penang, Singapore and Hong Kong, putting London in contact with Hong Kong in only 54 days compared with the previous 89 days. The later expansion of Western commercial interests in the East, with a growing trade with Japan, cargoes of rice from Siam and rubber from the new plantations in Malaya, meant increasing cargoes for more and more steamships.

The shipping entering and clearing ports of the UK expanded enormously over the decades after 1830. In 1834 the tonnage (excluding the coasting trade and that with Ireland) totalled 6.3m.; by 1860 it was 24.7m., and by 1890 74.3m. – an almost twelve-fold increase in under sixty years. By the last date over 70 per cent of the tonnage was that of British ships. Railways to feed the ports multiplied in Europe and the Americas – and even in the East, with 9,000 miles of track in India by 1880, and 17,000 miles in the rest of Asia ten years later. Over the world as a whole the 1840 total of less than 500 miles had mushroomed to 386,000 miles in 1890 (though much of it was in the United States). The Suez Canal, narrow as it was, saw 2.25m. tons of shipping pass through it in 1879–80, ten years after its opening, more than 75 per cent of it British. The shorter route to the East and to Australia made possible by the canal did much more for British shipowners than it did for the French engineers and investors who had originally conceived it, built it, and financed it.

In Britain new ports sprang up to meet the needs of more and larger ships. Cardiff, where one saw 'nothing but coal, coal dust or coal-blackened faces', ousted Newcastle as the world's greatest coal exporter, supplemented by nearby Penarth and, in due course, the new docks of Barry. Southampton, an important medieval port gone sadly to seed, was revitalized by direct railway links with London, and in 1842 both the Royal Mail and the P. & O. Lines made it their headquarters. Lack of good railway connections, or more fatally, the existence of railway competition, meant the end of many of the small ports which dotted the coastline. On the eastern side Whitby, Boston, King's Lynn and Southwold declined into somnolence, while in the south the sea had retreated from Rye in Sussex and sizeable vessels could no longer use its wharves; Minehead and other Somerset ports decayed sadly, as did Carmarthen, Aberystwyth, Lancaster, Ayr and Troon. At the growing ports there was much activity: harbours were dredged and extended, new docks were constructed, and warehouses, cold stores and railway sidings proliferated. The Port of London was equipped with many new docks – the Victoria, the Commercial Docks in Rotherhithe, the Millwall Docks in the Isle of Dogs, the Albert Dock, and last, the Tilbury Docks down river, dug out of the Essex marshes and opened in 1886. Liverpool, too, opened nearly 250 acres of new docks and constructed a vast sea-wall, and the Manchester Ship Canal took sea-going vessels right into Cottonopolis itself. Stone was the usual material for harbour works. The new structural material, concrete, came only slowly into use in Britain after extensive tests abroad, though the breakwater to protect the modern harbour works at Newhaven was built of nothing else.

Ships became bigger, faster, stronger, less prone to fire, less at risk from collisions and groundings. Lighthouses were modernized and rebuilt, like the new Eddystone which came into use in 1882. But there were still many lives lost at sea, despite the voluntarily provided lifeboats; in 1854 this resulted in the establishment of the Royal National Lifeboat Institution. In the nine years after 1878 nearly 6,000 souls were plucked from disaster by lifeboats, over 6,000 by rocket apparatus, and nearly 100,000 by the boats of wrecked ships and rescue vessels. There were numerous sea mysteries and disasters, almost all of them now forgotten. There was, for instance, the American clipper, *Bald Eagle,* employed in shipping Chinese coolies to Callao. The desperate Chinese rioted, were confined and shot down in the holds, to which they then set fire, and were at length burned to death as the fire rose, got out of control and engulfed the ship. And there was the notoriously unlucky tea-clipper, *Black Adder*, incompetently built and at first incompetently captained; she lost all her masts on her maiden voyage, survived a collision in the China Sea, struck an uncharted reef, and was finally lost at last at Bahia.

The first steam liner to be lost on the Atlantic run was the *President*, a paddle steamer of 2,350 tons, reputedly top-heavy and under-engined, which disappeared in a gale in March 1841. Then there was the Blue Anchor Line's big new steamship *Waratah*, which disappeared without a single trace – despite much searching – en route from Durban to Capetown in 1909, with the loss of 92 passengers and 119 crew. The disaster was never satisfactorily explained, as many other ships survived the severe weather of the time; but some former passengers had complained of her permanent list, once so pronounced that the water would not run out of the bathtubs, and of her violent jerking roll; and there was one nervous passenger who was so shaken by the list and roll on the passage from Australia, and by alarming visions that came to him, that he left the ship at Durban, wisely as it turned out. And there was, of course, the notorious *Titanic*, the 'unsinkable' liner driven at speed through a sea infested by icebergs to be lost on her maiden voyage, with its boats getting away half-empty and only 178 third-class passengers saved out of 706. There was a fatal flaw in *Titanic*'s design: she could stay afloat with four compartments flooded, but the fifth bulkhead only went up to 'E' deck, allowing the water to spill over. The ships of 1912 – which was when *Titanic* had 300 ft. of her side ripped open by a monster iceberg – were far bigger and far safer than the sailing vessels and little paddle steamers that had braved the Atlantic in the 1840s, but the designers of great new unsinkable steamships could not allow for human error, and the sea was still the sea.

* * * * * *

One factor encouraging the increased size and efficiency of steamships in the later Victorian era was the rise in emigrant traffic. Farmers, artisans, domestic servants, labourers and others had gone overseas to find a new life in previous centuries, but the numbers rose sharply in the mid-nineteenth century as the interior of America and new countries like Australia and New Zealand were opened up and their resources were publicized. The swelling of the populations of western Europe was making it less easy to find land and obtain work, and put pressure on already low wage levels. In some countries, though apparently not in Britain, political and religious factors played a major part and influenced the belief in a freer, more harmonious and rewarding life overseas. The ideas of Thomas Malthus concerning the inevitable growth of numbers also had some role: in Britain there was a widespread belief that the country was already overpopulated and that wages and living standards could not be improved unless there was a reduction in numbers; while in Ireland the great famine of the 1840s seemed to prove the cogency of Malthus's argument. Both private and government moneys were made available to pay the passage of poor emigrant families, and working people themselves established clubs and emigrant societies to raise funds for themselves. There were guidebooks and notices published in the newspapers concerning the fertile lands and good wages available in the new countries, and the facilities offered by ships and railways for getting there. There were even specialist periodicals, such as *Sidney's Emigrant's Journal*, which contained shipping notices, gave information on conditions abroad, reported the experiences and advice of previous emigrants, and gave answers to questions posed by would-be emigrants. Thus, 'female emigrants' were advised in 1849 that:

> for respectable domestic servants, for dairy-maids and girls accustomed to farm-work, the demand in Australia is almost unlimited. Young women capable of teaching reading, writing, and arithmetic, plain sewing & c., and willing to take

situations as nursery-maids may place themselves very comfortably and marry well . . .

In the colonies, a wife, although her husband may have ten thousand a year, must be ready, if she wants peace and comfort, to lead the way in all the domestic operations, great and small.' For servants are both ignorant and independent. Therefore, ladies thinking of Australia or the western states of America, and the bounteous crops of husbands there, must understand that, although a knack at writing verses has a charm in the honeymoon, and a piano in the bush is a very agreeable resource (and there are pianos in the bush), still, the salt of happy colonial life lies in the mystics of the pie and pudding, the roast and boiled; in the whole art of washing and ironing, in the secret of training a raw country girl into a light handy servant, of pulling down insolence and encouraging good humour.

In the early emigrant vessels the steerage quarters between decks were not only overcrowded and insanitary but also lacking in ventilation. As one shipowner of the time noted, the hatches, which were the only means of admitting fresh air, had to be closed in bad weather, though some ships had begun to be fitted with 'iron tubes' or ventilators, two forward to draw in fresh air, and two aft to discharge foul air. In 1855 and again in 1863 Parliament passed legislation to improve conditions for steerage passengers, and the new regulations provide a good indication of how bad things had been previously. No berth could be shared, it was ordered, except by married couples or women with children, and all unmarried males above the age of twelve were to be accommodated in the fore part of the ship; separate water closets were to be provided for women, and there had to be a satisfactory standard of ventilation. Improvement of the catering conditions eventually made it unnecessary for emigrants to provide their own food for the whole of the voyage.

The cost of the passage fell with the growth in emigrant numbers: in mid-nineteenth century some 20,000 to 30,000 Irish emigrants passed through Liverpool every year, joined by many others, including numbers of Scandinavians who had taken ship to Hull and then come by train

ALLAN LINE
ROYAL MAIL STEAMERS.

Ship.	Captain.	Ship.	Captain.	Ship.	Captain.	Ship.	Captain.
Sardinian	[illegible]	Caspian	Trocks	Peruvian	W. Richardson	Corinthian	J. Scott
Circassian	J. Wylie	Scandinavian	W. H. Smith	Moravian	J. Graham	Manitoban	H. Wylie
Canadian	McKenzie	Prussian	J. E. Dutton	Hibernian	F. Archer	Phenician	E. Scott
Polynesian	R. Brown	Austrian	J. Ritchie	Hanoverian	Grange	Waldensian	A. Woods
Sarmatian	A. D. Aird	Nestorian	R. S. Watts	North American	Miller	Saint Patrick	Stevens

The Splendid FULL-POWERED STEAM-SHIPS of this Line will be despatched as below.

LIVERPOOL TO QUEBEC, CANADA.

*S.S. CIRCASSIAN	Thursday, Sept. 11	*S.S. CASPIAN	Thursday, Oct. 9
‡S.S. CANADIAN	Tuesday, Sept. 16	‡S.S. PHENICIAN	Tuesday, Oct. 14
*S.S. POLYNESIAN	Thursday, Sept. 18	*S.S. SARMATIAN	Thursday, Oct. 16
†S.S. HIBERNIAN [illegible]	Tuesday, Sept. 23	†S.S. NESTORIAN [illegible]	Tuesday, Oct. 21
*S.S. SCANDINAVIAN	Thursday, Sept. 25	*S.S. CIRCASSIAN	Thursday, Oct. 23
‡S.S. MANITOBAN	Tuesday, Sept. 30	‡S.S. CANADIAN	Tuesday, Oct. 28
*S.S. PRUSSIAN	Thursday, Oct. 2	*S.S. POLYNESIAN	Thursday, Oct. 30
‡S.S. NORTH AMERICAN	Tuesday, Oct. 7		

LIVERPOOL TO NORFOLK AND BALTIMORE.

Calling at St. John's (Newfoundland) and Halifax (Nova Scotia).

S.S. NESTORIAN	Tuesday, Sept. 9	S.S. CASPIAN	Tuesday, Nov. 18
S.S. AUSTRIAN	Tuesday, Oct. 7	S.S. NESTORIAN	Tuesday, Dec. 2
S.S. NOVA SCOTIAN	Tuesday, Nov. 4		

And from Queenstown the following day.

Communication with HALIFAX, ST. JOHN, New Brunswick, PRINCE EDWARD ISLAND, and all the Gulf Ports, once a Fortnight.

* The Mail Steamers sailing from Liverpool on the Thursday call at Derry on the Friday for Mails & Passengers.

† TUESDAY Steamers for QUEBEC, via St. John's (Newfoundland) and Halifax, call at Queenstown on the Wednesday for Passengers and Mails, and accommodate Cabin, Intermediate, and Steerage Passengers.

‡ TUESDAY Steamers marked ‡ go Direct from LIVERPOOL to QUEBEC, and carry only Intermediate and Steerage Passengers.

Halifax, Norfolk, and Baltimore Steamers call at Queenstown on Wednesday for Passengers and Mails.

RATES OF PASSAGE from LIVERPOOL, LONDONDERRY, or QUEENSTOWN:

St. John's (Newfoundland)	£12 0s. or £15 0s.	Boston or New York	£16 16s. 0d. or £19 19s. 0d.
Quebec, Halifax, Norfolk, Baltimore	£15 15s. or £18 18s.	Montreal	£16 7s. 6d. or £19 10s. 6d.

Including everything requisite, except Wines and Liquors, which can be had on board.

[illegible]

THERE IS NO CHARGE FOR STEWARD'S FEES

A limited number of INTERMEDIATE PASSENGERS are taken in each Steamer at £9 9s. 0d. Children under Eight Years of Age, Half-fare; Infants, £1 1s. 0d. Intermediate Passengers are provided with Beds, Bedding, and all necessary Utensils, Wash-basins, &c. The accommodation is very inferior to Cabin, but is considerably better than Steerage. The Passengers get a better Table and a more Select Sleeping Compartment. [illegible] Adults sleep in Hammocks, and the Females and Children in rooms containing six berths each.

STEERAGE PASSAGE TO QUEBEC, [illegible], HALIFAX, [illegible], N.B., BOSTON, NEW YORK, [illegible], BALTIMORE, OR PHILADELPHIA,

£6 6s.,

[illegible] Children under Eight years of age, Half-price, and Infants under one year, £1 1s.

Passengers for ST. JOHN'S, Newfoundland, must only be booked by the Steamers advertised to call there.

Steerage or Intermediate Passages [illegible]

Steerage Passengers [illegible]

[illegible]

[illegible]

[illegible]

[illegible]

Baggage taken from the Ocean Steam-ships to the Railway Cars free of expense.

AN EXPERIENCED SURGEON IS ATTACHED TO EACH STEAMER.

Through Tickets issued to all Inland Towns in Canada and the States, as well as to San Francisco, Australia, New Zealand, Victoria, China, Japan, &c.

Intermediate and Steerage Stewardesses are provided by the Company to attend to the wants of Female Passengers and Children.

Return Tickets on favourable terms available by any of the above routes.

For particulars apply to ALLAN BROS. & CO.,

[illegible] James Street, Liverpool, and 85, Foyle Street, Londonderry.

September 8, 1873.

34 An advertisement of 1873 for the Allan Line of transatlantic sail-assisted steamships. Cabin passengers to Boston or New York paid £16.16s. or £19.19s. for their passage, including food; steerage passengers, provided with only a berth, paid £6.6s., and Intermediate passengers, with accommodation 'very inferior to Cabin, but considerably better than Steerage', £9.9s. (National Maritime Museum) across country to Liverpool. Ship accommodation was increased to meet the demand, and by 1880 the largest transatlantic liners carried some 300 cabin and 1,200 steerage passengers. Some of the latter were temporary

35 Emigrants leave to begin a new life: an illustration of the 1870s. At this time the Atlantic could be crossed in ten days or a little less, at a steerage fare of some £6–7.

visitors, skilled workmen who went out every spring to earn high wages in America, returning home in the autumn. They were joined on the return voyage by many disappointed emigrants who had disliked America or failed to make good there: according to one estimate they made up nearly three quarters of the passengers on the eastward voyage. There were many, indeed, who out of ignorance or undue optimism had grievously underestimated the difficulties of making a home in a new country. Robert Louis Stevenson, travelling by train westward across the Great Plains, recorded passing trains heading east loaded with people who leaned from the windows and cried 'Go back! Go back!'

The fares were not an impassable obstacle to emigration, except perhaps for those with large families and the very poor. Even at mid-century Australia could be reached for as little as £15, New Zealand for £18. Steerage fares across the Atlantic (without food) fell in the 1860s from £8.8*s.* to £6.6*s.*, and after 1883, because of fierce competition between shipping companies, to as low as £4.4*s.*, rising again in the 1890s to £5. Cabin rates were about double those for steerage. The total numbers emigrating from British ports are very roughly estimated as running between 100,000 in slack years to 200,000 in busy ones, rising after 1900 to reach an average of 460,000 in 1911–13. The occupations of those who left were naturally very varied, but included many building labourers, miners, general labourers and domestic servants. From the mid-1890s, however, their numbers were matched or exceeded by skilled workers, who indeed had always made up a sizeable proportion. Merchants and professional people ran at about 5–10 per cent of the total, though many of these were only temporary visitors to America. From the 1880s farmers and farm labourers made up a major element.

Reasons for leaving the homeland were almost as numerous as the emigrants themselves, though there was a general desire for economic betterment, set against a

36 The year 1900, when the Pacific Railway Company's *Lake Champlain* was photographed taking on passengers at Liverpool's landing stage, saw the beginning of an era of heavy emigration from British ports. Many of the emigrants were Irish, Germans or Scandinavians who had come to Liverpool to embark, but there were also many temporary visitors to America, especially among the cabin-class passengers. (National Maritime Museum)

background of some awareness of the high wages, cheap or free land, and the health-giving climate which had been portrayed with alluring and often much exaggerated publicity. Particularly influential in many persons' decision to emigrate were the letters of friends and relations who had already gone and established themselves. Professor Charlotte Erickson has made an extended analysis of such letters and has suggested many interesting conclusions about the motives of emigrants and their experiences. Ambition to improve one's conditions and social status were clearly significant, though it is perhaps a little surprising that so many emigrants, even those who were industrial workers and had no farming background, looked to the land as a better way of life. Those who were already farmers left for America to have the independence of their own land and an end to the paying of rent, tithes and taxes. Industrial workers in old and declining trades were pessimistic about the future at home and looked for a new security, even though farming meant hardship and isolation. Some, leaving in the 1830s and 1840s, feared a coming revolution and 'total destruction'. Others left to escape the worries and uncertainties associated with recurrent depressions in trade.

'Independence' was the great goal mentioned most frequently, while many emigrants unrealistically expected a life of greater leisure: 'Americans . . . live well and work little'. Nearer acquaintance was too often disillusioning. Getting a farm in America was seen, too, as a means of enabling a family to keep together as a unit instead of breaking up at home. To rural emigrants a new 'liberty' rarely meant escape from undue authority; rather low taxes and no tithe. Industrial workers more commonly felt the need to escape from what they saw as a tyrannical system of government, and welcomed the opportunity of living in a democracy where every man had his vote. As for choosing their new location, few emigrants seem to have been directly influenced by the propaganda of recruitment agencies, American state governments, railway and shipping companies, or land associations and guidebooks: prospective emigrants placed much greater faith in private links with relations or friends already there who were willing to help in the all-important matters of accommodation and work when they first arrived. And while many of the earlier emigrants took up industrial work in order to save up to buy a farm or to help relations to come over, in the second half of the century there was evidenced a more permanent attraction in industrial or commercial occupations.

There were those, too, who saved up in order to make their way home again. Life in the new country was seldom as rosy as it had appeared from a distance. The alien surroundings, the doubts and reluctance of the womenfolk, the enormous labour of farm-making in the wilderness, the lack of accustomed amenities and lower standards of comfort – all helped to discourage more than a few. But those who returned were still outnumbered, at least before 1914 by those just setting out. The worldwide commercial links established in Britain's industrial heyday, the growth of its shipping services, facilitated a human outflow which spread over many quarters of the globe. The workshop of the world shed some of its ambitious, its despondent, its socially conservative – for there were some emigrants who feared not the future of Britain but the loss of its past. Industrial Britain, with its unbridgeable gap between rich and poor, the social limitations inherent in its class structure, and its new environment of urbanized mass society repelled those hundreds of thousands who took their resentments, their unfulfilled dreams, away across the oceans.

Chapter Five

The Victorian Countryside

The villager of 1870, if he could return to his native hearth today, might not at first glance notice many changes. If he were there in early morning, before motorized milk floats and car-driving commuters were about, the centre of his old village might seem much as it was when he was a boy – church, chapel, inn, village shop, row of ancient cottages, all little changed. But just round the bend in the road there would be a strange red-brick school building which was not there before, and a cluster of more recent houses, still alien and unabsorbed into the rural scene.

37 A village scene from William Grundy's *English Views* of 1857. Notice the thatched roofs, the dirt road and complete absence of traffic. (BBC Hulton Picture Library)

He would notice the smooth, metalled roads which were formerly deep rutted mud in winter and thick layered dust in summer. Down the lane would be familiar old farmhouses with their timbered barns, but also much newer structures in ugly steel, concrete and corrugated iron. In the fields – now larger than they used to be, neater, and more often grassed – there would be unfamiliar livestock, black and white cows instead of the old shorthorns and local breeds, and novel machines, frightening in their noise, speed and power. Most striking, everywhere, would be the absence of the horse, the great means of power and transport of the Victorian age: no plough teams in the fields, no haywains, no carrier's wagon, doctor's trap or gentleman's carriage. The smithy, it might now be noticed, will have disappeared from its ancient site beside the bridge, as also the wheelwright's

38 The smithy at the Vulcan Arms, Cwmbelan, Montgomeryshire, about 1895. The blacksmith standing at the anvil was James Morris. The blacksmith was the last of the country craftsmen to decline as horses remained widely in use until the time of World War II, and the work of shoeing was often supplemented by the making and repair of farm implements and machinery. (Welsh Folk Museum, St Fagans)

shop that used to stand opposite. Gone too would be the butcher's yard, the saddler and harness maker, and the carpenter's workshop awash with ready timber, half-finished work and sawdust, with perhaps a newly completed coffin waiting on trestles in the back.

As for the things grown in the fields – well, they had always been changing: from grass to white crops, then to green crops, and back again to grass; from hops to fruit, and hops again; from potatoes to cabbages, and then to peas, swedes or mangolds. But some ground could never change: the poverty of the soil saw to that. Moorland sheepwalks, heathy wastes, and copse-crowned hills would be unaltered; Welsh mountain grazings, North Yorkshire moorlands, the wood-topped wolds of south Nottingham and neighbouring Leicestershire. Science has not been able to transform the landscape to that extent. The great variety of English farming conditions has remained, so that within a very few miles one could pass from lush alluvial pastures to deep clay ploughlands, from grassy chalk or limestone downs to fertile valleys rich in fruit and market gardens. There would still be the old striking contrasts: between the rolling Vale of Glamorgan and its neighbouring Black Mountain and Brecon Beacons; between chalk Wiltshire covered by great arable farms, and cheese Wiltshire with its compact dairy pastures; between the bleak limestone wolds of central Lincolnshire and the rich marsh grazings by the sea; between the Pennine wilds and the soft rolling grasslands of lowland Cumbria and Northumberland. The latter-day pilgrim to Canterbury would pass through the orchards and hop grounds to the south and west, to marsh directly east, and windswept arable plain of Thanet on the north-east – all within a very few miles of the ancient cathedral.

More influential in bringing about change than science-based agriculture, new breeds of livestock, or machinery, was the market. Victorian farming was essentially commercial, fundamentally geared to the demands of the urban population. True, there were still very many small

39 In the pre-motor car era the large village and country town boasted a remarkably extensive range of crafts and retail establishments. This photograph shows the saddler's shop of W. F. Francis at 13 Market Street, Falmouth, about 1910. (Museum of English Rural Life)

farms, as well as many thousands of holdings too small to be described as farms. But these were not surviving relics of a peasant subsistence culture: they, too, were concerned with trade, with specialized production where this was profitable on a small scale, as in dairying and pigs, potatoes, market gardening, fruit, hops and poultry; while many smallholdings were valuable adjuncts to some village or market-town business, for the keeping of the many thousands of horses used to pull bakers' vans, brewers' drays, coalmen's wagons, higglers' and cheapjacks' carts. Not a few country tradesmen combined their business with a little small-scale farming. Inns often had some acres of pasture attached to them, originally for the convenience of drovers collecting animals for sale, or passing through with herds on their regular route to market. Blacksmiths, wheelwrights, builders, shopkeepers frequently grew some fruit or vegetables for sale, dealt in poles and logs, or kept pigs, poultry, goats and bees. The farmers proper were sensitive, in greater or lesser degree, to the town demands for bread, meat, milk, cheese, eggs,

40 With the railways and the coming of rapid means of transport to distant urban markets developed the expansion of commercial fruit growing. Here strawberry pickers in Hampshire bring their filled baskets to be inspected and covered before sending to market. (BBC Hulton Picture Library)

fruit and poultry, as well as the great quantities of hay needed for the town horses, grain and hops for the breweries, wool for the woollen industry, hides for the tanneries and the making of boots, shoes and saddlery, local-grown hardwood for furniture-making, and timber for poles, posts, gates, fences, boxes and barrels – even straw for the Bedfordshire straw-hat trade.

Four continuing developments noticeably influenced the farmers' markets, pushing them in certain directions – some favourable to farmers, some adverse. Cities and towns were growing as the country's population multiplied, and an increasing proportion of people moved to towns to find a livelihood. An ever-increasing host of people came to depend entirely on what they could buy in shops and town markets, food that came from more or less distant sources. But this did not simply mean that all the farmers needed to do was supply more of the same. In the closing decades, especially, of Victoria's reign, living standards were rising substantially. More people could regularly afford meat at least once a week, and could buy larger quantities of dairy produce, salad stuff, apples, plums, cherries, strawberries, raspberries and chickens – articles of consumption closely related to income.

The railways, too, opened up more distant markets for farmers, and produce could be sent further afield with less risk of deterioration en route. Soon London's milk supply was being brought in from as far afield as the West Country and the Midlands, as well as from the home counties. The droving trade declined as more livestock were carried to market by rail, and country carriers found their local business hit by the spread of railways into country districts. The railways brought many other changes. Commercial travellers brought samples of town cloths and ready-made clothes round the cottages. Village people could get into town for Saturday evening shopping and amusement: country shopkeepers, tailors, inns and tradesmen all began to feel the pinch. Large villages which used to boast scores of tradesmen and craftsmen saw them dwindle away one by one, a process that was still going on with the growth of car ownership after World War II. Market towns found their very *raison d'être* under threat. Twice-weekly markets were reduced to opening only once a week, and then sometimes closed down for good. The scene described by Sir George Head in 1835 of the corn market held at the Hilyard Arms at Patrington in Holderness could not have long survived the coming of the railway age: each corn factor, he wrote, kept his separate room at the inn

> so that the farmers go from one to another, in order to drive their bargains, as it suits them . . . the staircase of the inn all the time is a thoroughfare, whereon the farmers continually stump up and down in their heavy boots, with a sample-bag in one hand, and, not unfrequently, a glass of hot gin and water in the other.

Lastly, there were the long-term shifts in prices: not merely the effects of runs of good or bad seasons, or of unusually damaging outbreaks of animal disease, that affected prices over short periods, but the sea-change brought about by the era of free trade inaugurated by the Repeal of the Corn Laws in 1846, and the subsequent rising flood of foreign competition. Already at mid-century livestock and dairy produce markets were considerably affected by the influx of Continental and Irish livestock and butter, cheese and bacon. To these were added fruit and vegetables – as early as 1850 the potatoes one could buy in Portsmouth had come over from France – and by the end of the century even hay, which landed in Liverpool forcing down the prices and profits of Lancashire farmers.

But most severely hit in the long run was wheat. At first the American and East Prussian grain was partially kept back by the cost of shipping it to Britain. Nevertheless, even before steamships improved in efficiency, and competition between steam and sail brought freight rates tumbling, the price of wheat was tending to drift slowly downwards. Then, from the 1870s, the cheapening of sea transport and the opening up by railways of the new wheatlands in the Americas, Australia and Russia combined to swell imports and send the price in Britain crashing. In the homeland King Wheat was dethroned: in 1873 it fetched 58*s*. 8*d*. the quarter (eight bushels), a price not to be approached again until well into World War I. Farmers found it almost impossible to grow it with profit as its price fell to as low as the miserable 22*s*. 10*d*. the quarter that it fetched at the nadir of 1894 – a price lower than that of barley, an almost unheard-of situation, and indeed only half the figure that was paid at the bottom of the last agricultural depression after the Napoleonic Wars. Imports of wheat and flour rose to reach over 100m. cwt. in the first year of the new sovereign, Edward VII – nearly eleven times the quantity imported in the year of Repeal. The wheat acreage, as a result, declined by over two million acres – 63 per cent – in the thirty-five years from 1869. Farmers still went in for grain; the barley acreage held up fairly well and that of oats actually increased; but wheat was largely unprofitable. In the eastern arable districts where wheat was the main cash crop farmers emigrated or retired, numbers bankrupted. Landowners sought new tenants from Scotland – where land was more highly rented – or from the West Country, men who had fresh capital and fresh initiatives, who were willing to convert run-down farms to grass and go in for milk for the London market. In consequence the area of permanent pasture used for grazing went up by some 3.5m. acres, or over a third, between 1873 and 1896, the conventional dates for the great agricultural depression.

Milk, however, was not the only saviour of English farming. Despite the competition from imports the swelling consumption of townspeople maintained the potato acreage and saw orchard land rise to eventually cover some quarter of a million acres. The cheapening of sugar, shipped from the West Indies, formed the basis of the new industry of jam manufacture. The area of commercial soft-fruit growing expanded and this became the era when Chivers, Robertson and Tiptree became household names. Market gardening and poultry production developed in favoured areas like the Vale of Evesham, the Sandy district of Bedfordshire, Sussex (which, oddly enough, was the home of the 'Surrey' capons), and a variety of areas round London. But livestock now formed the main support of British farming. While sheep numbers declined in the last quarter of the century with increased competition from imported mutton and wool, before recovering somewhat in the early years of the new century, cattle numbers rose steadily throughout. The nearly five million head of cattle (both dairy and beef) of 1867 passed the seven million mark in 1909, with three-fifths of that number being fattened for beef, and two-fifths in dairying. Consumption of liquid milk rose, but only slowly, though it was free of foreign competition: the amount drunk per head remained low, especially among the poorer classes, where it was used mainly in tea, coffee and cocoa. Price, the lack of a milk-drinking habit, large-scale adulteration by suppliers, the absence of any suitable place for storing it in working-class homes, and the convenient, if poor, alternative of canned condensed milk – all helped to keep down the level of fresh milk consumption. Beef, on the other hand, was another story. Here there was mounting overseas competition, especially after the introduction of refrigeration in sea-going ships and warehouses. With rising incomes many people were now eating beef regularly for the first time, though the meat was not the celebrated roast beef of old England but the cheap product of Argentina or Australia. However, the well-to-do, and the more discriminating among the better-off of the working classes, preferred the home-produced, if more expensive, alternative.

By shifting to grass, by going in for the products in rising demand and less subject to overseas competition, and by economizing on labour and other outgoings, farmers struggled to a more stable, if only moderately comfortable existence by the early years of the twentieth century. The graziers of the pastoral North and West had not really been depressed, if one judges by the moderate fall in the prices of livestock products as compared with the fall in prices in general. One of their most important costs, that of bought-in feeding stuffs, had fallen, though labour expenses rose and there were some years of very difficult seasons and disastrous outbreaks of epidemics among livestock. Accordingly, some historians have denied the very existence of a 'Great Agricultural Depression', at least for large parts of the country. But if they were not hit to the same degree as the arable men, the dairying and fattening specialists still saw difficult times. The prices of their products were under pressure, and home butter and cheese production declined as the imported alternatives (not forgetting 'butterine' and margarine) became cheaper and more efficiently produced. Certainly, by the cold logic of economic analysis they did reasonably well. But the environment was changing, foreign competition mounting, and if they were not depressed in terms of purchasing power, they still *felt* as if they were depressed. And that was what really mattered.

What happened to the individual farmer depended on circumstances, not merely circumstances of soil, climate and situation, but on what help his landlord could give him, his own skill in management, and mere prudence. A country rector, James George Cornish, noted that formerly, in the prosperous years before the depression, money was plentiful and many farmers could save. 'They did not have to make money, it was brought home and shot down at their doors.' Then when the hard times came:

> the wiser men weathered the storm while the unwise were wrecked. The former had been saving money during the good years and could draw on their bank balances. They had lived quietly and so needed to make little change in their home budget and they had not more land to farm than they could attend to well. With lower rents and extra care they managed to make both ends meet. One new thing many of them now

began: namely, the keeping of accounts. Formerly their bank passbooks were the sole record they possessed, and not one in ten had the foggiest notion of whether the corn or the cattle or the poultry were *each* paying their way.

The depression brought in a new era of more strained relations between landlord and tenant. Formerly the farmer had looked to his landlord to help him through bad times and to assist him in farming more efficiently by spending money on such basic improvements as drainage and new farm buildings and cottages. In return the farmer paid an increased rent, pledged his political support at election time, deferred respectfully to the landowner in social matters, in standards of conduct and in religion, and put up with the nuisance (where he was not a sportsman himself) of game preservation and the damage done to his fields by the hunt. If he was an enterprising, forward-looking sort of farmer (and many were not) he himself, his ideas enlarged by the farming journals and shows of the 'Royal', and some prodding from the agent, had gone in for new fertilizers like guano or superphosphate, had acquired some pedigree shorthorns, and experimented with new machines like reapers and hay tedders, steam threshing, and even steam ploughing. Thomas Aveling of Rochester in Kent, a manufacturer of traction engines, told an 1873 Select Committee that he believed there to be from 100 to 150 engines in Kent, and that as much as a third of the land in the county was ploughed by steam.

In this respect, as in some others, Kent may have been an exceptional county. Certainly by the depression years steam threshing and horse-drawn farm machinery, as opposed to that drawn by traction engines, had become commonplace. But economy now became the farmer's watchword. Machinery was increasingly used where it was more efficient and where labour had become scarce In some districts farmers claimed that the old-fashioned kind of skilled hands were unobtainable as well as more expensive, and blamed the schools for giving country children ideas beyond their station. Labour was cut back, and inessential work such as hedge-trimming or ditch-cleaning was put off or abandoned altogether. Many farms became sadly run down, the buildings dilapidated, the fields overrun by an all-devouring invasion of twitch. The Scots newcomers on the Essex clays sacked the old local hands as too slow and too wedded to the old ways, and ran their newly-established dairies mainly by the labour of the family. Landlords helped by cutting rents, sometimes drastically, and sometimes by paying for new cattle sheds and the bringing of water supplies into the new pastures. But many landlords were themselves strapped for cash and unable to do very much, and moreover were beginning to view their land as a distinctly unprofitable investment now that it had lost much of its political influence and social cachet.

The farmers saw that they were on their own. The landlords had not been able to prevent Repeal (where they had not themselves supported it), and now they were unable to put the clock back and re-introduce protection. The less realistic of the farmers still looked for the salvation of import duties, or seized on some minor irritations for the source of their difficulties – the burdens of tithe and rates, the question of compensation for unexhausted improvements, the inefficiency of the railways and their apparent neglect of the farmers' needs, the rising cost of labour, and the pernicious influence of the new rural schools brought in by the 1870 Education Act. The more discerning saw the basic need was to combine in order to bring pressure on government. Very occasionally in the past they had managed to put a farming spokesman into the Commons. Now they sought their own permanent organization, run by farmers for farmers, independent of landlords and fickle electors alike. The National Farmers' Union was founded in 1908, following an earlier county development, the Lincolnshire Farmers' Union. By 1915 the NFU could boast 15,000 members, mainly large-scale farmers, though this number represented less than one in ten of all the farmers in England and Wales. Its great days

41 With the triumph of free trade, the subsequent agricultural depression and decline of the landowners' political influence, the farmers broke away from traditional acceptance of landlord leadership. The first independent Farmers' Union began in Lincolnshire in 1904, and developed in a few years into the National Farmers' Union with a membership in 1910 of 10,000. (Museum of English Rural Life)

of power and influence were in the future, beyond World War I, in the era of renewed government intervention in agriculture from the 1930s onwards.

* * * * * *

The social structure of British agriculture at the onset of the Great Depression resembled a pyramid, very broad indeed at the base but tapering sharply to the peak. The census of 1881 recorded a total employment in agriculture, horticulture and forestry of 1,633,000 – some 384,000 fewer than were working on the land in 1851 when the labour force was at its maximum. Employment in agriculture continued to decline until by 1901 the number was down to 1,425,000, an overall fall of nearly 600,000 since 1851.

Of course, the great bulk of those employed were farm-workers: in 1881 the Census recorded under a quarter of a million farmers and graziers in England and Wales (the number of holdings of over 20 acres was given in 1885 as 212,000, with a further 36,000 in Scotland). Notwithstanding the old school of agricultural historians which claimed that enclosure and 'capitalistic' farming had between them destroyed the small farmers in the eighteenth century, there were in fact many small farms and holdings in every county of England and Wales. In 1885 only 4,767 farms of over 500 acres were recorded, as compared with total holdings of more than 5 acres of 338,715 – a mere 1.4 per cent, though of course they occupied a much greater share of the acreage.

What is certainly true is that the vast majority of farms were of small or medium size. While only 29 per cent of the acreage of England and Wales was in farms of more than 300 acres, 42 per cent was taken up by farms of 101–300 acres, and a further 23 per cent by units of 21–100 acres. Characteristically, the English farmer rented his land rather than owned it. In 1887–91, 82 per cent of occupiers were solely tenants, 14 per cent owned the whole of their land, and the remaining 4 per cent rented part and owned the other part of the land they farmed. The 85 per cent of the farm acreage that was occupied by tenants was held by landlords, the great bulk of it by a few thousand of them. Indeed, the 'New Domesday' survey of 1873 showed that four-fifths of the land was owned by fewer than 7,000 persons. Great estates of 10,000 acres or more, mainly but by no means entirely owned by titled aristocrats, covered more than a quarter of thirteen English counties, and in two, Rutland and Northumberland, reached a half or more of the county acreage. Some counties, such as Westmorland, Lincoln, Cumberland and Cornwall, could boast well over 250 country seats, and some smaller districts, such as the 'Dukeries' in northern

Nottinghamshire, were monopolized by great mansions and their parks.

The social structure of English agriculture can thus be defined fairly precisely in terms of three quite different kinds of people, with very different economic functions and vastly different incomes. There were the several thousand landowners of significance, men who owned land but did not usually farm it, except for the home farm by the mansion which served as a convenient source of fresh food for the house and perhaps as a laboratory for those owners interested in agricultural experiments. Below the landlords came the 200,000 or so farmers, who as we have seen usually owned little or no land and were in farming for a living – in good times often a prosperous one. Farmers varied greatly in the scale of their operations and hence in status: the greatest farming several thousand acres and living in houses that might be mistaken for those of the gentry; the small men, on the other hand, hardly distinguishable from better-off village tradesmen and craftsmen. Below the farmers were many thousand smallholders, market gardeners, fruitgrowers, poultry-keepers and the like, some of them combining this sort of business with a village trade or craft. The farmworkers, lastly, rarely owned or occupied any land other than a rented vegetable allotment or garden attached to the cottage. They relied to a great extent on the farmers for their income and were in no sense independent 'peasants' of the kind found over large areas of the Continent. They were essentially wage labourers, and though a few of them might progress to become smallholders or even small farmers, they generally lacked the means, the opportunity or the ambition to progress far up the farming ladder.

It might be wondered why successful tenant farmers, especially the larger ones, did not put their profits into buying land and so eventually make themselves independent of landlords. A few, in fact, did so, but the majority preferred to plough profits back into their working capital in order to be able to farm more efficiently or take on a

42 The staff of Home Farm, Newcastle on Tyne. As can be seen here, the majority of farm servants were young; the elderly man standing on the right was George Summers, the farm steward. (Museum of English Rural Life)

larger acreage. Others put spare money into cottages, local flour mills or implement works, or perhaps into railway shares. The main reason for this lack of interest in the purchase of land was that the return on it, in terms of rental value, was generally very low: only some 3 or 4 per cent when taxes and other outgoings were allowed for. Farm profits, on the other hand, were usually very much higher, though of course there were bad years as well as good ones. At any rate, throughout most of the nineteenth century the landlord-tenant system was never seriously challenged; landowners were content with their modest return, finding compensation in the political influence, social prestige and opportunities for sport that their estates afforded, while tenants, for their part, paid only moderate rents (which were abated in bad times) and enjoyed considerable security of tenure, even when they had no lease. Both sides recognized that efficient farming was to their mutual advantage, and landlords and tenants often co-operated in financing expensive improvements such as field drainage. Two of the farmers' main grievances, compensation for unexhausted improvements when they left a farm, and freedom to destroy hares and rabbits on their own holdings, received attention from the legislature in the 1880s, forcing reluctant landlords to fall into line with the more progressive.

Towards the end of the century, however, the situation was changing. When rents fell after 1879 many landlords found their estates highly unprofitable and began to put more of their land on the market to pay off debts or diversify into other investments such as railway shares and overseas stock. Land sales increased after World War I as the consequence of continuing low rents, higher taxation, and particularly the effects of crippling death duties when heirs were killed in the war and estates changed hands rapidly. On the farmers' side, they were presented with the opportunity of first refusal of their farms and the prospect of casting off a traditional subservience that was becoming increasingly irksome and outdated. As estates were broken up, more and more farmers became owners, exchanging a rent for a mortgage payment. The proportion of land owned by its occupiers went up considerably after 1920, and by 1950 had reached 38 per cent, continuing since then to well exceed 50 per cent, the highest figure in recorded history.

This trend has marked a very great reversal of landowners' former attitudes. Over the centuries much effort, forethought and legal ingenuity had gone into the building-up of estates, and keeping them intact once they had been established. Among the wealthier owners marriages inheritances were carefully managed so as to lead to more landed wealth accruing to the family. When small freeholders were selling up, the big owners were always in the market for any properties that would help round off their existing holdings, and especially to extend the main block of land around the principal mansion. It was every great owner's desire to be able to gaze out from his windows on no-one's land but his own, as far as the eye could see. The huge pleasure grounds and game preserves that were fashionable among *grands seigneurs* required large investments and continued expenditure on maintenance. The house and estate gave a family its sense of identity, a place in the county, perhaps a place in government and the making of policy. Country-house weekends were noted social occasions, sometimes politically influential, often leading events of the sporting calendar. Disraeli – no sportsman he – found country house visits tedious and time-wasting but inescapable: a statesman and party leader had to be on good terms with the leading nobility and gentry.

Country house life grew more expensive as old houses were extended and modernized, and as new ones were built on a more elaborate scale. Some of the great new houses were amazingly elaborate, with up-to-date forms of sanitation, bathrooms and lavatories, central heating, and gas, later electric, lighting. There were impressive halls in medieval style, billiard rooms, gun rooms and smoking rooms, separate stairs for the family, the nursery, the bachelors and servants – perhaps six or seven in all. Extensive servants' quarters catered for staffs that normally numbered from fifteen to forty and special rooms were provided for brushing, cleaning boots, polishing knives and filling lamps – even for the ironing of the morning newspapers. The consumption of coal was prodigious: Bulstrode Park, so Jill Franklin tells us, had forty-four fires burning on a typical November day, and in some houses iron railways were introduced to carry coal from the store into the basement, the one at Osmaston Manor having a length of 'about 300 feet with curves, turntables, etc.'.

The greatest establishments could only be maintained by the wealthiest of owners, particularly those whose estates included profitable coal mines, ironworks, docks, urban housing or seaside properties. Landlords with diversified estates and large non-agricultural investments could best weather the storms of the depressed years after 1879. Others, less fortunate, had to reduce their outlays, let off the grounds for shooting, part with outlying land or even sell up altogether and move to a fashionable resort as gentlemen in reduced circumstances. As Oscar Wilde truly expressed it, 'Land gives one position, and prevents one from keeping it up'. Numbers of the old properties that were sold, and many of the new ones that were built, were acquired by *nouveaux riches*, newcomers from the world of industry, commerce and finance, including such familiar names as Jesse Boot, the retail chemist, Colman of Colman's Mustard, Armstrong, the armaments king, Lipton the grocer, and Wills, the tobacco manufacturer. Some contemporaries welcomed this development – it was not entirely new – as broadening the composition of Britain's highest classes. Thus wrote Thomas Escott in 1879:

> There are typical country gentlemen in the House of Commons and in society, but the country interest is no longer the sworn enemy of the urban interest. Our territorial nobles, our squires, our rural landlords great and small, have become commercial potentates; our merchant princes have become country gentlemen . . . The great merchant or banker of today is an English gentleman of a finished type . . . His grandfather would have lived with his family above the counting-house, and regarded a trip to Hyde Park as a summer day's journey. As for the descendant, his town-house is in Belgravia or Mayfair. He occupies it for little more than six months out of the twelve, and during the rest of the year lives in his palace in the country, takes a keen interest in the breeding of stock, the cultivation of the soil, and the general improvement of his property.

But old-established landowners smiled contemptuously at the misguided efforts of the parvenus to impress high society. Lord Ashburnham (whose own family had risen mainly through a series of successful marriages in the early decades of the previous century) scornfully derided the fancy dress ball given by Sir Thomas Brassey, the railway contractor, at his newly-built 'French chateau', Normanhurst: 'A piece of purse-proud tomfoolery or tombrassery', with Sir Thomas himself 'acting as master of ceremonies, and shouting out directions to every one in a stentorian voice as if he had been on board of his yacht in a tempest', and Lady Brassey on 'a throne in the ball-room, upon a dais!'

The country gentry traditionally saw themselves as having a certain social role in the countryside, bearing obligations incurred as a result of their wealth, their large share of the land, and the possession of education and leisure. Leading gentry sat in Parliament for the county or a country town, served as magistrates and as Poor Law Guardians. The lesser squires accepted a more parochial role, kept an eye on affairs in the village, visited the school, organised an annual fete and sports; they helped out the villagers by witnessing wills, writing letters of recommendation and acting as trustees. Sir Baldwin Leighton, a prominent Shropshire gentleman, chairman of the County Bench of magistrates and of the Poor Law Guardians, recorded in his diary his visits to agricultural meetings, but also to the workhouse to visit the paupers suffering from cholera. He took an interest in the local cottagers, and 'spoke to one about children left at home while they were out to work'; he built a new farmhouse complete with water closet – clearly something of an innovation; and remarked on the change in manners that had occurred in his lifetime. Among gentlemen, he noted, drunkenness was now rare, and he recalled an occasion back in 1820 when the twelve men in a party drank thirty-three bottles of claret – besides champagne and other wine – and nine of them had to be carried to bed. The squires' ladies, too, were often active in good works, visiting the sick, providing medicines, and supplying coal and blankets to the poor at Christmas. Some of the more pious coupled their visits with prayers, hymns and the reading of a few pages of *Pilgrim's Progress*. One, a clergyman's daughter, Maria Charlesworth, also held an afternoon Bible class for the poor.

Some of the country clergy were themselves related to the squire, in whose gift the living might lie. Others were less well-born, and a number took a country parish as a rest from more arduous labours in a city. As ministers they were of all kinds – pious and conscientious, worldly and profligate. There were keen sportsmen who deliberately sought out livings where the hunting was good and the duties light, even to keeping their own pack of hounds. Quite a number, especially in the early decades of the nineteenth century, served as magistrates and were particularly prominent in the enforcing of the law and the running down of wrongdoers. There were notorious absentees who paid curates miserable stipends to fill their place in obscure backwaters while they luxuriated in distant society. Not a few were in conflict with the farmers of the parish over the tithes; and some fell out constantly with the squire over prickly questions of doctrine, the length of sermons and the squire's absence from service, the erection of new monuments in the church, and so forth.

Private box pews gave rise to much annoyance: in some churches they occupied much the larger part of the space, leaving only a few benches in the side aisles or gallery for ordinary folk. Often pews were unoccupied for months or years, and when there was any alteration disputes broke out over precedence and situation. At Horsmonden, in Kent, for instance, there were bitter quarrels when one family decided to send a carpenter to enlarge their pew at the expense of a neighbour's. In the church, all was strictly by social rank. The squire went up first to the communion rail, then came the farmers, and next the tradesmen, shopkeepers, wheelwright and blacksmith; last of all the farm labourers in their smock frocks. Joseph Arch, leader of the farm labourers' union, recalled that the wife of the clergyman at Barford in Warwickshire

> used to sit in state in her pew in the chancel, and the poor women used to walk up the church and make a curtsey to her before taking the seats set apart for them. They were taught in this way that they had to pay homage and respect to those 'put in authority over them', and made to understand that they must 'honour the powers that be', as represented in the rector's wife.

Reforming parsons, however, began to take steps to remove private pews, even to wielding the axe in person. Other departures from the past included the abolition of the old musical band which accompanied the hymns, and its replacement by an organ or harmonium: this might be for reasons of musical standards or, as has been suggested, because the band was sometimes too independent of the vicar. Another figure to go was the parish clerk who traditionally pronounced the responses; but parsons found it hard to persuade conservative congregations to speak up and take his place.

Great ugly iron stoves and hot water pipes were introduced to take off the chill in winter, formerly a powerful reason for the congregation staying at home on a frosty day. Attendance was best at the morning service, as a survey taken in March 1851 showed. Taking all churches, just over 25 per cent of the population attended then, with the later services attracting only a little over 17 per cent. Beside the winter cold there were many other reasons for absence. Fashionable families of the neighbourhood were away from the late autumn for the London season or might be touring abroad; farmers were likely to be absent in busy times or in bad weather when the lanes were deep in mud or snow; many labourers might be Methodists, or have no suitable clothes in which to come to church. Occasionally the squire, like Rider Haggard's father in Norfolk, made it his practice to stand in the porch to count the congregation as it left and to inquire why so-and-so had not come. The squire's own servants were under even closer scrutiny, and the labourers came, especially if they were elderly, for fear of losing the squire's or parson's approval and so being shut out from whatever charity was going. Numbers of working families preferred the more informal and democratic ways of the Wesleyan chapel, and it was not unusual for families to be seen at the morning service in the church and the afternoon or evening one in the chapel. Methodism brought the farmer, craftsman and labourer together, as much as the Church of England's respect for social niceties divided them. Where labourers served as lay preachers their role enhanced not only their own self-respect but the respect which their fellows, even their employers, had for them.

Conscientious priests did their best to ameliorate the labourer's lot and also bind them more closely to the Church by starting a school (even if only in a spare room in the rectory, in a farmer's barn or in the church itself); by organizing boot and coal clubs, by giving penny readings and lantern shows, and by frequent visiting of the sick. Not a few incumbents were instrumental in securing land for allotments which labourers could hire, and some were prepared to further invite the farmers' hostility by involving themselves in questions of wages, housing and sanitation. But neither Church nor Chapel could make much headway against superstition and pagan beliefs. A world of ancient customs survived in the nineteenth century concerning ghosts, devils, disease and death. Weird charms, sayings and ceremonies were invoked to ward off evil spirits, cure ailments or attract lovers: a diverse mass of ritual surrounded all the business of life and death. This paganism, together with the labourers' sense of social isolation – not to say the scorn they received from superiors – as well as mere indifference, kept many apart from the Church. On a Sunday in late Victorian times the villager preferred to spend his time in repairing his boots, digging his garden, walking with a band of kindred spirits to a pub in the next village, or simply sitting at home reading the sensational stories retailed in the Sunday newspaper. The Church neglected him and he neglected it. And in these same late Victorian years squire and parson were going downhill together. Rambling parsonages with over-extensive grounds, out of repair, and requiring cooks, maids and gardeners, became more and more of a burden as stipends and tithe compositions failed to meet outgoings. But while the squire could still afford his carriage, the parson, now less often so highly regarded as to sit on the Bench, was more likely to be seen on his bicycle.

* * * * * *

In standard historical accounts the farm labourers are often lumped together as one amorphous mass, alike in their poverty and hopelessness. This generalization, if convenient, does violence to the truth. There were, in fact, substantial differences in function, status and working conditions. Men in charge of animals, especially the herdsmen, shepherd, head teamsman and waggoner, had considerable responsibility, and in return were paid a little more, albeit for longer hours. In addition to ordinary farm-workers there were better-paid estate employees, game-keepers, foresters, and superintendents of woods and parks; and there were independent specialists like expert hedgers and ditchers, thatchers, mole catchers, farriers, water diviners and well diggers, who worked as farm labourers only when not engaged for their particular skills. There were in 1881 nearly 20,000 farm bailiffs or foremen, though these formed only a tiny proportion (2.25 per cent, in fact) of the 890,175 workers of all kinds on farms in England and Wales.

Some of the farm labourers, a declining number, continued to be hired and paid by the year as farm servants; they lived in with their masters, were generally young and unmarried, and made a habit of changing masters frequently, finding new employers at the annual hiring fairs or 'statutes'. By the later nineteenth century this type of employment was mainly to be found in the north and west, in remote areas where labour was scarce and livestock was the mainstay of the farming. The main body of men, the day-labourers, were hired and paid by the day, though often they worked for one farmer for long periods of years and lived in his cottage. The normal day was much shorter in the limited daylight of winter than in summer, when the hours might stretch from 6.00 a.m. to 6.00 p.m. with 1½ hours allowed for meals, and perhaps a 2.00 p.m. or 4.00 p.m. finish on a Saturday; more than a 60-hour week in summer, about 40–50 hours in winter. Days lost through heavy rain or snow might not be paid at all, though some farmers found jobs for the men in the yards and barns in bad weather.

Wages and perquisites varied regionally and locally. Summer and winter wage rates changed to allow for the difference in hours, and separate piece-rate agreements were often made with gangs of men for harvesting, and also for haymaking and jobs like hoeing. The actual rates varied from village to village, farm to farm. Regular labourers might have their cottage free, or alternatively paid a rent; there was often free fuel, use of a spare piece of ground for vegetables, and an allowance of milk, potatoes and bacon free or at a reduced price. The traditional daily allowance of beer or cider (varying from a quart to a gallon) was under attack in the later nineteenth century (as farmers disliked having the trouble of brewing it) and was eventually outlawed. Wives and older children were sometimes employed as well as the men, and in some areas farmers would not take on a man unless his wife were able and willing to help out on the farm.

Evidently, the pattern of farm earnings was complex and enormously varied, but some broad regional differences were clearly marked. In the Midlands and North, where nearby industries drew labour off the land and served to put a floor under farmworkers' wages, the rates were higher than in the more purely agricultural South. This difference was first brought to general notice by the leading agricultural expert, James Caird, in 1851: his map showed a dividing line across the country, roughly marking off those areas with coal from those without it.

In 1879–81 the highest average money wages were paid by farmers in the most northerly counties, in Cumberland, Westmorland, Northumberland, Durham, Yorkshire, Lancashire and Cheshire: the average figure was 16*s*. 2*d*. a week. The lowest average cash rate paid in the south – 12*s*. 4*d*., a difference of nearly a quarter – was in the South-West, in Somerset, Cornwall, Devon, Dorset and Wiltshire, followed very closely by the 12*s*. 6*d*. paid in East Anglia. It is interesting that as migration from southern agricultural districts became more marked, and especially as the northern industrial regions were hit by slump conditions in the years between the two wars, the regional difference was first gradually closed and then reversed. By the 1930s the former low-wage areas had become the high-wage ones.

Over the decades between 1850 and World War I there was a general tendency for average money wages to rise: from around the 10*s*. mark at and before mid-century to the 16*s*. 9*d*. national average paid in 1914. In the last quarter of the old century the real earnings of farmworkers rose considerably as consumer prices fell, while money wages continued to rise. The result was seen in a gradual, if uneven, improvement in housing, diet, and general living standards, and in the reduced number of women working regularly in the fields. By the end of the century it was said that a woman working in the open, hoeing or cutting roots, had become a rare sight. Observers, even in such a low-wage county as Dorset, remarked on such novelties in labourers' homes as stair carpets, bicycles, even pianos. But the improvement had started from very low levels, and farmworkers remained among the poorest paid of all workers. Through continued migration off the land and the introduction of wage regulation, earnings continued to advance from World War I onwards, though the average minimum wage in 1939 was still only 34*s*. 8*d*. (for an average week which had fallen from 58 hours in 1914 to a little over 50 hours), when men in comparable occupations, such as railway porters, road transport carters, builders' labourers and labourers employed by local authorities, all earned at least 9s. a week more.

Despite the slow improvement in earnings and purchasing power, the farmworkers' housing was often appalling, their diet inadequate and monotonous, and they lived always on the edge of disaster – disaster which became a reality if the breadwinner died or was incapacitated. Illness or accident – a fire, and the cottage burnt down, not so infrequent in the days of thatch – suddenly transformed a situation of poverty-stricken stability to one of desperate crisis, where the wife had to find some kind of paid work and the charity of relations, neighbours, squire and parson became vital. Fortunately, epidemic diseases were less rife, in general, than in the towns, though country workers suffered from painful and crippling rheumatic complaints. Frequent soakings in the rain, leaky boots, and damp and draughty cottages where clothes failed to dry overnight, were the daily experience in winter. Accidents were surprisingly frequent. Analysis of records of fatal accidents indicates a high number of deaths through drowning, as a result of accidents with horses and carts, and also from falls (especially in districts with numerous disused coal pits, quarries and other workings). A substantial number of people died from exposure, especially among the sick and elderly – and also the drunken.

Poverty was the background to much of the petty thieving – of potatoes, parsnips, firewood, poultry, even sheep – that was endemic in the countryside. And there was a great amount of poaching. Fortunately the age of the spring-gun and ferocious mantrap was over by the time of Victoria, but the game laws, somewhat less severe than earlier, were still in operation, and there were still some thousands of convictions every year. In the 1840s the new rural police were involved, for by 1841 twenty-four counties had established a force, though often consisting of very few men.

For country labourers the occasional purloined rabbit,

Figures 3 and 4 Two common designs for cheap, plain and utilitarian country workers' cottages that may still be seen in southern counties. The upper design was built about 1835, constructed with a deal frame and external weather-boarding. Each semi-detached cottage contained two rooms on the ground floor, one behind the other, with a full upper storey. The lower design was built some forty or fifty years later in brick, and had the front door opening on to a small kitchen from which a further door led to the parlour and a staircase giving access to the two bedrooms above. (John Woodforde, *The Truth about Cottages*, Routledge & Kegan Paul, 1969, pp. 121, 129.)

hare or pheasant eked out a meagre diet. However, there were again notable differences between North and South, the better-paid northern workers having the considerable advantage of cheap fuel, as well as higher wages. In the South the little meat or bacon that could be afforded was often reserved for the man, to sustain him in the fields, his wife and children subsisting on scraps, bread and tea. Vegetables could be had in season from garden or allotment, but too often the means, leisure, and even the knowledge for preparing inexpensive soups and stews were lacking. One clear advantage when the wife went out to clean someone's house, or the children had early morning jobs cleaning shoes and polishing knives at the vicarage or the doctor's, was that they got some food in the course of their work. Many country women and children, and the menfolk too in bad times, were undernourished, as was borne out by the results of medical examination of school children between the wars. Indeed, it may well be true that a main reason for the marked difference between farm wages in North and South during the nineteenth century was that the southern workers were too ill-fed to work very hard, and their lower pay reflected their lower productivity. Contemporaries pointed to the false economy of low wages, and remarked on the very slow pace of work, and slowness of wit, too, which marked labourers in many districts of the south.

In old age farmworkers' poverty was intensified. Some farmers kept on their old hands when they were past regular work, giving them odd jobs around the house and yards. Otherwise, there was before 1908 (when the Old Age Pension was introduced) only the help of relations, the chance of a little local private charity, perhaps an almshouse, or the public charity of the Poor Law. Destitute old people still able to live at home got a small pension of perhaps 2*s*. 6*d*. or 3*s*. 6*d*. a week from the Poor Law authorities, or otherwise were taken into the workhouse infirmary. George Sturt, the Surrey writer, recalled visiting his old gardener Bettesworth when he was taken from his

43 Housewives and two girls pose outside a pair of farmworkers' cottages about 1895. Cottages of this type, with their drab facades and blank side walls were built from about 1850 onwards, often in terraces. (Museum of English Rural Life)

cottage to the infirmary. There he found him 'wonderfully clean' and well cared for, in a cheerful and well-appointed room, but thoroughly miserable, longing for the independence, the poky, stuffy rooms and familiar squalor of his own little cottage and the 'worthless rubbish' that made it home.

Country workers' homes varied as much as did their wages and other conditions. Cottages might be newly erected, substantial houses, such as those which Lord Leconfield built in Sussex in 1893, with four bedrooms, a living room, kitchen and garden, and let at a rent of 1*s*. 6*d*. a week. Others, quite possibly more highly rented, were tumbledown two-room hovels, with a dirt floor, thatched roof and unglazed windows. A good deal depended on the local building materials and building traditions, whether timber, brick, stone or cob (a mixture of clay and straw) and whether, as in parts of Wales and the North, the animals were kept inside in one half of a 'long house'. Not all cottages were bad. It is interesting that emigrants to newly-opened areas of America often found conditions there inferior to those at home: 'it is by no means to be understood', wrote one, 'that an American log house equals in comfort and convenience a snug English cottage'. Moreover, many common items taken for granted at home were missing: fire irons, candlesticks, basins, pots, cutlery, feather beds, needles; while there was a want of stores, flour mills, forges and public houses within easy reach.

Generally speaking, cottages were larger, better built and better maintained on the estates of large landowners, though even there they varied greatly. Some great landowners, like the tenth Duke of Bedford, saw cottage improvement as 'among the first duties, and ought to be among the first pleasures, of every landlord': he built on a large scale and with the economy that mass production could achieve, and in 1849 sent his plans and quantities for publication in the *Journal* of the Royal Agricultural Society so that other owners could benefit from his experience. Others were less benevolent, or lacked the means to be so. Observers noted that the best cottages on Lord Leicester's estates in Norfolk were those by the approach to Holkham Hall, where they would be seen by visitors, the remainder being less well provided. Some owners, too, sacrificed the occupants' comfort for architectural effect, favouring 'Gothic' or 'picturesque' designs with tiny windows, sharply sloping roofs and massive eaves, involving much loss of useful space. Most irksome,

44 Many fruit and hop pickers were recruited in nearby towns and given temporary accommodation on the farms during the harvest season. The housing was often very rough and ready, not to say primitive, as this illustration indicates. (Museum of English Rural Life)

perhaps, was the strict control exercised by some owners over their 'close' villages. Lord Wantage, for example, allowed only one inn in his village of Ardington; this had to supply tea, coffee and soup as alternatives to stronger beverages. Control over tenants arose partly from a desire to keep out undesirables – vagrants, suspected criminals and the like – and also to keep the Poor Rates low; but the supervision tended to extend less justifiably into the cottagers' morals, daily habits and political allegiance.

The reverse of the landowner's close parish was the 'open' one. This was usually a large village where there was no resident squire and property was in many hands. There incomers were welcome because they added to the custom for the shops, pubs and crafts, as well as for housing. Tradesmen, publicans and shopkeepers with a few hundred pounds to invest ran up rows of cheap cottages. They were sometimes constructed with inferior materials and without adequate water supply, drainage and sanitation, soon declining into rural slums. Little better, if at all, were the cottages provided by farmers for the families of their men. Farmers often took a very restricted view of what was needed, especially as the men might change employer and cottage frequently; and in any case they were usually unwilling to risk the consequences of asking for repairs to be made. Housing legislation before 1914 made little impact upon the countryside and, moreover, the better houses tended to be pre-empted by the better paid, leaving the worst housing to be occupied by those who could afford least rent – the farmworkers.

At the end of the century conditions were still often very bad, and the shortage of decent cottages was one of the main reasons for young people wanting to marry and leave the countryside for the towns. Rider Haggard, on the tour of rural England which he made at the beginning of the present century, found some particularly bad cottages in Huntingdonshire: one, for instance, where:

> the bedroom in the roof, which was stopped with rags to keep out the rain, was approached by a steep ladder, the woman who led me there crawling upon her hands and knees into the apartment, where she slept with the daughter of a neighbour . . . This girl's previous bedroom had been shared with her father, a widower, in the next cottage. I should add that she was grown up.

Some others nearby were known as 'Eltisley death trap', because a large open ditch containing sewage and other refuse bordered the back walls. One of the sanitary problems of the countryside, indeed, was how to educate cottagers in the regular cleaning of earth closets, and the dangers of heaping great mounds of manure and garden refuse against the walls of the cottage. After World War I council building had some effect on rural housing, but in

1937 council houses constituted only about a tenth of the half-million homes occupied by agricultural workers. Of the remainder about 250,000 were privately owned, and some 200,000 were 'tied' cottages belonging to farmers and let to their workers.

In provision for education the countryside always lagged behind the towns, for not only did it have generally inferior school buildings and less well-qualified – often untrained – teachers, but also, in some villages, lacked any school at all. The 1870 Education Act, which enforced the building of a new school where existing provision was inadequate, was like later legislation mainly aimed at bringing the countryside into line with the more rapid progress of the towns. The 'Board' schools thus provided were not free, as is often mistakenly stated, and the fees for a large family were distinctly burdensome, even at 2*d*. a week: three children cost 6*d*. and that small sum was a substantial drain on an income of as little as 11*s*. per week. In some villages there was great opposition to the building of a Board school and a site was difficult to find. Farmers and middle-class residents opposed the new school on the grounds of expense, that working people did not really need educating, and that education would encourage the lads and girls to seek better jobs outside the village, so forcing up wages. The working folk themselves often opposed it, too, because compulsory attendance meant children were unable to help at home or work in the fields, and needed suitable clothes for going to a school where they would not be taught something profitable, like how to plait, or make pillow-lace.

Poor attendance, in fact, was a great problem in rural schools, especially when gleaning was still not finished and some crops, like apples and hops, were not harvested until September. Attendance could be bad throughout the year, however. Epidemics of measles, whooping-cough or ringworm kept children away. Boys played truant to earn a penny at the livestock markets, carrying meals out to the haymakers, planting potatoes, thinning turnips or weeding corn; girls were absent to look after baby when mother was sick or to take the place of servants away on holiday. There were many distractions: fairs, circuses, funerals, elections and processions. At the Horncastle Methodist Senior Mixed School average attendance in the years 1872–5 was only between 81 and 93 out of a school roll that totalled 133–6. Some of the children, also, were too poorly fed to benefit much from the instruction, or suffered from severe physical disabilities. The first report on medical inspection in schools in Lindsey, issued in 1909 by the Medical Officer of Health, showed that of 2,926 children between the ages of twelve and fourteen, nearly 44 per cent had defective vision, while almost as large a proportion were deaf in one or both ears or suffered from adenoids and tonsils; as many as 76 per cent had decayed teeth, and some 3 per cent revealed signs of tuberculosis.

Even when children attended regularly they were taught in classes which included pupils of widely different ages

45 Women gleaning ears of corn in 1903. By this date the traditional custom of gleaning the harvest field was long in decline, partly because of the farmers' restrictions, partly because of the passing away of home baking of bread. (Museum of English Rural Life)

and might be as large as a hundred or more. Given the circumstances, it is truly remarkable that devoted teachers managed to instil as much of the three R's as they did, though some lady teachers were not above having their own clothes repaired in the needlework class. By 1914 many things had improved: there were more qualified teachers and the regulations had been relaxed to allow a broader curriculum, while in larger places there were technical institutes and evening classes for those over school age. Yet the old hostility among the employer class remained: few rural schools were reorganized into junior and senior departments in the years between the wars, and when secondary education for all was enforced in 1944 it was a concept that was still strange and still resisted in some rural parts of the country.

Among the reasons for providing schools (by voluntary effort before 1870, by state intervention after that date) was the supposed effect of education in reducing poverty, violence, lawlessness and drunkenness. Reformers and government alike looked to the civilizing influence of the dispelling of ignorance. Certainly violence against the person declined from the 1860s, as did the number of outbreaks of arson, destruction of farm property, and maiming of animals. The 1860s may perhaps be seen as marking a turning point in the development of rural society: the acceptance by the labouring class of capitalist society with its acquisitive morality, its emphasis on order and regulation, and its use of the law to protect rights of property. Influential in the change were the slow improvement in wages and conditions, and the safety valve for rural discontent offered by the chance of migration to the towns or abroad. However, the old customs were still under attack, as such practices as gleaning the cornfields and collecting fallen wood, berries and mushrooms became increasingly treated as infringements of private property. And the old outlook by no means disappeared. At the end of the century there were villagers who still looked back to some mythical golden age when life was

46 'The Poacher', a photograph taken in 1890. Although the typical poacher was a young man in his twenties, there were many older habitual offenders sufficiently notorious to be widely known by name. Perhaps this was true of the man pictured here. (Hereford City Library)

better and people were free to use the land as they chose. Was not the earth and its fruits sent by God for all?

Before the 1860s discontent had been much more intense and more evident. Particular irritations, such as the spread of threshing machines which reduced the men's winter employment, helped to spark off major conflagrations like the Swing Riots of 1830–31, and in Wales a combination of grievances led to the Rebecca Riots some ten years later. Attempts to enclose commons where a large number of people had enjoyed rights of grazing and gathering fuel were the cause in the early 1830s of the alarming Otmoor disturbances. Such disputed areas were likely to see more than the average amount of poaching and general lawbreaking for long years after. Poaching, attacks on farmers, and arson were also widespread in areas of large-scale commercial farming, as in East Anglia, where burning farm buildings lit up the horizon on many a night in 1843–4. Many of these incidents were purely local and personal, the result of some labourer's dislike of a particular individual, a farmer who had turned him off, a Poor Law official who had refused relief, a squire who had ordered an eviction. Farmers saw their barns go up in flames and sat up with a gun to guard their stock and machinery, and unpopular landowners, parsons and Poor Law Guardians needed to take good care when out alone in the lanes on a dark night.

When the violence died away there still remained a great deal of poaching. Much of it was the work of organized gangs supplying local and distant markets. Casual poaching by individuals merely to fill the pot rose sharply in periods of bad trade when numbers of unemployed men from nearby industrial centres joined in the sport. Many of the depredations were the work of strangers in the neighbourhood, harvesting gangs, woodmen, road contractors' men and railway navvies. The typical poacher as he appeared in the magistrates' courts was a young man in his twenties, often a village craftsman or labourer; but there were many older, persistent offenders, sufficiently notorious to be widely known by name, and some villages, too, were infamous as the home of poaching gangs. The hatred between keepers and poachers persisted to the end of the century, and not infrequently led to violence and deaths. In some counties the keepers considerably outnumbered the regular police, who, however, had been drawn more closely into the issue by the unpopular Poaching Prevention Act of 1862 which authorized officers to hold and search suspects.

Vagrancy also remained a persistent problem in the

countryside. Vagrants were disliked and harried as supposedly responsible for much of the petty theft, house-breaking and poaching, though this was more probably traceable to local people. In practice, vagrants were not easily distinguishable from travelling harvesters, hawkers, and the men and women who had lost their jobs and homes and were honestly seeking work. The 'habitual vagrants' or 'tramps' proper were often workshy, refugees from strict workhouses, and men moved on by the Poor Law authorities. They followed regular routes across the country, sheltering in cheap lodging-houses, refuges, and the casual wards of workhouses, begging and stealing to survive, and occasionally taking a job for a day or two. If not so alarming a threat to property as people supposed, they were indeed numerous, the misfits and outcasts of a society that had become more demanding in its requirements of regularity, order and sobriety.

* * * * * *

The countryside of the end of the nineteenth century and the years before 1914 was still a scene of much distress and misery. Country houses stood empty or were converted to schools, nursing homes and offices; run-down arable farms had new and more economy-minded tenants; cottages housed families who, although rather less pinched than in the past, were still only barely managing to survive. The cohesion of rural society had long been under stress, and if the causes of the former violence and unrest had declined, there were now new stirrings of democracy and independence. Agricultural trade unionism, which flared up extensively in the 1870s, had not established itself and had now all but flickered out, leaving behind thwarted expectations and bitter memories. Landowners found government neglectful of the farming industry in an age when urban living standards depended more and more on cheap imports, while farmers, struggling to survive, began to combine to try and succeed where landowners had failed. Labourers moved increasingly off the land, and those who remained were less

47 The 1870s was the decade of the 'revolt of the field', the attempt by the farm labourers to organize in search of higher wages. The union movement began in 1872, gathered strength under Joseph Arch's leadership, but then declined under the pressures of farmers' lockouts, evictions of union men from their cottages, and internal disunity. By 1877, when the meeting shown here was held, the workers' movement was on its way towards ultimate collapse, not to be revived successfully for a generation. (Museum of English Rural Life)

respectful to their betters than used to be the case. So wrote an assistant commissioner in his report to the Royal Commission on Labour, set up in 1891:

The relations of employers and employed are marked everywhere by a want of cordiality, and in a great many places by mutual suspicion. The familiar and quasi-patriarchal terms upon which farmers used to live with their men are fast giving way to mere contractual relations. Things are at present in a transition stage; farmers resent the notion of men being independent of them and dread being left in the lurch at busy seasons. They begin to see that nothing but money will keep a man upon a farm, and money is more than ever difficult to get.

48 Access to land became a major political issue in the decades before 1914 when some reformers advocated the provision of smallholdings to stem the flight from the land, while others argued for the taxation of land values, and even land nationalization. Farm labourers deplored the large areas converted to game preserves or left uncultivated following the depression of the late nineteenth century, while builders complained of the difficulty of obtaining construction sites at reasonable prices. (Museum of English Rural Life)

Reformers discussed with concern the 'flight from the land' with its consequences for urban unemployment and shortage of housing, its effects on the newly-revealed decline in the national physique, and the future recruitment of armies and police. Controversial reports and enquiries proliferated, and a mixed batch of nostrums, smallholding Acts, parish councils, and labour colonies, were tried and found wanting: the farm labour force continued to decline. The process was inevitable, of course. Across the world industrialization and urbanization have involved the ultimate decline of the economy's rural sector, and in Britain, where the decline began early, it was running down very quickly in the later Victorian years – indeed, it has continued to do so to the present, when agricultural employment occupies less than 2 per cent of the national labour force. In the process the character of the village and its inhabitants was changed: land became increasingly subservient to the needs of industry and the urban population, the old hegemony of the squire declined, and social relationships became increasingly commercial and impersonal. But there were gains also: in independence, equality and living standards. Progress, after all, always works in both directions.

Chapter Six

Poverty and Wealth

The England of Victorian and Edwardian times exhibited very marked contrasts in incomes and living standards. Affluence and gracious living were contrasted with poverty and penny-pinching squalor. On the one hand were the fashionable squares, large houses, carriages and servants of London's West End, on the other the dismal, narrow, ill-kept streets, the endless rows of cramped, monotonous houses, litter-strewn alleys, noisome passages, workshops and yards of the East End. From Belgravia to Aldgate is only four miles: but in contrasting life styles they might well have been four thousand miles apart. East and West rarely met. The denizen of Whitechapel seldom had business in the West End, unless he were by trade a carter, hawker or sweep; and the patrician of Eaton Place or Grosvenor Square would perhaps never in his whole life venture beyond the bounds of the City into the wilds of Bermondsey, Bethnal Green or the Mile End Road. It is significant that in the early years of sanitary reform in the 1840s, middle-class people had to be given conducted tours of the East End slums in order to grasp fully the extent and seriousness of the public health problem.

The differences between the two Londons – which could also be found in the two Manchesters, Birminghams or Liverpools – may be illustrated in many ways. For one, let us take the availability of living space. The typical narrow-fronted, but high and deep, terraced house to be found in London's well-known squares had its basement rooms for 'domestic offices', with reception rooms and main bedrooms on ground floor and the floor above, and children's bedrooms and servants' rooms above those. Such accommodation – by no means the most luxurious – may be compared with the two rooms, 12 ft. square, which Mrs Pember Reeves found in Lambeth in 1913, housing a family of six. Or, in a more extreme case, man, wife and three children living in one room, 12 ft. by 10 ft., with one bed and a banana-crate cot. (This seems to have been a very common use for old banana crates.) Even the weather had different effects. In the West End a fine day attracted people out to shop or ride in the parks; in the East End the heat merely intensified the suffocating odours of rubbish-strewn back yards, and could give but little pleasure to tired, overworked women kept at home by their babies or bent on turning out the usual quota of work in some domestic trade. When Mrs Pember Reeves's visitor in Lambeth remarked on its being a lovely day one such woman responded: 'Lovely for you, miss, but it brings out the bugs something 'orrible.'

Another basis for comparison is diet. A glance at an Edwardian edition of Mrs Beeton shows the suggested family dinners as including in one week roast and cold lamb, stewed steak, veal cutlets, roast and cold beef, mackerel and salmon, to say nothing of salads and desserts. These were merely 'family dinners'; a complete dinner consisted of eight courses, four of which consisted of fish, an entrée, a joint and game. At the other end of the scale came the Lambeth housewife who had the home to keep and five persons to feed from an allowance of 19*s*. 6*d*; or in another instance eight to feed on 21*s*., and who spent upwards of 2*s*. 6*d*. a week on bread alone. There was meat, which absorbed between 2*s*. and 4*s*.; when money was short, it consisted of anonymous 'pieces' which ranged from 4½*d*. to 6*d*. the lb. Typical dinners in the home of a carter, whose wages varied between 19*s*. and 23*s*. 6*d*., included, in a good week, hashed beef, greens and potatoes (Sunday), cold beef (Monday), bread and dripping with cheese and tomatoes (Tuesday), boiled bacon, beans and potatoes on Wednesday, mutton chops on Thursday, sausages on Friday, and a pudding of 'pieces' to round off the week on Saturday. Bread, however, was the mainstay of breakfast and tea:

It is cheap; they like it; it comes into the house ready cooked; it is always at hand, and needs no plate and spoon. Spread with a scraping of butter, jam or margarine, according to the length of the purse of the mother, they never tire of it as long as they are in their ordinary state of health.

The diet was particularly inadequate for children. The only milk they knew was the separated variety which came in cans priced at 1*d*., 2*d*., 3*d*. or 4*d*., according to size, and bearing on them in large red letters the legend: 'This milk is not recommended as food for infants'. The lack of fresh milk derived from the same cause as the cramped housing conditions and uncomfortable clothing: it was too expensive.

Milk costs the same, 4*d*. a quart, in Lambeth that it costs in Mayfair. A healthy child ought to be able to use a quart of milk a day, which means a weekly milk bill for that child of 2*s*. 4*d*. – quite an impossible amount when the food of the whole family may have to be supplied out of 8*s*. or 9*s*. a week.

But it is not easy to generalize about diet: it varied not only with income but also regionally and seasonally, and with individual taste and the housewife's skill and knowledge. Quantities of food bought tell us nothing about quality or the nutritional value of the dishes that resulted. On a more scientific basis Dr Oddy has analysed the information in diet surveys made towards the end of the century to show that the energy value of the diets in the 'servant-keeping families', at 3,256 calories per day, was over twice that of families living on less than 18*s*. a week (1,578 calories), with other income groups falling in between these two extremes. The consumption of protein in the servant-keeping families was well over twice as great as in the under-18*s*. category, fat more than three times as great, iron well over twice, and calcium over four times. Only in consumption of carbohydrates was the gap narrowed, to an advantage among the servant-keeping families of a modest 65 per cent.

There were many other possible contrasts beside housing and diet: health, medical care, longevity, education, leisure, security. Perhaps one of the most telling was life in old age. The well-to-do business or professional man who had been able to save on an ample scale from his very moderately taxed income, enjoyed retirement in a pleasant villa in the country, or in an upper-class resort like Bournemouth, Folkestone or Harrogate, more economically perhaps in a comfortable hotel in Aix, Lucerne or Baden-Baden. For him there were interesting company and attractive surroundings, good food, servants, amusements. By contrast, the elderly poor, with no property, no savings, no relations to care for them, faced the bleak charity of the Poor Law. George Lansbury, the social reformer, became a member of the local Board of Guardians in Poplar, a crowded dockside parish of East London, in 1892. There he saw and recorded the unpleasant aspect of relief in the old type of workhouse:

> The place was clean: brass knobs and floors were polished, but of goodwill, kindness, there was none . . . Officials, receiving ward, hard forms, whitewashed walls, keys dangling at the waist of those who spoke to you, huge books for name, history, etc., searching, and then being stripped and bathed in a communal tub, and the final crowning indignity of being dressed in clothes which had been worn by lots of other people, hideous to look at, ill-fitting and coarse – everything possible was done to inflict mental and moral degradation.

A lack of knowledge of how the other half lived heightened misunderstanding, suspicion and distrust. The 'toff' in contemporary eyes was autocratic, supercilious, unimaginative and rather lacking in intelligence; the industrial employer was hard, unfeeling, unscrupulous; the working man sometimes honest but stupid, otherwise lazy, unreliable, drunken. It was in many respects a hard age, when deprivation, preventable sickness and ignorance aroused

less notice and much less outrage than they were to do in the mid-twentieth century. Poverty and unemployment were generally regarded as the natural consequences of fecklessness and drink, of personal moral failings rather than, at least in part, the result of impersonal economic forces, the trade cycle, the maldistribution of wealth, the limited view of the role of the state. There were among the upper classes the 'scientific' reformers, such as those of the Charity Organisation Society (1869), who thought indiscriminate giving to be ineffective or positively harmful, an encouragement to idleness and vice, and wished to see private relief organized on a more systematic and logical basis. They had begun by attempting to co-ordinate the work of the charitable societies and Poor Law, but went further to try and reform the very spirit of society, as an alternative to socialism. The COS popularized the method of casework and helped found the profession of social work. And there were many earlier and later individual charitable societies which did much good, such as the YMCA, Church of England Children's Society, Dr Barnardo's Homes, the Children's County Holiday Fund, the National Institute for the Blind, the Boys' Brigade, and of course the Salvation Army.

Such bodies sought to help the innocent and convert the sinners. They did not, and could not, deal with funda-

49 and **50** Scenes in Poplar Workhouse, 1905. 'The place was clean', wrote George Lansbury, 'brass knobs and floors were polished, but of goodwill, kindness, there was none . . . everything possible was done to inflict mental and moral degradation.' (Tower Hamlets Library)

mental causes of social ills, low and irregular earnings, disease, unemployment. Money was the religion of both ambitious and cautious; drink the nirvana of the hopeless and careless. Many of the small employers had themselves risen by dint of unremitting toil and thrift, and like the naval and military warrant officers who had come up through the ranks, were often the hardest taskmasters. For millions of housewives, life was a constant 'study' of money, of how to pay the bills and feed a family on a weekly income of a pound or less. They were not helped by husbands who, like D. H. Lawrence's coal-miner father, kept back the same amount each week for beer and baccy regardless of how short time or a poor seam reduced the earnings.

Social divisions were not confined of course to the crude dichotomy between rich and poor. Within the ranks of manual workers there were clear distinctions of income and status among the unskilled, semi-skilled, and skilled. The skilled often earned twice as much or more than the unskilled, a margin which put him in quite a superior, if still recognizably 'working-class' style of life. Then one

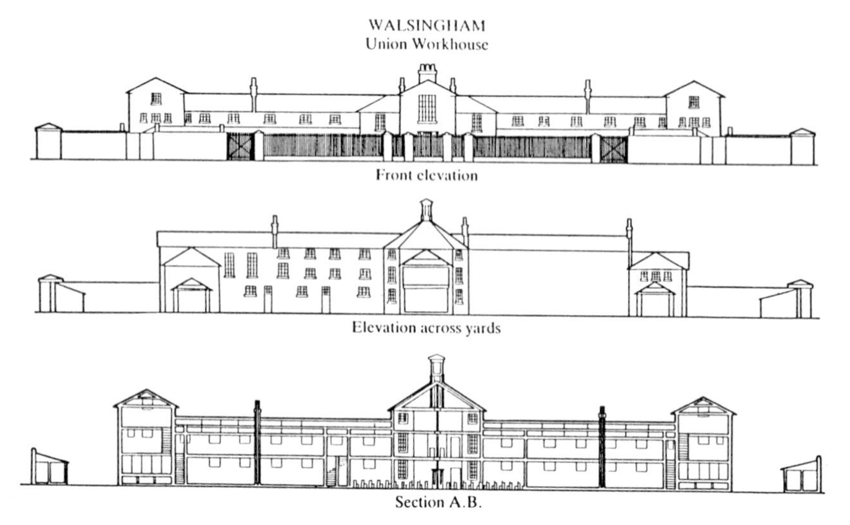

Figure 5 Elevations and section of the workhouse built for the Walsingham Union, Norfolk. This was one of the many new workhouses built as a result of the Poor Law Amendment Act of 1834, this particular one providing accommodation for 250 paupers at a cost of £5,900. (Anne Digby, *Pauper Palaces*, 1978, p. 76.)

entered the multifarious groups which stood between the artisan and labourer and the middle and upper classes: the shopkeepers, workshop masters and petty business men, commercial travellers, school teachers, clerks and bookkeepers, publicans, superior domestic servants and hotel staff, and many more – the world from which so many of Dickens's characters were drawn, the world of the 'shabby-genteel'.

The fluidity of society, the general absence of occupational barriers, meant that many people assumed a number of very different roles in the course of a lifetime. They had perhaps worked at one time in a factory, tried their hand at keeping a shop, run an undertaker's business, even owned and taught in a little private school. Sergeants and petty officers, retired from army and navy, had an ambition to keep a pub, or took employment as hotel porters or commissionaires, bank messengers or guards, workhouse masters or court bailiffs. And there were not a few who combined an inoffensive occupation by day with criminal activities by night. The underworld was extensive and widespread, with certain concentrations in the notorious rookeries, congested slum areas, which lay close to the commercial centres of London, Birmingham and Manchester. The dock areas of Liverpool and Newcastle, Cardiff and East London had evil reputations, but even more infamous were the great rookeries of the 'Holy Land', situated between New Oxford Street, Great Russell Street and St Giles High Street; or 'The Nichol', an insanitary nightmare whose sagging houses had to be supported by great beams, and which had grown like a malignant tumour on the body of the once respectable silk-working district of Spitalfields. There a variety of doubtful trades could be found, the 'shops' of fences and forgers, the homes of hordes of beggars, whores, and many, many children. There were cheap lodgings for the broken-down clerk, the drunken attorney, disgraced clergyman; cellar dwellings for itinerant Irish or newly-arrived European Jews, dosshouses for tramps and thieves down on their luck. These were anthills of misery and vice: a warren of narrow alleys, dark passages and inter-connecting houses so dense and so complex, and withal so dangerous that wanted men could vanish there and defy the police almost indefinitely.

On the border territory of the 'Holy Land' stood the brilliantly lit and palatial gin shops of Drury Lane, Covent Garden and Clare Market, whose customers faced an agonizing choice between such rival attractions as 'The Cream of the Valley', 'The Out and Out', 'The No Mistake', 'The Good for Mixing', 'The Real Knock-me-down', 'The Celebrated Butter Gin', 'The Regular Flare-up', and other equally enticing concoctions. Close by and sharply contrasted with such flashy and intoxicating delights were, as Dickens described,

> Wretched houses with broken windows patched with rags and paper: every room let out to a different family, and in many instances to two and even three – fruit and 'sweet stuff' manufacturers in the cellars, barbers and red-herring vendors in the front parlours, cobblers in the back; a bird-fancier on the first floor, three families on the second, starvation in the attics, Irishmen in the passage, a 'musician' in the front kitchen, and a char-woman and five hungry children in the back one – filth everywhere – a gutter before the houses and a drain behind – clothes drying and slops emptying from the windows; girls of fourteen or fifteen, with matted hair, walking about barefoot, and in white greatcoats, almost their only covering; boys of all ages, in coats of all sizes and no coats at all; men and women, in every variety of scanty and dirty apparel, lounging, scolding, drinking, smoking, squabbling, fighting, and swearing.

Within the criminal community were to be found the same differences of function and gradations of status as were evident in the reputable workaday world. Each branch of the criminal trade was subdivided among various specialists. Thus among the broad category of thieves were the 'mobsmen', light-fingered gentry who relied on manual dexterity and included 'buzzers', who stole handkerchiefs, 'wires' who picked ladies' pockets, 'prop-nailers', the takers of pins and brooches, 'thimble-screwers' who wrenched watches from their guards, and 'shop-lifters' who purloined goods while pretending to examine articles. The category of thief known as 'sneaksmen' included 'drag-sneaks', specialists in taking goods or luggage from carts and coaches, 'snoozers', who slept at railway hotels and decamped with passengers' luggage in the morning, 'till friskers' who emptied a till during the shopkeeper's absence, 'snow gatherers' who took clean clothes from the hedges where they were drying, and 'cat and kitten hunters' who collected pewter pots from the spikes of area railings. The 'swell mobsmen' frequented places of public entertainment, sometimes specializing in services at the more elegant churches and chapels, especially when there were charity sermons. There were, too, the footpads, cracksmen, confidence tricksters, 'magsmen' or travelling operators of gambling games, gentlemanly 'macers' or gambling sharps, and 'shofulmen', the coiners and their agents and distributors.

Fraudulent beggars abounded, as well as honest ones: those with forged testimonials, and the fake blind and lame, with supposed wounds concealed under filthy bandages; those who stood in the streets half-naked in cold weather to arouse sympathy, the 'shallow lay'; those who hired children to beg with them or independently, paying 3*d*. a day for a normal child, and from 6*d*. upwards for a crippled one as being much more profitable. Not all these practitioners were male, though men predominated in most trades. There were female thieves, accomplices and beggars, and many of the prostitutes looked out especially for clients befuddled by drink, so they might make off with their money, watches and rings. The women hid the money in their stays, their hair, stockings, and 'where decency forbids to name', as one account has it. Some even swallowed it if there was immediate fear of the constable's arrival. If necessary they would take 'opening medicine' to secure its early reappearance.

Certain fashionable parts of the metropolis were notorious for the numbers of prostitutes who frequented them: the Haymarket, Regent Street, Portland Place – noted particularly for 'a French detachment of voluble habits' – and the Burlington Arcade, modestly described as the 'counterpart of an Eastern slave market'. Strolling along the Strand in the evening 'every hundred steps one jostles twenty harlots; some of them ask for a glass of gin; others say, "Sir, it is to pay my lodging" '. Clients were led to 'disreputable coffee-shops in the neighbourhood of the Haymarket and Leicester Square where you may see the blinds drawn down, and the lights burning dimly within, with notices over the doors that "beds are to be had within" '. Mayhew, in his *London Labour and the London Poor*, carefully classified the prostitutes, his third-class category consisting of servant girls, daughters of labourers, and some of a still lower class:

> Some of these girls are of a very tender age – from thirteen years and upwards . . . Many of them are dressed in a light cotton or merino gown, and ill-suited crinoline, with a light grey or brown cloak, or mantle. Some with pork-pie hat, and waving feather – white, blue or red; others with a slouched straw hat . . . Some have a look of artless innocence and ingenuousness, others very pert, callous and artful.

Piccadilly Circus was 'always an offensive place to pass, even in the daytime; but at night it is absolutely hideous, with its sparring snobs and flashing satins, and sporting gents and painted cheeks, and brandy-sparkling eyes, and bad tobacco and hoarse horse-laughs and loud indecency'. 'It is indeed a striking sight', remarked the *Saturday Review*, 'one which no foreigner who wishes to study our national morality . . . ought to overlook.'

The slums, too, had their quota of streetwalkers, and 'red light' districts could be found in every town of any size. So bad was the situation in the garrison and dockyard towns that Parliament resorted to special measures in an attempt to control the situation. Contagious Diseases Acts were passed in the 1860s providing for inspection of prostitutes reported to be transmitting disease, and those in or near important naval and military establishments were made subject to regular medical checks. The Acts, however, proved difficult to operate, partly because of the problem of distinguishing professional prostitutes from the promiscuous wives and widows of soldiers and sailors; and it was complained that the powers of blackmail which unscrupulous constables and brothel keepers already had over prostitutes were greatly extended by the new regulations. A campaign begun by the Ladies' National Association, in which such prominent figures as Florence Nightingale and Harriet Martineau were involved, was taken to a successful conclusion by the zeal of the Association's secretary, Mrs Butler; and the Contagious Diseases Acts were repealed in 1886. Before this a new Act of 1885 made procuring and brothel-keeping illegal and drove prostitution under cover.

It continued to thrive, of course. In towns of importance the demand from residents was very considerably supplemented by that from tourists and casual visitors, business men, commercial travellers, and countrymen in town for a market. Cheap railway travel brought in many newcomers, and the women of the town made a point of meeting the arriving trains. The supply originated in a variety of factors: the near starvation wages of some female workers – domestic servants, charwomen, dressmakers, seamstresses, milliners, hotel employees and country girls; the maids and waitresses discharged by employers for theft, disease or drunkenness, and unable to get another situation without a reference; overcrowded and unhappy homes, bad parental example, seduction, lack of education, and, of major importance, drink. The combination of streetwalking with picking pockets was not only a matter of opportunity: it was the result, too, of the need to get money for drink. Frances Finnegan's study of prostitution in York shows this link of thieving with prostitution very clearly, and also notes that half of the city's prostitutes came from outside the city, and that two out of every five of the clients were visitors: 'respectable gentlemen' in York on business, as the newspaper put it, or farmworkers from the neighbouring district.

Among the concerned there was always some awareness of the seriousness of poverty, disease, crime and immorality. Charles Dickens, Lord Shaftesbury and a number of other well-known figures had joined in Edwin Chadwick's public health campaign in the 1840s; and in the next decade Henry Mayhew accumulated his enormous body of material on 'London Labour and the London Poor' which was published in the *Morning Chronicle,* and was followed by similar inquiries in the provinces. About the same time Mary Carpenter, both literary and practical reformer, was publishing her books on *Ragged Schools, Reformatory Schools,* and *Juvenile Delinquents.* Later reformers looking back, like Beatrice Webb, detected a new tide of interest which began to flow in the 1880s. There was, she wrote, a belief arising then in a social utopia which the new discoveries of science would help bring about, a 'religion of humanity' in which the impulse of self-subordinating service was transferred from God to man. There developed a new spirit of scientific inquiry into social problems, a purposeful urge to ascertain the facts, and to find new and more appropriate remedies.

This new awareness was fed by the revelations published in books, pamphlets and newspapers. The writer, George Sims, brought social questions to notice under such striking titles as *The Black Stain* (about the exploitation of children), and the Revd. Andrew Mearns with his *Bitter Cry of Outcast London*. In July 1885 W. T. Stead, the editor of the *Pall Mall Gazette*, published in his paper a series of sensational articles in his 'Maiden Tribute of Modern Babylon' campaign. Stead was concerned to show how easy it was for young girls to be taken from their homes and shipped over to Belgium to be incarcerated in one of the licensed brothels there. To prove his point, Stead himself purchased a girl, Eliza Armstrong, kept her in London in the charge of a woman of his acquaintance, and arranged for the couple to travel across the Channel and back again. The government, however, so far from showing disquiet, decided to make an example of the upstart editor and prosecuted him. It appeared that Stead had purchased the girl from her mother, and since she was not the legal guardian he was convicted of abduction and sentenced to three months' imprisonment. His associates received even heavier sentences, though General Bramwell Booth of the Salvation Army, who was also involved in the affair, was acquitted.

Then a few years later, in 1888, another celebrated scandal filled the press. A series of six (possibly seven) unsolved murders occurred in a limited area of the East End, in and around Whitechapel, between August and November. The victims were all prostitutes, women alone in the streets at the dead of night, and because the corpses were expertly mutilated and organs removed, the unknown perpetrator was dubbed 'Jack the Ripper'. Murder was regular newspaper fare, and the Victorian era provided a rich crop of celebrated cases, from that of Maria Marten (the 'murder in the red barn' – which took place in 1827 but became a staple of later melodrama) to the case of Dr William Palmer, racing enthusiast extraordinary, who may have murdered as many as sixteen people; the beautiful Madeleine Smith, suspected of disposing of an inconvenient lover; Charles Peace, homicidal house-breaker and collector of other people's violins; Florence Maybrick, acquitted of extracting arsenic from flypapers to end the life of her hypochondriacal husband; and Dr Thomas Cream, who a few years after the 'Ripper murders' killed off a number of prostitutes with the aid of strychnine. And there was of course the famous Charles Bravo case, which included among its many doubtful elements poison by antimony, the possibility of suicide, the secret motives of the wealthy wife and her relationship with an elderly former lover, a fashionable homeopathic physician.

All these celebrated cases attracted enormous interest, but the 'Ripper murders' were in a class apart. They were particularly grisly, particularly difficult to solve – the police seem never to have got near a solution (though a number of homicidal maniacs were under suspicion, one of whom was picked out of the Thames on 31 December). They affected that unmentionable twilight class, the women of the streets, in a particularly unpleasant part of London. Newspapers brought to readers' attention the squalor and misery of conditions in the East End, the night life which revolved round drinking dens, cheap lodging houses and prostitutes. The murderer was never found, though theories abounded then and have done ever since: he was a perverted surgeon or medical student (because of the murderer's evident anatomical knowledge) whose life had been blighted by some prostitute and was bent on taking revenge on prostitutes in general; he was a Jewish butcher (the district abounded with Jews); he was a sailor from a foreign ship which sailed away and never returned (explaining why the murders ended so abruptly); he was a member of the royal family (which would explain the apparent incompetence of the police). Certainly, at any rate, respectable families reading their papers in their parlour in Kensington or Regent's Park had their eyes opened to the nature of life in the *terra incognita* which stretched beyond the bustling realm of the Bank of England and Tower Bridge.

* * * * * *

Almost at the end of Victoria's reign came a much more significant revelation of the nature of urban life. This arose from the recruiting figures for the Boer War. It became known that between 1897 and 1901 as high a proportion as 26.5 per cent of men volunteering to join the army in the towns of York, Sheffield and Leeds had to be rejected outright on medical grounds: the main defects were physical under-development, active disease, such as tuberculosis, defective vision, and deformities. A further 21 per cent of the volunteers did not meet the army's physical standards, but these men were accepted provisionally to see if a short spell of army life would bring them up to standard – which, perhaps surprisingly, it frequently did. There was much public concern over the figures, and the fear was expressed that Britain might be unable to mount a large army in a future major war. In consequence, an inquiry was set afoot in 1904 by a body with the extraordinary title of Committee on Physical Deterioration. This reviewed the field of poverty, inadequate nutrition, bad housing, defective public health, which had already been examined by a number of recent private investigators. The committee placed emphasis on the deleterious effects of overcrowding, adulteration of food, and limited educational facilities upon the intelligence and physique of the poorer classes. Particularly telling was the fact that in working-class areas of towns the infant death rate might be double that of the better areas, and that as high a proportion as 1 in 5 of working-class babies died within the first four weeks of life.

This contrast in infant death rates was associated with another difference, the size of families. One reason for the high mortality among working-class families was that they had more babies: by 1911 the wives of unskilled workers had nearly twice as many babies as did wives whose husbands were members of the professions or higher business ranks. Larger families meant overcrowding in the home, more strain on the mother, and an income that was increasingly stretched with each new arrival. Middle-class families could easily afford their babies, and moreover generally took care that the number was limited and did not become a burden. The decline in the middle-class birth rate had been going on for some decades before the turn of the century, and it continued to fall thereafter, so that the number of births per 1,000 women, which had been 119 in 1911, had fallen to only 94 in 1931. Possibly this trend owed something to the feminist movement and to the airing of views on family limitation: the latter was an issue popularized by the Malthusian League and given much publicity by the trial in 1877 of Charles Bradlaugh and Annie Besant for re-issuing a work on birth control, first published in the early 1830s, the circulation of which immediately shot up by leaps and bounds. It has also been suggested that the fall in the birth rate was a reaction to the fall in the number of infant deaths in middle-class families, a recognition of the fact that it was now very likely that every conception would mean a child who survived infancy to require bringing up and educating.

The question has also been raised whether there were sufficient career openings for the sons of middle-class families at the end of the nineteenth century. Controversy has arisen over whether middle-class employment kept pace with population growth, and the figures do suggest in fact that numbers in the Church and the law certainly fell behind, though there was compensation in the rapid expansion of medicine and dentistry, literary careers, scientific pursuits and architecture. Such evidence refers to the major professions and the upper middle class. There was undoubtedly a big expansion in the size of the lower middle class, the group which Professor A. L. Bowley, the statistician, described as containing persons with small salaries, profits or earnings in forms other than wages. His category included clerks and others in the distributive wholesale and retail trades, and the younger and less successful persons in teaching and other minor professions.

The traditional middle class, those in the major professions, together with superior civil servants and the more important businessmen, some managers of firms, and the gentleman farmers, shared a certain background

51 The home of the wealthy: an impressive room in Hafodines Hall with elaborate arches supported on marble pillars, and fireplace to match; grand piano in the background. (R.C. Ancient & Historical Monuments in Wales)

in education – generally public school, but also to a surprising extent lesser scholastic establishments – a common outlook and morality, a belief in hard work, discipline, thrift, and the maintenance of a well-defined code of behaviour, which extended to manners and dress. There was much concern to avoid anything which might harm the reputation of the family; anything scandalous, which if it was impossible to avoid then certainly had to be hushed up. Great emphasis was placed on keeping up appearances, of maintaining conventions of respectability which became remarkably limiting and hidebound. They could not begin to compare, however, with the leading landlowners and their vast incomes from agriculture, mining and urban ground rents; nor with the successful financial entrepreneurs of the City of London, the great figures in banking, insurance, commodity dealing and property speculation; nor yet with the magnates of shipping, the colonial trades, brewing and tobacco, the newly-risen industrialists – the Thomas Brasseys and Alfred Morrises – and the later press barons, car manufacturers and owners of multiple stores.

An upper middle-class family occupied a substantial ten- or twelve-room house in a superior residential district, often with enough ground to provide room for a croquet lawn and tennis court, and perhaps a paddock for the children's pony. At least three indoor servants were employed as well as a gardener, together with a groom and coachman where a carriage was kept. The indoor servants were almost all women: in the Hampstead of 1901 there were 80 female domestics to every 100 occupiers. Already at this date, however, the finding of servants was becoming more difficult as young girls increasingly preferred a career as a school teacher, post-office clerk, typist, shop assistant or factory worker. Life as a domestic servant was often hard, with very long hours, severely restricted freedom, and tedious and unpleasant duties such as laying fires, blackleading grates, carrying innumerable scuttles of coal and cans of water up endless flights of

52 The home of the wealthy: kitchen and kitchen staff at Minley Manor, Hants. The chef studies his recipes while a female assistant draws a pair of game birds. (National Monuments Record)

stairs, emptying slops and chamber pots, washing dishes, scrubbing, sweeping, dusting and polishing. One relief was that the cleaning of the boots and knives and running of errands was the province of a boy who came in daily for an hour or two before school, and again perhaps after school. Much of the servant's regular work had to be performed in dark and damp basements, and the nights were spent in bleak attic bedrooms, sleeping on a narrow, specially made servant's bed (costing about 25s.), with a lumpy flock mattress and coarse, unbleached calico sheets, surrounded by a suite of cheap 'servant's furniture' consisting of toilet table, washstand, chest of drawers, towel horse and chair, which was commonly advertised for sale at some £3 or £4.

It was to economize on servants' time and to keep up

with the times that brushing and sweeping were lightened, first by the patent carpet sweeper, and then the portable version of the electric vacuum cleaner which became available after 1905. But many tasks still had to be performed by hand, the furniture polished with Ronuk or Johnson's, the brass with Bluebell, the silver with Goddard's. In the afternoon one servant, at least, freshly clean and smartly dressed, had always to be on hand to answer the door to callers, to say whether the lady of the house was at home, to receive cards, and to serve tea if the visitor were a family friend and thus invited to stay for more than the formal fifteen minutes. In summer the family went off with some of the servants to a rented house in Brighton or Bournemouth; and at home as long as the evenings were fine there were local diversions at the golf club, cricket or tennis club. The family always changed for dinner as a matter of course, even when no visitors were expected, and the evening was spent in reading the papers, the *Strand Magazine*, *Punch*, or a new novel by Rider Haggard, Anthony Hope, or H. G. Wells. When guests were entertained there was bridge, perhaps billiards for the men, or songs at the pianoforte, and young ladies were asked to bring their music with them.

The income needed to sustain this way of life need not be very great, a thousand or two, or just several hundred pounds, since food, servants, fuel, workmen and public transport were all cheap and taxation was low. Brides came with dowries and inheritances, and spare capital invested in sound stocks produced a valuable supplement to a moderate professional income. Government bonds, it is true, yielded rather under 3 per cent, but money placed in railway shares, public utilities and property, especially abroad, could produce over twice as much. Death duties made hardly any impact on inheritances before the modest reforms carried out by Harcourt in 1894, and even then produced a total revenue for the government of less than £20m. before 1910.

But most fundamental to the middle-class ability to save,

and indeed to their whole way of life, was the very limited burden of income tax. After its first introduction to help pay for the wars against Napoleon, this unpopular innovation was struck down along with the *Grande Armée* at Waterloo. Then, after a long hiatus, Peel saw fit to revive it in 1842 as a temporary measure to help wipe out the Whig deficit which he had inherited and to provide elbow room for reforming the tariff. It was fixed at 7*d*. in the pound of all incomes over £150, a threshold which effectively exempted the great majority of the working classes. The tax proved to be a great revenue raiser, which was precisely one of Gladstone's objections to it: it was, he said, 'an engine of public extravagance'. Moreover, it encouraged immorality among taxpayers: 'a tangled network of man traps for conscience'. For two years, in 1875 and 1876, the tax fell to the almost derisive level of 2*d*. in the pound (under 1 per cent), and in 1874 Gladstone had fought an election, unsuccessfully, on its abolition. For the rest of the century the rate remained at 8*d*. or below, and then the Boer War, naval expansion, and Lloyd George's social reforms put it up at first to 1*s*. and then to 1*s*. 2*d*. In 1905–6, with exemption on the first £160 of income and reduced rates on further increments, and with the standard rate at 1*s*., the lower middle-class gentleman with £300 a year paid an average 5·6*d*. in the pound, a total of £7; his better-off superior with £600 paid 9·6*d*. or a total of £24. Income tax, though a useful contribution to government revenue, still produced only a little over a fifth of the total, completely dwarfed by the £72m. (out of £153m.) provided by customs and excise.

Such a low burden of income tax meant that even among the upper middle class disposable income was almost as large as the gross income received. The more well-to-do, at least if they were moderately careful, could easily find an ample margin for saving and investing. It is significant that total bank deposits, under £700m. in the early 1890s, rose to over £900m. by 1908 (and so rising by much more than did the price level); while exports of money capital for investment in the Empire and the Americas also increased markedly, reaching a total of some £200m. a year, equal to about a tenth of the whole national income. Cheap government, low taxation, an expanding economy at home and abroad, cheap labour, and cheap food and manufactures all contributed to the comfortable standards of the middle class. But not to them alone. Such circumstances contributed, too, to the great comfort of large numbers of better-off working-class families who spent a very high proportion of their modest income on food, fuel, and clothing and other mass-produced goods. They could do well at a time when flour was under 1*s*. a stone, potatoes came at ½*d*. a lb., milk at 1½d. a pint, eggs at 1*d*. each, cheese at 8*d*., British beef 8*d*. a lb. and frozen beef and mutton at 4½*d*–5½*d*., tea at 1*s*. 6*d*., sugar at 2*d*., and coal at 1*s*. a cwt.

* * * * * *

Below this moderately comfortable section of society stretched the ranks of the poor, primarily the families of unskilled workers who struggled to make ends meet on 'round about a pound a week', to use the phrase of Mrs Pember Reeves. Below them came the very poor, with lower and less regular incomes, and below them still, the destitute. How numerous were the poor? This was a question which puzzled inquiring minds in the later nineteenth century and led to a series of investigations which became pioneer models of social survey. There was, first, a difficult problem of definition, for 'poor' was and remains a relative term (many of the present-day poor in the United States run cars – they have to in order to find work or to pick up their relief pay from an office on the other side of the city). There are, indeed, official Poor Law figures for England and Wales, but these merely show the tip of the iceberg for they included only those who had no source of income and were desperate enough to seek the rather limited compassion of the authorities. For what the figures are worth, they show that the percentage of the population classed as paupers was actually falling, from 5.3 per cent in 1851 to 2.4 per cent in 1901, the latter figure indicating some 780,000 persons receiving public relief. Beyond these 'official poor' were an uncounted number of people not so destitute as to enter a workhouse or seek a Poor Law dole, but positively and recognizably in poverty.

The first modern investigation was set afoot by Charles Booth, London representative of the Liverpool-based Booth shipping line, producing, said *The Times*, the 'grimmest book of our generation'. Booth's solution to the problem of definition was to take together both income levels and conditions of life. He placed the inhabitants of London in a series of categories, of which Class A consisted of the hopeless poor, made up of occasional labourers, loafers and semi-criminals; Class B was the very poor, those mainly engaged in work of a casual nature, such as the dock labourers of East London; and Class C, the poor who had low intermittent earnings affected by seasonal and other factors, such as building labourers, stevedores, and the like. Above these came Class D, whose incomes were small but regular, and Class E with regular standard earnings above the level of poverty. 'By the word "poor",' wrote Booth, 'I mean to describe those who have a sufficiently regular though bare income such as 18*s*. – 21*s*. per week for a moderate family, and by "very poor" those who from any cause fall much below this standard.' He found that in the great city of London, reputedly the world's wealthiest, 1.25 per cent of the population fell into Class A, 11.25 per cent into Class B, and 8 per cent into Class C. Altogether, 30.7 per cent of London's people, nearly one in three, were either on his poverty line or fell below it. As to the causes of this enormous deprivation, Booth found that the great bulk of it – 85 per cent at his estimation – arose from a combination of low pay and lack of regular work associated with large families and the consequences of sickness. Only 15 per cent was due to character defects, idleness, drunkenness, thriftlessness.

Booth's inquiries, begun in 1886, ranged widely over

all aspects of the problem, including housing, education, drink, betting, and religious and social influences. It took him seventeen years to complete, and involved the publication of seventeen large volumes, the final one appearing in 1903. His findings sparked off much controversy and inspired a number of similar if smaller investigations, most notably that by Seebohm Rowntree. Booth's survey could be criticized on the grounds that London, with its large numbers of casual labourers, beggars and criminals, was untypical of the country's major cities, and that by obtaining much of his information at second hand through such people as school attendance officers, policemen, and clergymen, it suffered a bias towards over-emphasis on hardship and bad conditions. Rowntree chose to study poverty in York, a much smaller city, and one where his own family's chocolate factory was a leading employer. It was a natural choice, but while York might not suffer from the large numbers of casual workers who inhabited large parts of London, it was still not a typical factory town; and it might be contended that in an industrial town proper, where there were many factories giving regular employment, poverty might well prove to be lower.

Rowntree's study, largely conducted by door-to-door visits made by paid investigators, was carried out in 1899–1900, and was of a highly detailed character. Rowntree based his poverty line on the maintenance of 'bare physical efficiency'. Using recently discovered knowledge about vitamins and nutrition, he calculated what income was necessary for a family of given size to buy sufficient food, clothing and other necessities, pay their rent and meet other essential outgoings, assuming the strictest economy and plainness of diet. 'No allowance', he emphasized, 'is made for any expenditure other than that absolutely required for the maintenance of merely physical efficiency'.

And let us clearly understand what 'merely physical efficiency' means. A family living upon the scale allowed for in this estimate must never spend a penny on railway fare or omnibus.

They must never go into the country unless they walk. They must never purchase a halfpenny newspaper or spend a penny to buy a ticket for a popular concert. They must write no letters to absent children, for they cannot afford to pay the postage. They must never contribute anything to their church or chapel, or give any help to a neighbour which costs them money. They cannot save, nor can they join a sick club or Trade Union, because they cannot pay the necessary subscriptions. The children must have no pocket money for dolls, marbles, or sweets. The father must smoke no tobacco, and must drink no beer. The mother must never buy any pretty clothes for herself or for her children, the character of the family wardrobe as for the family diet being governed by the regulation, 'Nothing must be bought but that which is absolutely necessary for the maintenance of physical health, and what is bought must be of the plainest and most economical description.' Should a child fall ill, it must be attended by the parish doctor; should it die, it must be buried by the parish. Finally the wage-earner must never be absent from his work for a single day.

On Rowntree's stringent basis, the minimum weekly income necessary for a family of five, mother, father, and three children, to maintain bare physical efficiency was 21*s*. 8*d*., a sum made up of 12*s*. 9*d*. for food (based on the lowest current prices and a diet 'less generous as regards variety than that supplied to able-bodied paupers in workhouses'); 4*s*. for rent; and 4*s*. 11*d*. for clothing, light, fuel and other essentials. No fewer than 7,230 persons, almost exactly a tenth of York's population, had incomes so low as not to meet this bare minimum. This condition Rowntree

53 and 54 Drink was widely considered one of the great social evils of the late Victorian and Edwardian eras, creating domestic strife and violence, causing public disorder, and making low wages less than adequate for supporting a family. Seebohm Rowntree found spending on drink to be a major source of deprivation in his investigation of poverty in York, and some benevolent employers banned the public house from their model industrial and agricultural villages and established temperance clubs for their workpeople. (Manchester Polytechnic Archives of Family Photographs)

described as 'primary poverty'. But there were over 13,000 other persons, nearly 18 per cent of the population of the city, who lived in a state of 'secondary poverty'; i.e. they had enough income to meet Rowntree's physical efficiency level but because of spending too much on drink, betting or gambling, or because of ignorant or careless housekeeping, still failed to escape from a state of need. Though their definitions and methods were different, and there were obvious differences between the main sources of working-class livelihoods in London and York, the findings of Booth and Rowntree were remarkably similar, Booth estimating 30.7 per cent of the population of London as living in poverty, and Rowntree 27.84 per cent of York's much smaller population (in a later and rather more prosperous period).

As for the causes of secondary poverty, Rowntree believed the great problem to be drink: he was unable to form a close estimate of the average spent on drink by

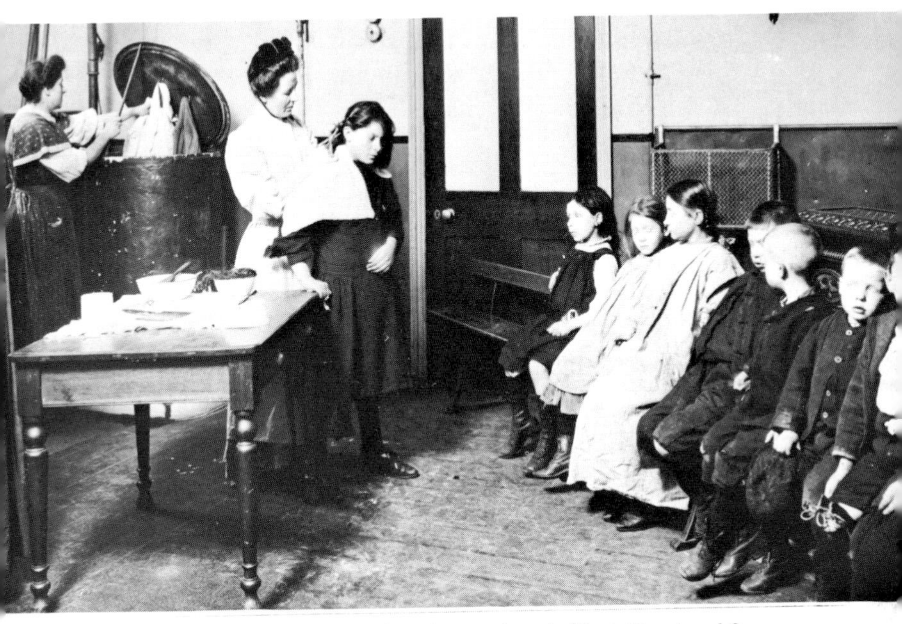

55 and **56** Intimate scenes at cleansing stations in Finch Street and Sun Street, near Finsbury Square, on the eve of World War I. The children's hair is cut and their heads inspected for nits, their clothing disinfected; and boys are stripped of their rags and bathed from tip to toe by severe-looking matrons. (Greater London Council)

working-class families, but accepted a national estimate of 6*s*. 10*d*. a week as probable, pointing out that even the sum of 6*s*. represented as much as a sixth of the average family income of working people in York. In regard to primary poverty, Rowntree found that in York the principal cause, by far, was simply that wages were too low. The family's chief wage-earner, usually an unskilled labourer, was in regular work but at wages insufficient to maintain a 'moderate' family (i.e. one of not more than four children). The average wage for unskilled workers in York was in fact only 18–21*s*., while as we have seen he had calculated that at least 21*s*. 8*d*. was necessary for a family of two adults and three children to maintain physical efficiency. The next major cause after low wages was largeness of family (i.e. more than four children), which accounted for 22 per cent of those in primary poverty, compared with 52 per cent arising from lowness of wages. Thirdly, the death, illness or old age of the family's chief wage-earner was the cause of 21 per cent of the primary poverty. Other causes – irregularity of work and unemployment – were relatively insignificant, accounting for only about 3 per cent and 2 per cent respectively. Here, especially in the small importance of irregularity of work, was a major contrast with Booth's findings in London.

Poverty meant inadequate diet, bad housing, poor health and a high death rate. Rowntree collected much detailed information on these matters, providing, for example, the actual sample diets of some typical families. Diets tended to be particularly poor and variable in quantity where casual or irregular employment was the rule, though it happened that this was not a prevalent problem in York. But in that city over a fifth of all the houses had no separate closet, while in the worst area a total of 58 closets served the needs of as many as 353 houses: 35 of these houses actually had only three closets between them. Water supply was also deficient, a factor which discouraged cleanliness of both the person and the home. A total of 442 houses had to share as few as 30 water taps, and this deficiency was not exceptional, for as many as 2,229 houses of the city were served by the meagre total of 155 taps. Again, in working-class districts there were numerous yards, paved and unpaved, odorous with overflowing ashpits and piles of refuse, and suffering often enough the unpleasant smells of adjoining slaughter-houses and hide and skin businesses.

It is hardly surprising in these circumstances that in the poorest area of York the death rate, at 27.78 per 1,000 in 1898, was over twice as high as in the best part of the city (13.49 per 1,000), and over 50 per cent higher than the average for the whole city. As many as 247 out of every

1,000 infants born in the worst part of the city died before reaching the age of 12 months, as compared with 94 infant deaths in the servant-keeping class, and 176 over the whole population of York.

Rents of working-class dwellings were high in relation to incomes, relatively higher in fact than for the middle classes. As Mrs Pember Reeves pointed out, middle-class families of £500 or £2,000 a year paid some sixth or eighth of their incomes away in rent, rates and taxes, while the families of the poor, with an income of £62.8*s*. (24*s*. a week) paid as much as one-third, mainly in rent. A high proportion of income went, too, in drink, as Rowntree noted. The public houses and beershops did well out of the poor: York boasted 338 such establishments, 1 to every 230 members of the population – a higher proportion than, say, Cardiff (1 to 458) or Leeds (1 to 362), but lower than Northampton (1 to 167) or Manchester (1 to 183). Rowntree's observers kept watch on a slum pub for 17 hours on a Saturday in July 1900 and noted a total of 550 persons entering the house during the day, 119 of them women, and 113 children – and this in an area which contained thirteen other public houses, three of which, and a working-man's club, were within a hundred yards. By the time of Rowntree's survey pubs were less used than formerly as meeting places for football clubs, trade unions and friendly societies, though they still served a valued social purpose. Music, singing, a warm, brilliantly lit and gaudy atmosphere attracted customers, especially the young:

> The company is almost entirely composed of young persons, youths and girls, sitting round the room and at small tables. Often there are a considerable number of soldiers present. Every one is drinking, but not heavily, and most of the men are smoking. At intervals one of the company is called on for a song, and if there is a chorus, every one who can will join in it. Many of the songs are characterised by maudlin sentimentality; others again are unreservedly vulgar. Throughout the whole assembly there is an air of jollity and an absence of irksome restraint which must prove very attractive after a day's confinement in factory or shop.

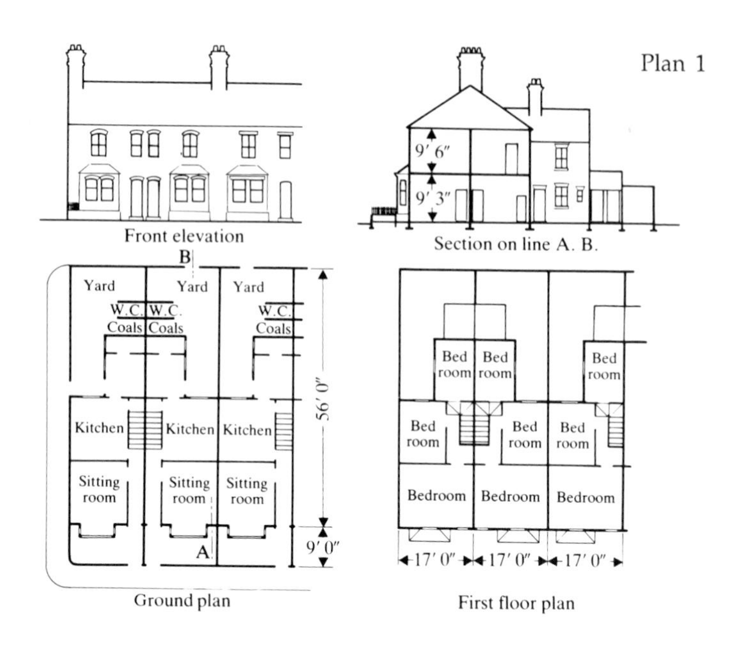
Plan 1
9′ 6″
9′ 3″
Front elevation
Section on line A. B.
B
A
Yard
Yard
Yard
W.C.
W.C.
W.C.
Coals
Coals
Coals
Kitchen
Kitchen
Kitchen
Sitting room
Sitting room
Sitting room
56′ 0″
9′ 0″
Bed room
Bed room
Bed room
Bed room
Bed room
Bed room
Bedroom
Bedroom
Bedroom
17′ 0″
17′ 0″
17′ 0″
Ground plan
First floor plan

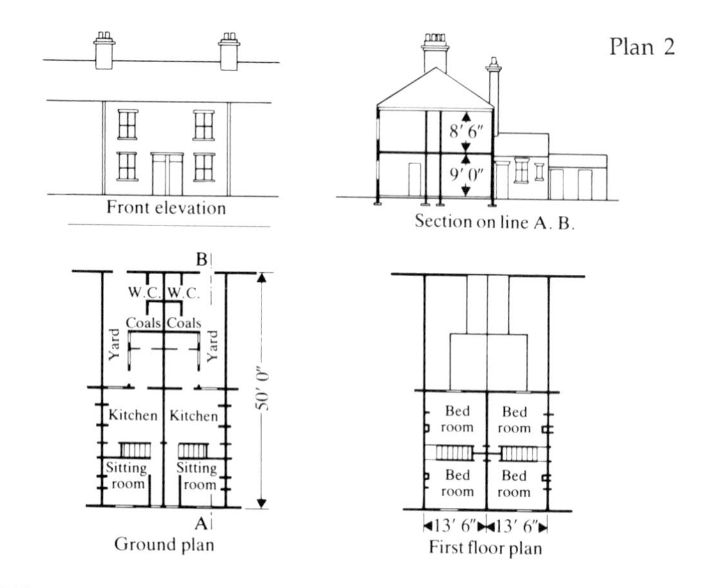
Plan 2
8′ 6″
9′ 0″
Front elevation
Section on line A. B.
B
A
W.C.
W.C.
Coals
Coals
Yard
Yard
Kitchen
Kitchen
Sitting room
Sitting room
50′ 0″
Bed room
Bed room
Bed room
Bed room
13′ 6″
13′ 6″
Ground plan
First floor plan

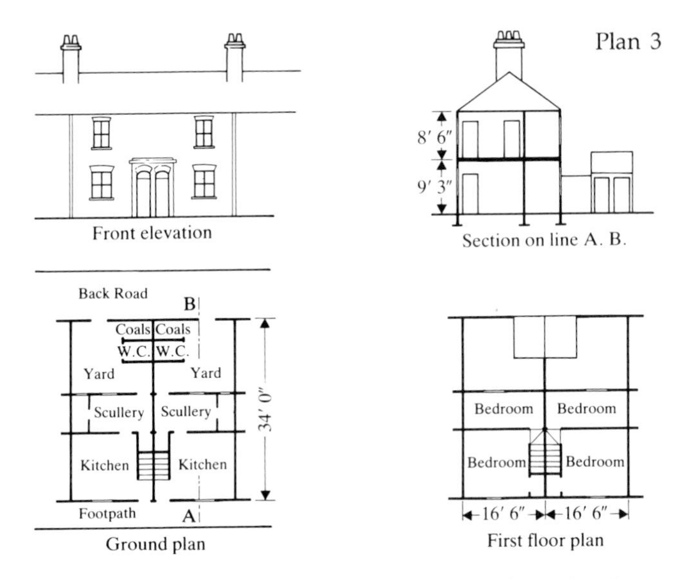

Figure 6 The plans of the three categories of working-class house investigated by Rowntree in 1899. Plan 1 illustrates 'the comfortable well-to-do artisans' in the newer parts of the city. Few of these houses boasted a bath, and some were provided with a midden privy rather than a water closet. Plan 2 shows the houses 'for the most part four-roomed, principally occupied by families in receipt of moderate but regular wages' – the majority of York's working class – to be found in the older and 'dull and dreary' streets. In these houses midden privies were more common than water closets, and some of the houses lacked a scullery. The third plan refers to the remaining smaller houses inhabited by about a quarter of York's working class people, 'the struggling poor'. Many of these houses had only two or three rooms, and very few more than four; numbers could be described only as slums 'situated in narrow alleys paved with cobbles, others in confined courts'. (From B. Seebohm Rowntree, *Poverty: A Study of Town Life*, (1902 ed), pp. 146–53.)

Pawnbrokers and moneylenders, as well as publicans, played an important part in the lives of the poor. Pawnbrokers charged a relatively moderate rate of interest, typically 1*d*. on 2*s*. (which, however, works out at over 200 per cent on an annual basis). In Liverpool it was not uncommon for the whole of the family's Sunday clothes to go in every Monday and be redeemed every Saturday, whether the need for cash were desperate or not, the pawnshop serving as a kind of extra-mural wardrobe. Sometimes, however, and especially when money was needed for drink, the pawning extended to bedclothes, essential clothing and furniture, leaving the home bare and comfortless. The moneylender, often a woman, had no security and too often charged exorbitant rates, 1*d*., 2*d*. or even 3*d*. per 1*s*. per week, the last representing 1,300 per cent p.a. Furthermore, some moneylenders kept small shops, and to obtain 2*s*. in cash a woman might have to take a shilling's worth of stale fish or bad meat, making the total debt 3*s*.; sometimes the purchase had to be thrown away uneaten for fear the husband might guess where it had come from.

Among the poor a funeral was a great event which ran away with ill-spared funds. A great show was put on, and any insurance money that might be due from a benefit club was lavished together with other spare cash on the black hearse, black horses with their nodding black plumes, and black-garbed professional mourners. A widow would boast 'I put him away splendid', though her home might be bereft of food and her children in rags and lacking boots. Another would say she had 'buried him with ham', meaning that the assembled company had been regaled with sandwiches of the best description. A funeral, indeed, provided one of the few opportunities in her life for a poor woman to hold open house, provide hospitality and impress the neighbours. Betting, of course, offered a much more frequent diversion. In a working-class district it was the shops, rather than the pubs, that acted as agents for the bookmakers, particularly the barbers, tobacconists and newsvendors; while a good deal of the money was passed in the streets as men went to and from work. The £5 fine that a magistrate could impose was hardly a deterrent, merely an overhead that the bookmaker expected to have to meet. Then came the excitement of the result:

See the sudden life in a street after a great race has been run and the newspaper is out: note the eagerness with which the papers are read. Boys on bicycles with reams of pink paper in a cloth bag on their back, scorching through the streets, tossing bundles to little boys waiting for them at street corners. Off rush the little boys shouting at the tops of their voices, doors and factory gates open, men and boys tumble out in their eagerness to read the latest 'speshul' and mark the winner.

* * * * * *

It is easy to become obsessed by the extent and nature of late Victorian poverty, more particularly when it is seen as contrasting sharply with the record of industrial innovation and commercial success, the growth of the national wealth and upper- and middle-class affluence, the age of the Pax Britannica. There were the poor certainly, but there were also the millions of working men and women whose conditions stood comfortably above the poverty level, people who could afford days by the sea, buy books, flowers and other little luxuries, and still save a pound or two towards a rainy day. The personal accounts of a London typist kept over a 52-week period in 1909–10, included in a report made by the Board of Trade's Labour Department, are revealing in this respect. The woman lived at home and paid 10*s.* a week for her board and lodging, which left her 15*s.* for her fares to work, extra food out, dress and all other items. Her fares to the city cost 3*s.* 2½*d.* a week, extra food 6*s.* 7*d.*, and dress only a little over 2*s.* (The low cost of dress arose partly because some items were run up at home, but more because many major ones were cheap in the shops; a new coat for 21*s.*, a pair of walking boots for 8*s.* 11*d.*, a pair of kid gloves for 2*s.*) From the remaining 3*s.* a week and an annual Christmas Box from her boss of £1.10*s.*, the typist was able to go away on holiday for a fortnight, make fairly frequent visits to theatres, picture galleries and concerts, go roller skating and purchase records for her 'talking machine', subscribe to a literary society, purchase 11 books in the course of the year and take the *Windsor Magazine* regularly, as well as buy birthday and other gifts, Christmas cards, flowers and small miscellaneous items, and contribute to one or two charities.

The better-off working class enjoyed diets which showed some, though not marked, improvement over those of the poor. More bread, cereals, meat and fats were eaten, if only about the same quantities of potatoes and milk. Many of this better-off class were still poorly nourished, perhaps because of dietary ignorance, because of preference for tasty rather than less palatable but more healthy foods, because of a certain prejudice against fruit, vegetables, salads and milk, or simply because the main object was to spend as little as possible on food and have more money for clothes, drink, and amusements. The homes of this class were frequently stuffed to overflowing with furniture, china and pictures. There might be a showy brass bedstead inlaid with mother-of-pearl, an over-large sofa, and a piano which took up a whole wall of the front room and was never played – but, as one pitman's wife said, did well for the purpose of 'cooling the bread'. There were pets, cage birds, homing pigeons, dogs, and in the North especially, many men who owned a cornet, trombone or euphonium and played in the works band.

One advantage of the better-paid wage earner, the man on about 30s. a week or more, was that he could more readily afford to belong to a friendly society; and by the mid-1880s at least 4m. did so. The Manchester Unity of Odd Fellows had already 260,000 members and an income of £340,000 as early as 1848. Less than forty years later this society numbered over 600,000, and its rival, the Foresters, even more. These were the big friendly societies, concerned much more with sickness and accident benefits than with funeral allowances, though Lancashire was the home territory for the burial clubs, so much so that in the Stockport area over half the population was insured for burial in 1853–4. The Blackburn Philanthropic Burial Society had as many as 130,000 members by the early 1870s, when total burial society membership may have been about 750,000. There were numerous small local friendly societies and village clubs – public house 'free-and-easies' – for labourers who thought a club no club at all unless it offered feast, fire and beer. Many of these were short-lived, or survived only through evading obligations by declaring claimants' membership to have 'lapsed'. Even the big societies, like the Odd Fellows, were not immune from losses caused by embezzling secretaries or suddenly vanishing treasurers. Eventually the Friendly Societies Act of 1875 brought down the rotten societies and forced the survivors to put their house in order.

In 1910, on the eve of the coming of National Insurance, the various types of societies could boast a combined membership of some 13m. and funds running into the scores of millions; though it has to be said that very many of the small societies – and numerous branches of the larger ones – were deficient in their funds and actuarially unsound. It was the case, indeed, that a high proportion of societies were rescued from pending insolvency by the intervention of the state with its National Insurance scheme. At all events, millions of people, the great majority of them ordinary wage earners, enjoyed some degree of social security through membership of a friendly society, or through a trade union which offered similar benefits. Millions more were insured through the profit-making industrial assurance companies, such as the Prudential, or the Collecting Societies like the Royal Liver and the Liverpool Victoria. National Insurance, when it appeared in 1911, shored up and built upon this old-established voluntary and private basis, and extended assistance with the risks of life to those who formerly had not the income or the prudence to provide it voluntarily for themselves.

As working people's purchasing power improved in the later nineteenth century, and hours of work were shortened to provide for many a free Saturday afternoon, so there was more scope for leisure. In the earlier decades of the century the pub was the great focus of social life. This

57 Clubs played an important role in the lives of working men, providing their members with facilities for political discussion, social functions and recreation, and also a sense of fellowship and degree of privacy that was not offered by the public house. Here is the scene at the laying of the foundation stone of the Isle of Dogs Progressive Club in Pier Street, E.14, near the Millwall Docks. (Island History Project)

was not only for the beer, the warmth, the company and entertainment, but because for many years the pub served as the working people's only meeting place, a forum for discussion and an outlet for grievances, the place where friendly society and trade union business was transacted, and the unemployed could hear of jobs. Subsequently the pubs lost some ground as friendly societies and unions found other premises, and as some paternalistic employers deliberately kept pubs out of their factory towns and model villages, providing meeting halls, sports grounds and libraries in lieu. The working men's clubs originally sponsored by the employing class were soon taken over by the members, and numbers of clubs lost their temperance aspect as it was found that only beer could guarantee a faithful membership and solvency. Most clubs, in fact, were a sort of private pub, providing facilities that most pubs lacked, newspapers, social functions, and facilities for billiards, cards and dominoes. Such clubs have continued to the present, particularly in the North, as 'vigorous centres of a popular, post-music-hall brand of floor shows and bawdy entertainment', as Professor F. M. L. Thompson has succinctly remarked.

Pubs continued to flourish if only for the company and entertainment they offered, and especially so in slum districts; and were often, apparently, most attractive to the young. The 1830 Beer Act allowed the setting up of 'beer shops', some of which gained an unsavoury reputation as resorts of doubtful characters, though the granting of licences was strictly controlled. From 1872 the opening hours of pubs were restricted, although they remained very liberal by present-day standards, stretching from 5.00 a.m. to after midnight in London, and from 6.00 a.m. to 11.00 p.m. in the provinces. Rowntree's observers had noted how men and women desperate for drink were to be seen even at 6.00 a.m., waiting patiently for the house to open, and in the evenings the pull of the pub was irresistible to senses and muscles dulled by long hours of monotonous factory work, or as an escape from a comfortless cramped home in a dreary back street.

But life was not necessarily restricted to irksome toil and beery relaxation, and there were many families who supported their church or chapel and never entered a pub, who joined temperance clubs, took up hobbies, cared for their pets, were anxious for their children to get as much as possible out of school and not read comics or spend their time playing in the street. Sport, both amateur and professional, was a great outlet for energy which found no fulfilment in work or home. Cricket, horse-racing and rugby all had their devotees, but it was soccer that became the ruling passion in the lives of millions of young men. For some it was the local church team, or works or club team in which they played, for others the famous professional teams whose fortunes were followed with minute attention. By the late nineteenth century a league match could draw 20,000 or 30,000 spectators, while race crowds ran at about half these numbers, except for the major bank holiday events which drew their 70,000 or 80,000. Football lost its early veneer of middle-class respectability, its association with 'muscular Christianity', as it became professional and commercial, and as crowd behaviour not infrequently proved alarming, with violence, assault and vandalism a not infrequent element of a Saturday afternoon. The races, it is true, could also see some violence, especially when punters revenged themselves on welshing bookies by horse-whipping, or tarring and feathering them, or merely by throwing them in the river. But it was football, especially in the North, that aroused the strongest emotions. It was 'something more than a game', as it was said in the early 1890s; 'it awakes local patriotism to its highest pitch'. The professional clubs soon realized the need to cater for the different elements which made up their supporters, the respectable artisans and tradesmen, the foremen, clerks and businessmen, by building stands and introducing differential prices, 1*s*. 6*d*. or 2s. for admission to a covered stand, 6*d*. for those who could afford only the price of entrance to the ground.

For family outings the day by the sea was encouraged, as we have already noted, by cheap railway fares and the initiative of Sunday schools, temperance clubs and paternalistic employers. Northerners favoured Blackpool, Scarborough or Morecambe, Midlanders Cleethorpes, Skegness or Yarmouth, Londoners Brighton, Margate or Southend. For the working folk in the Midlands, furthest from the sea, a trip to an inland beauty spot, such as Matlock or Buxton, might be a cheaper alternative. Savings clubs enabled families to put some money by for a day's excursion, or even for a whole week as employers began by the late 1880s to close their works for an annual break in summer, a development which occurred first in the textile towns of Lancashire. By the 1890s whole communities in the cotton areas 'had a deserted appearance at the

Wakes, with shops closed and churches having to join forces to raise even the semblance of a choir for Sunday services', as John K. Walton remarks. As we have noted, there were also many irregular illicit holidays, a product of nationwide industrial indiscipline, as workspeople absented themselves to attend fairs or parades, watch an important match, or simply take a day off. Such casual holiday-making tended to work against the early introduction of a regular annual week's break, and absorbed savings that might have paid for a visit to the seaside.

Thus nineteenth-century working life was not all monotonous routine and dull uniformity, a matter of going from home to work in the morning and back home at evening, and then the oblivion of the pub. There was a varied mosaic of activity, rich in regional or purely local idiosyncrasies, a richness that was witness to the native intelligence, independence, individuality and aspirations of a working people who, indeed, rarely saw themselves as a hopeless proletariat crushed by unfeeling capitalism into one mindless, spiritless mould.

Chapter Seven

The Age of Reform

The Age of Reform was the title given to E. L. Woodward's volume in the Oxford History of England covering the period 1815 to 1870. The succeeding volume, by R. C. K. Ensor, was simply called *England 1870–1914*. The titles, in fact, might well have been juxtaposed, for reform, of course, did not stop short in 1870. Indeed, it could be argued that post–1870 reform was more extensive, more far-reaching, and far more effective; and that the earlier period was only the opening phase in the long, gradual process of creating a more humane, more just and more egalitarian society.

Nineteenth-century reform reached into many obscure corners of contemporary life as well as affecting the major issues of political equality, education and social welfare. But the achievement of greater political equality was one of the most striking changes, for over the course of a little over half a century the proportion of adults accorded the right to take part in elections was raised from something like 1 in every 20 to approaching 1 in every 3. Nevertheless the move towards democracy was gradual and cautious, and such pressure to short-circuit the process as came from the Chartists in the 1840s – universal male suffrage was a key point of the Charter – made no lasting impression.

Throughout the nineteenth century and down to 1918, in fact, the franchise was restricted to males, and to those males who could make some minimal claim to property. The last major Victorian reform, that of 1884, brought the property qualification in the counties in line with that which had existed in the boroughs since 1867, and raised the size of the electorate from about 2.6m. to some 4.4m. (28.5 per cent of the adult population). Earlier the electorate had been much smaller. The first Reform Act of 1832 had merely got rid of the worst absurdities of the old unreformed Parliament: the unrepresented industrial towns; the infamous rotten boroughs like Old Sarum, an ancient city site deserted in the early middle ages; and Dunwich, a port submerged by the sea in the twelfth century. The country towns were, however, still much over-represented. The effect on the franchise was mainly to introduce a more uniform basis of electoral qualifications, but added only a little over 200,000 new electors to the 435,000 (5 per cent of adults) who had held the franchise in 1831. The next reform in 1867 was much more sweeping, and apart from a further redistribution of seats, added nearly 1m. new voters, consisting mainly of the better-off skilled artisans and tradesmen in the boroughs. The electorate in England and Wales then consisted of nearly 2m. out of a total adult male population of well over 5m.

One other change of significance was the Secret Ballot of 1872, which abolished the old public hustings at which each voter appeared before the magistrate to cast his vote. Thus was made obsolete the disgraceful scenes wittily described by Dickens; the party-controlled public houses in which supporters got their free drink; the giving of green parasols to the supporters' good ladies; the locking up of electors to prevent the other side from getting at them; the strident processions and uproarious mobs; though no doubt there continued the kissing of electors' babies and the offering of vague promises (rather unlikely to be fulfilled) should the candidate be returned. Some farm tenants and house-occupiers in the towns remained unconvinced that the ballot was now really secret. There lingered a deep suspicion that landlords and employers could get to know how one had voted and might take their revenge. And for long enough there were those newly-enfranchised working men who never voted at all, holding that politics was for the 'high-ups', those who understood the matter, and not for the likes of themselves.

If the spread of the ideals of the French Revolution, liberty, equality, fraternity, formed the background to the reform of Parliament, and the growth of a substantial class of sober, sensible and literate householders among the working classes made possible the extension of the franchise to the majority of adult men, there was one large element of society that was totally excluded. Some few females, and their male champions, had been putting forward women's claim to the vote since before Victoria's accession, but their efforts – limited and somewhat feeble as they were – bore no fruit. One might have expected that the coming of a queen to the throne would have proved auspicious to the cause, but there was no support to be had in that quarter: the claim for women's rights 'on which her poor feeble sex is bent', wrote the Queen, was a 'mad, wicked folly . . . forgetting every sense of womanly feeling and propriety'. The Queen's strongly expressed sentiments were supported and elaborated by eminent persons, some of whom at least might have been expected to know better. An American theologian wrote that if women were given the vote a physical transformation would follow: they would become 'thinner, sharp-featured, lank and dry'. Mrs Linton, Lord Leighton's sister, went even further, claiming that enfranchised women would lose the power of love. T. H. Huxley, the biologist, referred to the difference in mental and physical endowment, the average woman being inferior to the average man. Charles Darwin believed that women's superior strengths in powers of intuition, rapid perception and imitation were, in fact, characteristics 'of the lower races and therefore of a past and lower state of civilization'; and there was of course the 'scientific' evidence that the female brain was 5 oz. lighter than its male counterpart, and the strong presumption that it was the political faculty that was missing.

58 and **59** Alternative views of the typical suffragette: 'Fancy' and 'Fact', drawings by Charles Lane Vicary, 1907. (Museum of London)

It was left to Disraeli to point out the absurdity of refusing women the vote in a country where a woman was on the throne, peeresses could sit of their own right in the Lords, and any woman could own land, be a lady of the manor and thus hold her own manorial courts, and take office as a churchwarden and overseer of the poor. Had he written later in the century he might also have added that women could vote for and be elected to Boards of Guardians, and serve on the councils of counties and local authorities. However, there were in fact some practical difficulties in the way of bringing women into the franchise. One was that since the right to vote was based on possession of property before 1882 only relatively few women, and those mainly elderly spinsters and widows, could be enfranchised; and why should they 'be exposed to the impertinent intrusion of agents, canvassers and candidates – to be besieged alternatively by the adulation of fools and by the insolence of bullies?' Moreover, to the Liberals, such an addition to the electorate possessed little charm, for spinsters and widow ladies living in houses of their own were only too likely to vote Conservative. And the women themselves were divided: some highly intelligent and famous women of the day opposed woman suffrage, including Mrs Humphrey Ward, the novelist, Gertrude Bell, who helped found the state of Iraq, and no less a radical than Beatrice Webb, the Fabian Socialist.

And so once a year, year after year, a Woman Suffrage Bill was regularly introduced into Parliament, and each year was equally regularly rejected. That of 1897, supported by a monster petition bearing 257,796 signatures, was defeated by a margin of 71 votes. But it was just about this time that female restiveness came to the boil, not only through frustration over the franchise but also because of more general impatience with the restrictions on daily life that Victorian respectability imposed on young ladies. There was, wrote one such young lady in *The Nineteenth Century* in 1894, a desire 'to develop our Personality (with a very big P)', a need to

> satisfy the cravings of our souls for something beyond the commonplace . . ., an equally intense longing to frequent music-halls and possess latchkeys . . . and to remove the lingering prejudice against women smoking in public . . . She considers it hard that she cannot walk the length of two or three – even five or six – streets to visit a friend, without having first provided herself with an unhappy maid or attendant of some description, presumably to prevent her from losing her way or getting run over.

And, not least, if a girl were 'permitted to follow the natural bent of her mind, she would not be impelled by boredom and discontent into marrying the first person, whether congenial or not, who appeared on her limited horizon'.

The unfulfilled aspirations of intelligent women and their impatience with the apparent stalemate in the polite and futile manoeuvrings of the 'constitutional' women's movement led by Millicent Fawcett, led to a split in the ranks. Encouraged perhaps by the enfranchisement of women long before this in Kansas, and more recently in New Zealand and Australia, a militant movement was launched in 1903: the Women's Social and Political Union, led by Mrs Emmeline Pankhurst. In addition to the diminutive Mrs Pankhurst, the new organization found another standard bearer in another Emmeline, Mrs Pethick Lawrence, a London social worker. The two Emmelines were ably supported by Mrs Pankhurst's two daughters: Christabel, a law student who served as her mother's influential lieutenant, and Sylvia, who had studied art and now involved herself in spreading the cause among the women of London's East End.

The campaign of the militants, dubbed 'Suffragettes' by the *Daily Mail*, began modestly with a verbal protest from the Strangers' Gallery of the Commons as a new Suffrage Bill was in danger of being talked out. It escalated to more headline-worthy incidents, including the smashing of shop windows in Oxford Street and the firing of stones from a catapult at office windows in Victoria Street from the vantage point of the open top of a double-decker bus. There followed the damage of putting greens with acid, the wrecking of the orchid house at Kew, the firing off of an old Crimean War cannon captured from the Russians, and the burning down of railway stations. A bomb, for which Mrs Pankhurst claimed responsibility, wrecked part of Lloyd George's new house in Surrey, and in court one suffragette hurled a directory at the magistrate (and missed at six feet), while another preferred an inkwell as missile. Some WSPU supporters chained themselves to the railings of Buckingham Palace, Mrs Pankhurst tried to invade the palace itself, and there was an abortive attempt to storm the House of Commons, using a furniture van as a Trojan horse. Much controversy arose over these events, and also

60, **61** and **62** The demand for woman suffrage met with both sympathetic and hostile responses in the years after 1903 when Mrs Emmeline Pankhurst launched the militant Women's Social and Political Union. (Museum of London)

over the forced feeding of imprisoned suffragettes who went on hunger strike – where tubes were forced into the mouth or nostrils through which was poured a mixture of Valentine's meat juice and lime juice cordial, or alternatively Benger's Food or beef tea. But the most notorious incident was the death of Emily Davison who fell in the path of the king's horse, Anmer, at the Derby of 1913. (King George judiciously inquired after the condition of his injured jockey, while Queen Mary inquired for Miss Davison.) The funeral procession in central London of the sacrificial suffragette was marked by enormous pageantry, as thousands of women marched in groups dressed in black, purple and white, and carrying purple irises, red peonies and laurels.

To some extent the actions – some would say 'outrages' – of the suffragettes tended to harden opinion against their cause. Incensed reactionaries demanded stronger government action and harsher penalties, and some wits proposed that the contumacious females should be deported to St Helena, or alternatively to the remote islands of Rum, Eigg and Muck, and – generally approved as most appropriate – the Isle of Man. But the tide was running in favour of reform as in the ten years after 1907 women were given the vote in five more countries, including Norway, Denmark and the new USSR. World War I showed that women were not afraid to staff hospitals and drive vehicles on the edge of battle, and were quite capable of taking over from men in public transport, munitions factories and on the land. Thus the war confirmed women's new independence, courage and self-reliance, and helped pave the way for the inevitable. The Reform Act of 1918 was passed hastily as the war ground to a finish. In two respects it was a sweeping measure: the property qualification was at last abolished and all adult males given the vote; and women also were allowed to vote, provided they had reached the age of thirty – when they might be considered as having attained the age of discretion. However, only 1 of the 17 women who offered themselves as candidates at the ensuing election was returned: she was a Sinn Feiner and never took her seat. Of the unsuccessful, Christabel Pankhurst, standing at Smethwick, did best, polling over 8,000 votes. The last act in the drama came ten years later, in 1928, when by an apparently unauthorized announcement, the government found itself committed to bring women's suffrage into line with that of men.

* * * * * *

The widening of the franchise held certain implications for the state's role in education. Private schools run for profit, together with charitable institutions, had helped create the class of educated skilled artisans that was enfranchised in 1867. But this was clearly not the end of the road, and the further extension of the franchise depended on provision of at least a basic minimum training in the three R's for all male adults. In the famous ironic and misquoted phrase of Robert Lowe, Vice-President of the Education Department, 'we must educate our masters'. Down to 1870 the state's part in education had been confined to providing funds (beginning in 1833) to help finance the two major voluntary bodies providing schools, the National (Church of England) Society and the British (Nonconformist) Society. Controversy over the nature of the religious teaching to be given in publicly financed schools had long held back more rapid progress and the adoption of a more positive role by the state. Nevertheless, as early as 1833 the Factory Act of that year had required factory children to be given part-time schooling, while the workhouses had their own schools for pauper children. The rest was left to voluntary effort and private enterprise. The consequence was an enormously wide range of institutions stretching from the famous public schools such as Eton, Harrow, Winchester and Rugby (the term 'public' arose because these schools accepted pupils from all over the country), to local grammar schools, Sunday schools, charitable institutions such as the ragged schools and the classes held by parsons in a spare room of the rectory, down to the craft schools which taught pillow lace, straw plaiting, knitting and sewing, and the little dame schools, mentioned earlier. Anyone so minded could open a school; no qualifications were required, and often a school was combined with some other business, such as that run by

Mr Wopsle's great-aunt in Dickens's *Great Expectations*. A report to the Newcastle Commission of 1858–61 noted schools conducted by:

domestic servants out of place, discharged barmaids, vendors of toys or lollipops, keepers of small eating-houses, of

63, 64, 65 and **66** Scenes from (1) Farnham Royal School about 1892, and (2) (3) and (4) Manchester schools about 1911–13. Beginning in 1870, a succession of Education Acts gradually raised the minimum school-leaving age and in 1891 abolished fees in rate-supported schools. But even in 1914 many working-class children ended their school years at the age of thirteen, and others attended only part-time between the ages of eleven and thirteen. (Museum of English Rural Life; Manchester Polytechnic Archives of Family Photographs)

mangles, or of small lodging houses, needlewomen who take in plain or slop work, milliners, consumptive patients in an advanced stage, cripples almost bedridden, persons of at least doubtful temperance, outdoor paupers, men and women of seventy and even eighty years of age, persons who spell badly (mostly women, I grieve to say), who can scarcely write and who cannot cipher at all , . . None are too old, too poor, too ignorant, too feeble, too sickly, too unqualified in every way, to regard themselves and to be regarded by others, as unfit for school-keeping.

A school-room might be too small even for the children to be able to sit; in one the children were 'as closely packed as birds in a nest and tumbling over each other like puppies in a kennel'; in another, 'the children sit on the floor, and bring what books they please; whilst the closeness of the room renders fuel superfluous, and even keeps the children quiet by its narcotic effects'.

The Education Act of 1870, following hard on the heels of the Newcastle Commission and the franchise reform of 1867, was a landmark, though more for what it portended than for its immediate effects. The prime object was to 'fill the gaps' in the voluntary and private system, which in part meant the formation of elected School Boards to build rate-supported schools in areas where existing provision was inadequate or totally lacking. As a result 1.5m. new school places were provided, though the majority came from the churches not the Boards. The Act, contrary to common belief, did not introduce elementary education – the Newcastle Commission found that 2.5m. children were already attending some kind of school – nor did it make elementary education compulsory – many Boards failed to use their permissive powers in this respect. Nor did it make the schools free, except for very poor children. Many children continued to leave school at the age of 11, and, as before, girls continued to stay on longer than boys who could more often find work at an early age. Subsequent legislation raised the minimum leaving age by gradual steps, but it took World War I and the 1918 Education Act to bring it up to 14 years, and to abolish the system of 'part-timers' whereby children who reached a certain standard could go to work part-time. In the meanwhile two major changes had been brought in: school fees in rate-supported schools were abolished in 1891; and the 1902 Act recognized the existence of 'Higher Grade' or separate senior schools for older children (over 11) which some progressive authorities had established.

From 1870 down to the present it could be said that much of the legislation was concerned with compelling the backward areas to come into line with the standards of the more progressive, whipping in the laggards. Higher grade schools had existed for thirty years before the 1902 Act; numbers of children were staying on till the age of fourteen before the Act of 1918; and similarly, many children were already in secondary schools before the famous Butler Act of 1944 announced the era of 'secondary education for all'. The English school system developed piecemeal as a series of responses to changing circumstances, with the state belatedly recognising the changes which had occurred and enforcing a degree of conformity, rather than attempting to reshape the system from any coherent set of principles. The 1944 Act, for instance – again contrary to what is generally held – required all authorities to provide some form of secondary education, but said nothing specific about what types of secondary schools should be provided.

The 'system' – if a haphazard collection of different types of schools can be honoured with that description – developed along unplanned lines, building on what had already been created by private and local initiative. The effective result was that lines of development ran along distinct class divisions. The publicly provided primary and secondary schools catered for working-class children (treating girls and boys equally, somewhat remarkably) who were seen as needing only a basic training in the three R's, together with a smattering of history and geography, some glimmerings of religious instruction, some needlework for the girls, woodwork for the boys, and little more. They would then leave school knowing sufficient to exercise adequately the right of franchise and to be acceptable in low-paid jobs in factories, shops and domestic service. The brighter boys might take up apprenticeships and graduate into the ranks of the skilled workers; the more intelligent girls might train as nurses or go to night classes to learn shorthand and typewriting. Above this level came the schools concerned with the children of the lower middle classes (and also a relatively few 'scholarship' children from working-class families). Pre-eminent here was the grammar school, often an old establishment rescued from decline and stagnation by the burgeoning demand for middle-grade clerks in the civil service, local government, banks and commercial offices. The institution of nationally recognized school-leaving examinations conducted by the universities (the School Certificate examination began in 1917) provided employers with a ready-made standard of competence; and the supply of this kind of well-educated material was supplemented by the better private schools which catered for parents who desired a degree of exclusiveness, polite speech, and manners, but could afford no more than the local 'Greyfriars' or 'Ashdown House'. Third, and most prestigious, came the public schools and their associated preparatory schools. Here the fees, and the difficulty of getting in, ensured an upper middle-class and aristocratic clientele. From these schools came the governing élite, the politicians, the judges, top civil servants, army and naval officers, and the directors of large companies.

Whether such an educational 'system' was good for the economy may be doubted: it directed too many of the best brains into the professions, and encouraged an attitude of disdain towards trade, industry and technology. Socially it was certainly divisive, and for long into the twentieth century, when income had largely ceased to be the basis of class distinction, it was education that determined who was and was not the gentleman. But it met the needs of the time, as needs were then perceived. The upper classes took a very limited view of what kind of education was appropriate to the working classes, and many agreed with Lowe's famous dictum:

> The lower classes ought to be educated to discharge the duties cast upon them. They should also be educated that they may appreciate and defer to a higher cultivation when they meet it, and the higher classes ought to be educated in a very different manner, in order that they may exhibit to the lower classes the higher education to which, if it were shown to them, they would bow down and defer.

In other words, the lower classes should be just sufficiently educated to know that they were not well-educated!

Such an attitude, somewhat modified, long persisted: even as late as 1943 an expert committee produced, in the Norwood Report, the remarkable argument that children not only fell into the three recognizable types of 'academic', 'mechanically minded', and 'essentially practical', but also conveniently fell into them in the same proportions as grammar, technical, and ordinary secondary schools existed. By sheer good fortune, without any foresight or planning, the country had managed to produce the right schools and in the right numbers!

The same class divisions, the same conservatism, the same preference for the classical education and disdain of the technological, infected higher education. New Chairs in scientific subjects made but a tardy appearance at the two ancient seats of learning, which were even more remarkably backward in their attitude to women students, who were first admitted but not examined, and then examined but not awarded degrees, and finally granted the right of receiving degrees only at the beginning of the 1920s. The red-brick universities which began to appear in the course of the nineteenth century were, by contrast, much more utilitarian institutions, considerably tainted by their humble origins and by their association with commercial cities and generally middle-class qualities. And despite the growth in institutions, university education remained confined to a small élite – under 13,000 students in 1908–9, still under 41,000 in 1935–6. University graduates made only a limited impact on the realm of industry and commerce, partly because of the businessman's reactionary prejudice in favour of the family relation, the gifted amateur, the practical man who had worked his way up through the firm.

Technical colleges, too, came late to Britain, and faced a long upward struggle towards respectability. Their forerunners, the Mechanics' Institutes, were numerous by the 1850s and were particularly strong in the industrial districts. They combined the holding of popular lectures, often on scientific subjects, with reading rooms, libraries and social functions, and offered classes where young workers could improve their education. Some of these institutes developed into important technical colleges, the outstanding example being the London Institute which eventually became Birkbeck College and was incorporated into the University of London. There was a growth also of specialist colleges for chemistry, mining, art, and agriculture, while Quintin Hogg succeeded in transforming his Working Men's Institute into a Polytechnic with premises in Regent Street.

But the big advance came only in the 1880s when a royal commission, alarmed by the industrial progress of Germany and the United States, advocated the establishment nationally of both technical colleges and technical schools. And very fortunately, at just this time, the government happened to be embarrassed by a surplus of money arising from the compensation originally intended for the owners of public houses that had been closed down by an Act of 1890 – the 'whiskey money'. The new technical colleges, however, found it difficult to attract full-time students. As late as 1928, contrary to the experience of Germany and the United States, the great bulk of British technical college students attended only in the evenings. The colleges never acquired high public esteem, and this was particularly so when their courses competed with those offered by a university in the same town; another serious and continuing problem was the inadequate basic education of many of their evening students. In 1939 the country's total output of qualified mechanical, electrical and civil engineers was only a little over 2,000, of which the universities supplied over a third. Lukewarm support for technical education, the lack of openings for qualified engineers and other scientists, and the scorn with which science and technology were held in certain circles of society were no doubt contributing factors to Britain's declining economic strength and slow rate of change in the century after 1850.

* * * * * *

Although in popular mythology the century before 1914 has acquired an image of rampant capitalism, an era when the industrial juggernaut carried all before it and crushed its hapless labour force into unrelieved hunger, misery and enslavement, the extent of reforming activity was in fact wide-ranging and far-reaching. It was indeed an age of ever-increasing government intervention, when central investigation and control replaced the too often palsied hand of local initiative and brought at least some degree of action, order, and improvement. The principle of inspection, carried out by full-time professional civil servants to ensure that legislation was as effective as it could be, displaced or supplemented the unpaid magistrates and amateur parish officials – their enforcement of the law had been, it is true, often enthusiastic and frequently cheap, but was also frequently lax, inefficient, wasteful or merely non-existent. The idea of inspection had been applied first in the Factory Act of 1833 – which thereby became the first effective Factory Act – and in the New Poor Law of 1834, when there were newly-elected Boards of Guardians to be advised and newly-built workhouses to be regulated. Inspection was soon applied more widely, so that there appeared inspectors of mines, of schools, of public health, of lunatic asylums, of safety provisions on ships. And the inspectors did more than enforce: they discovered what deficiencies existed in the law, what further measures were needed, and what evils were still unremedied, and campaigned to rectify them. This was true, for instance, of factories, where the regulations were eventually extended to cover all classes of worker and also the guarding of dangerous machinery. And in the new century the law also came to embrace the infamous 'sweated trades' and the hours and conditions of overworked shop-girls.

Many of these reforms owed much to the devoted work of individual reformers who campaigned long and hard for the redress of some formerly unregarded grievance. The early factory legislation owed much to Richard Oastler and his letters on 'Yorkshire slavery', and to his associates like Parson Bull, the Tory MP, Michael Sadler, and the Earl of Shaftesbury. Shaftesbury was also much involved in improving the plight of the climbing boys whose daily chimney sweeping work was painful, dangerous, and even fatal; in the regulation of slum housing and insanitary common lodging houses; and in the control of private asylums to which wealthy families consigned deranged and otherwise inconvenient relations. Shaftesbury joined with Dickens and Edwin Chadwick, the Benthamite author of the New Poor Law and 1833 FactoryAct, to campaign for public health reforms, specifically the efficient removal of nuisances, the securing of clean water supplies, and the creation of an effective system of sewage disposal. The subsequent Public Health Act of 1848 perhaps owed more to the frightening toll made by the invasions of Asiatic cholera than to the activities of the reformers, but in any event the concern about town conditions was so lukewarm that the Act was allowed to lapse at the conclusion of its five-year term. Then Chadwick turned his attention to the grossly over-used and insanitary urban burial grounds – there was one in Rotherhithe which was so densely packed with coffins that the level of the ground had risen perceptibly – and he also advocated the introduction of a national burial system. He obtained a little success over the closing of the worst cemeteries but none at all on burials; it is remarkable, perhaps, that no socialist government so far has yet taken up his idea.

New regulations concerning railway safety followed after increased fatalities from accidents, as shipping controls followed disasters at sea. Railway companies were eventually required to install the block signalling system and automatic vacuum brakes, and ships sufficient life-boats. Merchant navy officers were required to be properly qualified and the frequent overloading of vessels was checked by Samuel Plimsoll's safety mark which after 1876 had to be painted on the hulls of all ships.

As regards the living standards of the poor, a most notable omission was the lack of any regulation of wages (apart from the Coal Miners' Minimum Wages Act of 1912, which followed a national coal strike). Hours, working conditions, safety became increasingly regulated, but not wages. A national minimum wages act, however, would have been difficult to apply, might well have led to the substitution of women in men's jobs, and led to higher unemployment among the unskilled. But an important departure came in the Workmen's Injury Compensation Acts which rescued the incapacitated workman from dependence on the often inadequate humanity of his employer.

Apart from the intervention in working hours, the safety and sanitary conditions of the workplace, the most important single factor affecting the workman, his wage, was left to the practice of the trade, or where unions existed, to the free bargaining between employers and the men's representatives. The history of trade unions is complex and controversial, but the major steps torwards their full acceptance as legitimate and respectable organizations followed on the work of the leaders of the 'model unions' of skilled workers (such as the Amalgamated Society of Engineers) in the third quarter of the century. The unions acquired legality (including peaceful picketing) and protection of their funds in legislation of the first half of the 1870s. Subsequent parliamentary Acts were the consequences of hostile legal decisions – the famous Taff Vale and Osborne judgments – and effectively placed the unions in an exceptionally privileged position inasmuch as they could not be sued by employers for breach of contract.

Meanwhile, union organization had spread beyond the ranks of skilled artisans to embrace many unskilled workers: this was signalled by the strikes of the match girls in 1888, the gas stokers in the following year (which secured a reduction in daily hours from 12 to 8), and in the same year, 1889, the great London dock strike for the 'docker's tanner'. The movement now fell into the hands of the more radical leaders of the big unions, the miners, dockers and railwaymen who formed a powerful 'Triple Alliance'. Nevertheless, one should not exaggerate the power or influence of unions. Total membership, even as late as 1900, was only 2m. out of a total national labour force of over 16m., and the membership had been very much smaller a decade or two earlier. The major reforms of the nineteenth century had come from members of the middle and upper classes, rather than from organized labour or from radical visionaries such as Robert Owen and Chartist leaders like Feargus O'Connor. There had been a big improvement in living standards – a rise of two-thirds in real incomes in the thirty years after 1870 – but the major factors here were cheap food and cheap factory-made consumer goods rather than union activity. As a share of national income, the proportion of income arising from employment, at 48 per cent, stood only about where it had stood since the model unions were established in the middle of the century. Wages had as yet made no gain on the half of national income which was held by rents, interest and profits.

The significance of the union movement was more for the future than for any of the advances achieved before 1900. But it was in that year that the unions joined with the Independent Labour Party of Keir Hardie, the Social

Democratic Federation, and the Fabian Society of radical intellectuals such as Sidney and Beatrice Webb, and the writers Bernard Shaw and H. G. Wells, to form the Labour Representation Committee. This alliance, six years later, blossomed into the new Labour Party, with the unions as paymaster; and only eighteen years later on the new party was called upon to form a government, albeit a minority one. It was under the pressure of the Labour party, unions, and Fabians that the Liberal administration which came into office in 1906, and which numbered Lloyd George and Winston Churchill among its leading spirits, carried out a great programme of reforms. These included, among many others, the introduction of Old Age Pensions (1908, at 5*s*. a week for a single person, 7*s*. 6*d*. for a married couple; applicants having a recent criminal conviction were disqualified); of employment exchanges (1909, designed to reduce the unemployment arising from lack of contact between employers and unemployed); and the National Insurance Act of 1911, which brought compulsory state insurance against sickness and unemployment to some 2.25m. people. There were, too, reforms in trade union law; regulation of sweated trades, mines and shop workers; the provision of school meals and medical inspection for school children; and the allocation of special places in grammar schools for children from elementary schools – the beginning of the controversial 'eleven plus'.

It was this same Liberal government that resisted all the ploys of the suffragettes and delayed the extension of the franchise to women until the end of World War I. But long before this there had been some significant improvements in the legal and social status of women. The Act of 1857 established the Divorce Court and allowed women to sue for divorce. However, the rights under the new law were expensive to exercise, and legal separation became the more usual resort of women who wished to leave their husbands. From 1882 the property of women no longer automatically became that of their husbands on marriage, and was thenceforth protected by law. Further legislation

TO PRINTERS' LABOURERS

AND OTHER WORKERS IN THE PRINTING TRADE

We, the Printers' Labourers, are on strike for a wage of **20s. per Week** and 6d. per hour overtime. We appeal to the Machine Minders and other workers to aid us in obtaining our just demands.

Our present wages vary from **12s. to 14s. per week,** and many among us have wives and families to sustain. We work on an average fifty-four hours a week, and

SEVENTY-FIVE HOURS TO EARN £1.

How, and under what conditions do we work? In heated cellars where gaslight replaces daylight; amidst perpetual din; breathing a stifling, filthy atmosphere. We have to keep eye and hand ever on the alert to KEEP STROKE with the machines we tend.

Our kind, respectable Christian employers would not put their pet cats and dogs in the styes where they condemn us to pass our best working years. Above are the demands for the toil which destroys our health.

We appeal to all fellow labourers to join us. Do not listen to the specious talk of interested foremen and employers who "promise to favourably consider your demands." They want time to work off urgent orders. If you on strike are selfish enough to go in because a few employers grant concessions, you help to ruin the cause. Will you purchase your gain at the expense of our defeat? Show the same spirit as our comrades in other industries are displaying.

STRIKE!!

STRIKE ALL TOGETHER!!

Stand Together and Win

Printers' Strike Committee,

RED STAR COFFEE HOUSE, CLERKENWELL GREEN.

GEORGE EVANS, *Sec.*
GEORGE WALDEN, *Treas.*

STRIKE COMMITTEE MANIFESTO 1889

67 and 68 From the 1880s the trade unions became more militant in their efforts to improve wages and working conditions. In the dramatic year 1889 the Printers' Labourers went on strike to raise their wages from 12–14s. to 20s. for a 54-hour week, but this strike was overshadowed by the great Dockers' Strike of the same year when the dockers, led by Tom Mann and John Burns, demanded an extra penny an hour to raise their hourly rate from 5*d*. to 6*d*. (National Museum of Labour History)

THE GREAT PENNY STRIKE;
OR, THE BLOATED CAPITALIST AND THE AUTOMATIC DOCK LABOURER.

gave a mother guardianship of her infants upon the death of the husband, and entitled married women to maintenance in case of desertion. Then, from 1907 women could take part in local government, and after the Sex Disqualification Removal Act of 1919 could qualify and practise as solicitors or barristers.

The Church of England, of course, was one of the institutions which kept its doors firmly shut against women. It had become however, somewhat grudgingly, more liberal towards other churches. In 1828 it had agreed to the repeal of the old Test and Corporation Acts which had formerly restricted the activities of dissenters, and had accepted, much less willingly, Catholic Emancipation. There followed a Church Pluralities Act forbidding a clergyman to hold more than two livings – some had found four or five a useful number in the past – and the compulsory commutation of tithes into a money payment varying with the price of corn.

Internally the unity of the Anglican Church was split by the Oxford movement or 'tractarians', whose members sought to revive the authority of the Church and attack religious indifference. It was an intellectual movement, intensely religious, and as Sir Llewellyn Woodward said, evidently out of touch with the rapidly changing real world of Stephenson and Chadwick. And it was greatly weakened when John Henry Newman, one of its leading figures, was received into the Roman Catholic Church, taking many of his followers with him. External challenge came from the growth of scientific knowledge and its propagation through learned societies, popular lectures, and the meetings of the British Association. Most devastating was Darwin's *Origin of Species*. The whole of the first printing – 1,250 copies – was sold on the day of publication in 1859. To the public the phrase of Herbert Spencer, 'the survival of the fittest', summed up the Darwinian theory. The denial of any sudden creation of man, and the demonstration by geologists of the age of the earth, forced a reconsideration of the fundamental significance of Church doctrines, and particularly affected Evangelicalism, one root of which was literal stress on the Bible. The rationality of science further weakened the grip of religion on the people. Already, as a survey of March 1851 showed, only 26 per cent of the population attended any church at the most popular of Sunday services, the morning one – a total of 61 per cent for all three Sunday services. England, a Christian country, had become a land in which a high proportion of its people were indifferent or even hostile to its established Church.

Society was becoming increasingly hedonistic. The strict keeping of Sunday as a day of rest, devoted to religious observance, might have been noted with awe and some discomfort by foreign visitors but was in fact never universal. In the later nineteenth century it declined with the innovation of 'the weekend' among the rich, and the railway excursion among the poor. In high society the Prince of Wales created one of the first breaches by giving Sunday evening dinner parties at Marlborough House; his well-known penchant for self-indulgence, his gambling and womanizing, introduced a moral standard remote from that expected of national figures. The age moved on to the 'naughty nineties', typified by a relaxation of taboos, by the vulgarity of the cheap press and popular amusements, by such scandals as the Oscar Wilde case. Family prayers began to decline, first in aristocratic households, then among the middle classes.

The Church was in retreat. Its revised version of the Bible failed to gain wide acceptance. Evangelicalism 'failed to restate its positions in conformity with either the new science or the new history'. Few first-class honours men now entered the Church, except those graduating in theology. Lay headmasters began to be appointed at public schools. Rival careers in the law, the Civil Service, education, and business drew off the best brains, in part because intellectuals no longer felt religion to be a central concern in their lives, and the poorly-paid work of a parish priest failed to attract. Clerical stipends went downhill along with the price of corn in the agricultural depression after the 1870s. The same rival careers also affected recruitment to the Nonconformist churches. Church attendances fell away, though they were still far above later levels. A census taken in London in 1902–3 showed that less than 1 in 5 of the capital's population attended any form of

Sunday service. Nonconformity held its support better than Anglicanism, while the very poor (except the Roman Catholic Irish) did not even attend a local mission. The Victorian Sabbath could no longer be kept up. The National Sunday League campaigned successfully for Sunday recreations to flow into healthy channels, organized Sunday railway excursions, and in 1896 achieved the Sunday opening of London museums and art galleries.

The stresses and strains of the nineteenth century exposed another highly conservative institution as being much in need of reform: the British army. The terrible blunders and gross incompetence of the Crimean War had demonstrated the urgent need for change, but it was 1868, fourteen years after the Charge of the Light Brigade, before major changes were brought in by the very able Secretary for War, Edward Cardwell. The Iron Duke's opinion was still invoked by conservative officers to ward off the abolition of flogging, but this was a step, along with short service engagements and the discharge of known bad characters, which allowed Cardwell to recruit a better type of man to the ranks. A higher hurdle, and again one approved by Wellington, was purchase as a means of obtaining officers' commissions and promotions. This had obvious vices. Aristocratic youths bought commands for which they had no training, and looked with contempt on career officers who had actual fighting experience in India. The old type of aristocratic officer was typically a sportsman in uniform, and as Lord Wolseley later testified, was 'entirely wanting in military knowledge'.

Only a few of the younger officers believed in reform, but fortunately the Franco-Prussian war of 1870–1 came to Cardwell's aid, demonstrating that the old amateurism, the reliance on classic British 'muddling through', were no longer adequate. Abolition of purchase opened the door for Cardwell to go some way with much needed reform of the command structure. He also based infantry regiments in individual districts of the country, so that in time they became identified with a particular county as the

'Durhams' or the 'Dorsets'; he also re-armed them with the breech-loading Martini-Henry rifle and metallic cartridges – though so great was the conservatism of the ordnance officers that they insisted on going *back* to muzzle-loading cannon! Thus the British army was dragged, reluctant and protesting, into the modern age. Without Cardwell's reforms the military successes of the next twenty-five years would have been impossible.

Further important army reforms were undertaken by Haldane, the Liberal Secretary for War in 1905–12. Most crucial was the long-deferred creation of a general staff, but Haldane also recognized the home establishments so that an Expeditionary Force, completely equipped and with reserves, could be mobilized readily in time of war. The result was that in August 1914 some twenty divisions, complete in all arms, were rapidly placed in the field. Reserves, soon required to make good heavy initial casualties in Belgium and France, came from his reorganized Territorial Force, while the old volunteer corps at public and secondary schools was converted into the Officers' Training Corps. And all this was done at no increase in cost to the Exchequer, indeed with some saving of money, the army estimates of 1914 being half a million less than before Haldane took office.

Reform and modernization of the navy, however, was necessarily expensive. The prime reason for this was the changes in technology. The old wooden ships had been good for a life of sixty years, but the rapid revolution in materials, propulsion and armament after mid-century meant that warships quickly became outdated, and indeed obsolete vessels only ten years old were floating death-traps if matched against the most modern warship. After 1866 no large wooden hull was laid down, and the 'iron-clad', a wooden ship protected by armour, was soon outmoded by armoured iron hulls, as the new rifled, breech-loading 9-inch guns of 1865 put paid to old naval cannon. Most of the new ideas – armour, turrets, breech-loaders, mines, torpedoes, submarines, and naval scout aircraft – came from abroad: the senior service was nothing if not conservative. The first British ironclad, the *Warrior*, was launched in 1860; then, following the foundering in 1870 of the three-masted *Captain* in a gale in the Bay of Biscay, sails were abandoned – though a First Sea Lord had once complained that since the arrival of steam 'he had never seen a clean deck, or a captain, who, when he waited on him, did not look like a sweep'.

The first all-steel battleship, the *Collingwood* of 9,500 tons, appeared in 1886. She boasted two pairs of 12-inch breech-loaders, and also a secondary armament of 6-inch guns and quick-firers designed to beat off torpedo boats armed with the Whitehead torpedo which had been developed in the 1870s. A new pattern of big 12-inch guns, using cordite instead of gunpowder, and having much higher velocities, was carried by the *Magnificent* class in the 1890s. But the major development, coming shortly before World War I, was the appearance of the *Dreadnought* class. These were bigger vessels, and faster too – the first turbine-engined ships in any navy. *Iron Duke*, for example, completed in 1913, displaced 25,000 tons and carried ten 13.5-inch guns as well as sixteen 6-inch. The *Dreadnought*'s power and size compelled the Germans to follow suit, and also to widen the Kiel Canal to take comparable ships, a long and costly operation. It was to meet the German threat that Admiral Fisher, the innovating First Sea Lord, produced not only the *Dreadnought* but also reorganized the disposition of the fleet, creating a new Home Fleet, based on the Nore, and a new Atlantic Fleet based on Gibraltar, thus pulling part of the Mediterranean Fleet out of that sea.

The expense of maintaining naval superiority with larger, faster and more heavily armed ships, and of having to scrap outdated vessels continually, was enormous. The naval estimates, under £13m. in 1886, went to £26m. in 1900 and to nearly £49m. in 1914. Only a small part of this massive increase represented improved pay and conditions for officers and ratings, though there had been some important changes here, too. The false economy of keeping a large number of officers on half-pay in peacetime was abandoned, and promotion was speeded up: no longer were newly-appointed Admirals at the Nore well into their seventies. Training establishments were instituted, and after 1853 the men were signed on for continuous engagements and no longer paid off and discharged after each commission: thus the press gang faded out of history, along with the infamous cat o' nine tails and keel-hauling.

* * * * * *

The political, social, military and naval reforms of the period to 1914 could not be carried out without reform and expansion of the government's own machinery. For an age often supposed to be marked by *laissez-faire*, the increase in the numbers involved in public administration was remarkable. By 1911 the 40,000 males and 3,000 females of 1841 had swollen to 271,000 and 50,000 respectively. This more than six-fold increase was, indeed, vastly greater than the rate of increase in the country's population, and reflected both the enormous expansion and increased complexity of governmental activities and the replacement of amateur part-time administrators by full-time professionals.

The Civil Service in the mid-nineteenth century was itself much in need of reform. True there had been a gradual abolition of sinecures, the institution of a rule that the person who held an office should actually perform its duties; and departments had given up casting accounts in Roman numerals while the Treasury (after a disastrous fire) had ceased to keep its records in the form of notches carved on elm wands. Still, as late as 1808, the clerks of the Stamp Office had to be admonished to forgo their disputing of politics during office hours, to refrain from bringing their dogs to the office and from wearing their hats all day, and to end their habit of erupting into singing, fencing and rioting on the completion of business.

Certainly the old patronage system had something to be said for it: after all, it had brought to the fore men like Chadwick and Henry Taylor, and had put able and conscientious officials like Horner and Tremenheere into the factory and mines inspectorates. But the times were hostile to old-fashioned amateurism and nepotism. Already in 1813 Haileybury College (with the Reverend Thomas Malthus on its staff) had been established for the training of the East India Company's officials in the subcontinent, and in 1833 an Act prescribed selection by examination of nominated candidates for the home Civil Service. But such examinations could be rigged: and indeed the Treasury was supposed to keep around two duffers – 'the Treasury idiots' – to provide suitably feeble competition for favoured candidates.

It was only after 1854, following the shameful absurdities of the Crimea – Florence Nightingale's woefully equipped hospital, the delays in issuing winter clothing to the troops freezing in the trenches before Sebastopol, the shipment of boots all for the left foot – that patronage was completely abolished and selection made by open examination. The Trevelyan-Northcote Report of that year denigrated the stultifying effects of years of routine chores, the mechanical promotion by seniority, and the necessity of going outside to find men capable of filling the highest posts. Recruitment for these top places, it was argued, should be by competitive examination at a level equal to the highest anywhere in the country, with the emphasis on classics and mathematics – this with an eye to the old universities, and reflecting the belief that the liberal education, rather than professional training, provided the best basis for high administrative posts. There was much opposition from those who saw the public service as a convenient means of support for friends and relations, and progress was slow. Would a man of ability 'submit himself to an arduous examination in order to earn a post so ill-paid, obscure and subordinate'? The Queen herself complained that when recruited by examination civil servants would cease to be gentlemen, while *The Economist* sneeringly argued that much of the work required only very mediocre faculties:

> You have work to do demanding only conscientiousness and plodding industry – work quite within the reach of dullness to perform. You have numbers of young men reliable but dull – men who are up to this work, but who would be up to no other; quite fit to copy, to register, to file – quite unfit for anything beyond. The country abounds in such: is it not wise to use them?

It was 1870, indeed, before open examination was made obligatory throughout the service, and the Treasury acquired control of departmental organization and of the rules for the testing of candidates used by the Civil Service Commission which had been established in 1855. Another minor revolution came with the arrival of the lady with the typewriter: slowly the copyists faded away, though the record they left behind them, 'the old copy-letter book with its damped flimsies and smudged copies of hand-written letters, did not disappear until the 1914–18 War'. Though thrown open to all talents, and with selection conducted by an authority independent of the department concerned, it is remarkable that the leading figures in the Civil Service were drawn from the same social class, and often from the same families, as the great politicians they served. 'Ministers preferred to have as the permanent chiefs of their departments men of the same social standing as themselves, whom they had known at Eton or other great public schools or at Oxford and Cambridge, and who, by kinship or marriage, belonged to their world.'

The forms of local administration inherited by the nineteenth century were various; the unpaid justices and town magistrates, the farmers and tradesmen who acted as parish officials, the select vestries and improvement commissions. Their powers were often uncertain, confused and overlapping, their work often slack and ineffective. But as a means of local government the system was cheap, and it had the great advantage of making use of local interest and knowledge. Jeremy Bentham and his followers had, however, little time for such amateurism. They believed in professional central control, and the creation of local units large enough to permit specialization, and thus efficiency. The Poor Law of 1834 began the change, replacing over 14,000 parish administrations by under 700 unions of parishes under elected Boards of Guardians, and in the following year the Municipal Corporations Act substituted 179 new elected municipal councils for old corporations. The Public Health Act of 1848 provided many towns with elected Boards of Health, while in the next generation the Act of 1875 put public health powers in the hands of the councils and made mandatory the appointment of public health inspectors throughout the country. Meanwhile new police authorities appeared from the 1830s, Highway Boards in 1862, and School Boards in 1871. Then, in the same year of 1871, the Local Government Board was established to take over central administration of both the Poor Law and Public Health.

Thus the administrative powers of the old forms of local administration were gradually abolished or whittled away, though the major transformation for the county justices came only with the institution of elected county councils in 1888, and district and parish councils in 1894. The change was far from a complete revolution: justices, for example, still sat ex officio on Boards of Guardians, and many of the old county families were to be found still active under the new guise of county councillors. The large cities became county boroughs with powers similar to those of the counties, while smaller towns retained their more restricted authority. In the towns, however, the councils came to consist largely of local businessmen and shopkeepers: the professional class stood aloof, and this may be one reason, as Ensor supposed, for economy forming the watchword. The great object was to keep down the rates, and so nineteenth-century towns slowly became better built, more adequately paved, cleansed and lighted, and also somewhat more sanitary (though slums and epidemics still abounded), but also hideously ugly, drearily monotonous and, with rare exceptions, characterless.

From the chaos of new authorities and powers created by the piecemeal changes of the nineteenth century emerged the basis on which relations between the central government and local authorities have come to be established: inspection from the centre and grants-in-aid of approved services. New and more comprehensive functions could not be provided without more money. Between 1830 and 1870 the local authorities' receipts from rates in England and Wales doubled, from £8m. to over £16m., while central government contributions rose from under £100,000 to £1,255,000. Education, health, housing, roads, police and a hundred other services continued to expand and draw more heavily on the public purse. By 1914 the rates were bringing in £71.3m., to which a further £22.6m. was added by the grants of the central government.

* * * * * *

Sixth-formers used to be taught (and perhaps some still are) that the nineteenth century was the age of *laissez-faire*. The concept of the economy as a self-regulating mechanism best left alone, and the view that the least government was the best government, were used to explain the mid-century shift to free trade and also the limited nature of government intervention in factories, public health, and other social questions. In the sense of leaving the economy free to work of itself, and the people free to seek their own self-interest, *laissez-faire* might be better applied to the eighteenth century; while the bonfire made of antiquated laws in the early part of the nineteenth betokened a belated recognition of the uselessness of retaining on the statute book legislation that was neither enforced nor enforceable.

The general tenor of the economic theory of the period, it is true, did encourage the belief that inexorable economic laws applied to supply and demand, to wages and to

69 The creation of new bodies for local government was one of the outstanding reforms of the sixty years from 1835. County councils were inaugurated in 1888, and District and Parish Councils in 1894. The municipal councils, formed in 1835, gained additional powers and responsibilities, and supervised the slow improvement in the conditions of English towns, dominated very often by local businessmen and shopkeepers. Here is the Poplar Council of 1902–3. (Tower Hamlets Library)

population, and made government attempts to intervene not merely futile but positively harmful. Economic thinking was amplified by the belief that free enterprise made for progress and prosperity, and that low taxes allowed money to 'fructify' in the pockets of the people, as Gladstone had it. So, it was argued, came the Repeal of the Corn Laws, the abandonment of the Navigation Laws, the removal of restrictions on formation of joint-stock companies and the adoption of limited liability, the haphazard construction of a railway network consisting of competing lines. *Laissez-faire* was certainly the background to these developments, and certainly influenced people in power. But *laissez-faire* was also used to make respectable opposition to any intervention which might threaten a vested interest, as the owners of slum dwellings, directors of inefficient water companies, and proprietors of night-soil businesses opposed public health reform. But the economists did not speak with one voice, and some even held that certain forms of government intervention, for example on behalf of factory children, were justifiable.

More significant was the fact that the freeing of trade, shipping, and companies was very much in the interests of the industrial and commercial class which was exerting increasing political influence. Indeed, the Repeal of the Corn Laws has long been interpreted not as a measure to cheapen food – there was little surplus corn to come in – but as an essentially political attack by this class on the landed interest which still contrived to retain political power after the limited reform of 1832. Governments then, as now, were swayed by current political circumstances. Peel believed that abandonment of the Corn Laws was a necessary sacrifice worth making in order to stave off demands for a further reform of Parliament. Politics was, as always, the art of the possible, and sometimes the balance of advantage lay in taking a *laissez-faire* line, sometimes the opposite.

And though *laissez-faire* informed much of the thinking of the age, it was not all-pervasive. There were many influential people who rejected the philosophy, and clung to the old-fashioned view that it was the responsibility of the governing class to remedy grievances and root out evils. They faced a number of factors which operated to make reform piecemeal and slow. Opposition from vested interests ensured a cautious approach: there was the sanctity of private property to consider, and the innumerable pitfalls in interfering in a long-established web of patronage and private interests, of rights to local control of local affairs. The question of cost was also a major obstacle. It was an age that believed cheapness in government to be a prime virtue, and so Gladstone would boast of saving the miserable salary of a clerk, and quibble with the Queen over the cost of the Albert Memorial. To have a chance of going forward any reform had to be cheap – witness the minuscule staff of the 1848 Central Board of Health.

Then there was the question of inadequate knowledge. The nineteenth-century pace of change was unprecedentedly rapid, the problems new, or at least on a much greater scale than hitherto. The spate of royal commissions and committees of inquiry indicates the extent of ignorance and (often) a willingness to investigate, if not always to act; while in some fields, such as public health, reform was held back by insufficient understanding of causes and, equally, of effective remedies. Specialists were needed who were scarce or had to be specially trained: medical officers of health, nurses, civil and sanitary engineers, factory inspectors and teachers. The government itself, as we have seen, was woefully inadequate in its own Civil Service, and new forms of local administration had to be devised and established.

The age achieved much. It might have achieved more, if only the limitations on reform had themselves changed more rapidly. An informed public opinion was required, one that was conscious of the need for greater government action and was not held back by religious scruples, by constitutional quibbles, or by the belief that too much help was bad for the moral fibre, would weaken the impetus to self-help. There had to be a willingness to shoulder higher taxation – not merely the regressive indirect taxes whose burden fell heaviest on the poor, but the direct taxes which hit the incomes of the rich. Thus the budget of 1909, which raised the standard rate of income tax to 1*s*. 2*d*. in the pound (it had been 1*s*. 3*d*. during the Boer War, but this was now peacetime), and more significantly introduced a new 'super-tax' of 6*d*. in the pound on all incomes above £5,000 (to be levied on the amount by which such incomes exceeded £3,000). This was Lloyd George's 'War Budget': 'It is for raising money to wage implacable warfare against poverty and squalidness'. The House of Lords insisted on throwing the budget out, and so brought about the constitutional crisis which resulted in its being formally shorn of any power over a money Bill.

From the perspective of the 1980s the figures that aroused this storm seem paltry. But it was the precedent, the breach in established tradition, which mattered. Only a few years later World War I, with its standard rate of 6s. in the pound and super-tax also of 6s. was to make the issue an academic one. The raising of the threshold of the acceptable level of taxation was one consequence of the war that was to be of enormous significance for the future building of a Welfare State.

Chapter Eight

The Old World Dissolved

World War I marked the end of the old Britain, the beginning of the new. Life was never quite the same again. The war brought terrible loss and suffering, but also a greater degree of democracy, reforms in education and housing, and a generally more egalitarian society. It was also a landmark in changing Britain's place in the world, writing *finis* to the Pax Britannica, exposing the shortcomings in Britain's economy, ending her role as the world's chief lender of capital, and putting the former workshop of the world on short time. After a brief re-stocking boom which lasted only until 1920, Britain entered on an era of industrial depression which, with ups and downs, was to last for the next twenty years. When by the middle 1920s other countries had recovered and enjoyed something of a boom, Britain's run-down staple industries had not regained their former markets and were the main factor in the 1.2m. to 1.5m. unemployed. (This represented some 10–12 per cent of the labour force, while in the ten years before the war the figure fluctuated between 2 and 10 per cent.)

It is difficult to estimate the precise role of World War I in Britain's post–1920 level of unemployment. The war certainly checked temporarily the country's economic progress, although by 1920 income and production had recovered to the levels of 1913. The war also hastened trends unfavourable to Britain which had been developing for some time earlier, and contributed to the failure of exports to recover fully after 1918. In particular, the war had provided the opportunity for other producers, notably

70 Armistice Day, 11 November 1918, celebrated by a mixed crowd of civilians and men and women in uniform. (BBC Hulton Picture Library)

the United States and Japan, to take over more completely our former markets in South America and the Far East. But the picture is complicated by the fact that in any event the traditional British exports would have lost ground. They were no longer in such high world-wide demand, partly because of competition from new producers, partly because of new technology and the development of substitutes. Oil and electricity became powerful rivals to inefficiently mined British coal, and between 1924 and 1930 the proportion of coal-miners out of work quadrupled to over 28 per cent. Shipbuilding collapsed earlier, in 1921, when massive post-war launchings produced a world

71 and **72** The motor industry was one of the new and thriving ones in the inter-war years, and following the lead from America, pioneered the techniques of mass production and the assembly line: two scenes from the Ford works at Dagenham showing early Model T production. (Ford of Britain)

overstocked with ships. In April 1921 3.3m. tons were under construction in British yards, eighteen months later only 1.1m. tons: orders for 300 ships were cancelled in 1921. Unemployment in the industry rose to over 28 per cent and stayed there. In steel there was over-production and a good deal of technological backwardness, resulting in unemployment in the industry rising to 20 per cent, and then to over 30 per cent. In 1912 Lancashire exported nearly 7m. yards of cloth; in 1924 only 4.5m. yards, a figure which was to decline even further. By 1930 45 per cent of cotton hands had no work.

The problem was that the unemployment was not the

result of a severe but temporary drop in the trade cycle, and would disappear when conditions improved, as had happened throughout the nineteenth century. World trade as a whole did recover after World War I, and indeed increased in the middle and later 1920s, but Britain's exports, nevertheless, ran at only about three-quarters of the volume achieved in 1913. True, there were new and expanding industries, notably electricity supply and engineering, motor vehicles, bicycles, aircraft, rayon, hosiery, plastics, chemicals, stainless steel and scientific instruments. They accounted for a growing share of total production, but still only a fairly small one: 16.3 per cent in 1930, and a rather smaller proportion of the export trade. Moreover, most of the new industries' plants were located in the more prosperous Midlands and South of England, and not in the depressed regions of the North, South Wales, Scotland and Northern Ireland. The bulk of the unemployment in the 1920s was of a structural kind, caused by the permanent shrinking of old, large industries, and thus slow to cure; the new industries, apart from being located elsewhere, employed mainly semi-skilled workers, a large proportion of them women. Hence the persistence of the unemployment problem in the inter-war years.

Yet there were some bright aspects of the industrial scene. The basis was laid for important export industries of the post-World War II future, especially motor vehicles, electricity, and aircraft. In their structure the exports of 1938 were not very different from those of 1913, still dominated by steel and engineering products, coal, ships and textiles, but those of 1950 and afterwards were markedly different. Further, industrial productivity grew at a substantially higher rate between the two wars than it had done since the heyday of the mid-Victorian boom. This important development was by no means solely due to the growth of the new industries; it was a feature too of the depressed staple trades, where the reduction in markets involved the closing down of surplus capacity, obsolete mines, outdated steelworks, antiquated shipyards and old-fashioned textile factories, and the concentration of production in the more efficient units, a process known as 'rationalization'. Where new, modern equipment was installed, as in car factories and electricity supply, the growth of productivity was remarkable.

To the structural unemployment of the 1920s was added the cyclical decline of the slump of the early 1930s. Unemployment rose sharply from the 10–11 per cent plateau of 1927–29 to hit 16 per cent in 1930, 21.3 per cent in 1931, and 22.1 per cent in 1932, subsiding only slightly to 19.9 per cent in 1933; it did not fall below 11 per cent again until 1937, and both 1938 and 1939 were higher, at 12.9 per cent and 11.5 per cent respectively. (These figures are of course national averages. In the depressed areas the figures were over twice as high, and in some black spots unemployment amounting to 40, 50, 60 or even 70 per cent of the local labour force was not unknown.) With the near collapse of the world economy in the early 1930s the volume of British exports sank to a new low, averaging only about half the 1913 figure in 1931–3. The subsequent years were better, but exports were still lower in 1934–9 than they had been at any time in the 1920s. A major reason for the poor performance of the export trade was the fall in world commodity prices which had the effect of reducing the incomes of some of Britain's best customers, for example Canada, Australia and New Zealand. They suffered severe balance of payment difficulties and were thus obliged to restrict their import of British goods.

Whether the policies of the government went far towards relieving the depression, or made it worse, is a complex and controversial issue. In the 1920s the government followed a policy of deflation and cut expenditure, and in 1925 put the currency back on the gold standard at its former pre-war parity ($4.86 to the pound). According to the great contemporary economist, John Maynard Keynes, this in effect over-valued the pound by about 10 per cent, meaning that the prices of British exports were that much dearer than they would otherwise have been, and consequently more difficult to sell. It must be said, however, that in view of the French determination to retain their exchange-rate advantage, and the resurgence of competition from German industry, it is doubtful how far a lower exchange rate for sterling would have helped British exports. And the return to gold did have the effect of cheapening imports and of creating exchange stability which contributed to business confidence.

To offset any exchange-rate handicap either the costs of production had to come down, including wages, or more of the overseas markets would be lost and unemployment increased. Though the return to the pre-war parity was a factor in bringing on the crisis in the coal mines and the General Strike of 1926, there was in fact no general fall in wages. There was, however, unrest in the mines after the cutting of wages which led to the General Strike, and a prolonged coal stoppage which followed the collapse of the strike. But despite the impotence of the unions after 1926, average weekly wage rates remained virtually unchanged throughout the middle and later 1920s, at about twice the level of 1900, and a little less than twice the 1913 figure. A small fall did occur in the early 1930s, but by 1937 this had been recovered, and indeed the rates rose to above the level which held before 1931.

In the crisis years of 1931–2 Britain came off the gold standard, and in common with other countries devalued the currency and resorted to more complete measures of protection against imports. In a world awash with trade restrictions and competitive devaluations the fall in the value of the pound could make little difference to the level of British exports. Protection, too, had little impact on employment levels, because most of the new industries were already protected. The domestic economy was perhaps now better insulated from external disruptive forces, and control of food imports made it possible to introduce a new era of regulated prices for farmers, though with relatively small effect on their incomes during the 1930s. However, the bank rate, and therefore the cost of borrowing, was low in the 1930s, and so helped in the growth of certain industries, most notably building, which experienced a boom in the middle and later years of the decade. Measures designed specifically to help the depressed areas of the old industries came late, and were in any case on too small a scale to make much impression. Rearmament, forced on the government by the growing threat of Hitler's Germany, began in 1937 and had some influence in such industries as aircraft, engineering and shipbuilding, but again came too late to have any major impact on conditions before 1941. Indeed, there were still 1m. unemployed in the first full year of the Second World War, 1940, and nearly 400,000 (6.6 per cent of the work-force) in 1941.

One final aspect of the inter-war economy is still relatively little known, and indeed does not form part of the

73 In the more prosperous parts of the country, at least, the retail trade did well in the years between the wars as customers' purchasing power increased. The Co-operative Society's stores, such as those shown here at East Ham in April 1929, were favoured by many people, partly because of the 'divi' or discount on purchases which was regularly paid out to members. (BBC Hulton Picture Library)

popular image of these two black decades. Living standards, despite high unemployment, actually rose. The precise extent of the improvement is difficult to measure, but that there was a rise is in no doubt; some authorities put it as high as 30 per cent, though perhaps 20 per cent is a more reliable figure. The main factor here was not money wages: as we have seen, these remained nearly constant for most of the period, and working hours – slightly over 46 hours a week in manufacturing – did not change greatly. Prices however fell considerably after 1920, and in the years 1923–39 were only about half as high again as those of 1913, while earnings were nearly twice as high. Particularly significant in most people's living standards was the low level of food prices. The obverse side of the over-valued pound of the 1920s and of the poverty in the 1930s of countries like Canada, Australia and New Zealand was the cheapness of their products in the British markets. Industries in Britain suffered from reduced exports, and the ranks of the unemployed swelled, but living was cheap. Another factor in the improved living standards was the increased productivity of industry, especially those using new technology. In the competitive conditions of the period greater efficiency meant low prices. So, in the 1930s one could buy a new house for under £300, a new car for well under £200, a bicycle for £3.19*s*.6*d*. One could go down the high street on a Saturday evening – shops stayed open till 9.00 p.m. – and buy a nice little joint of Argentine beef for 2*s*. 6*d*., seven pounds of potatoes for 6*d*., confectionery at 2*d*. the quarter, have a fish and chip supper for a shilling, and round off the evening with a seat in the cinema for 9*d*.

* * * * * *

The depression of the 1920s and 1930s was a true deflation: though output in general rose, prices fell and unemployment was heavy. It was quite different from the 'stagflation' we have known since the 1970s, when output has been static, unemployment higher than for much of the inter-war period, and prices have risen inexorably. Momentous in the inter-war depression was the sudden world crisis of 1931, which finally put paid to any hopes of getting back to pre-war 'normalcy'. The origins of the crisis are disputed, and were certainly a complex combination of both monetary and 'real' factors. Some authorities point to world over-production of foodstuffs and raw materials which caused prices to begin to sink in the late 1920s. Others would place the onus on basic weaknesses in the apparently prosperous American economy of the 1920s, the stock exchange mania and subsequent collapse, which in turn led to a sudden cessation of American lending abroad. The cutting off of America's loans helped to bring about the collapse of the world monetary system. Under the gold standard, trade deficits were supposed to be eased by transfers of gold; but the huge gold reserves of the New York and Paris markets were kept locked up in the vaults, and London did not have the gold necessary to save the day. Debtor countries which relied on loans to balance their books were forced into deflationary policies designed to raise exports and diminish imports. The world was swamped with unsold goods and prices collapsed, some by as much as 40 per cent in the winter of 1929. The reduced capacity of primary producing countries to import hit the export trade of the industrial countries, and so spread the deflationary disease even further.

The crisis came to a head in the summer of 1931. On 11 May the Austrian Credit-Anstalt bank closed its doors; German banks had invested heavily in Austria, and to save its banking system the German government froze all foreign assets. The strain of providing funds was thus transferred to the one major financial market still allowing free transfer of gold, London. Gold and foreign exchange began to flow out of London at an alarming rate, £4m. a day. The Bank of England might possibly have ridden out the storm but for a political crisis which blew up on the publication of the Report of the May Committee, on 1 August. This report severely criticized the policies of the Labour Government, and advocated economies which included cutting £67m. from payments to the unemployed. This cut in unemployment relief became the symbol of the government's willingness to tackle the emergency, and it threatened to split the cabinet. The one alternative was to protect the currency by leaving the gold standard, devaluing the pound, and instituting exchange control to safeguard the remaining reserves. But Snowden, the Chancellor, held fast to the Gladstonian creed of 'economy, free trade, and gold': there was no devaluation and the government broke up.

In the National Government which followed,

MacDonald and Snowden remained as Prime Minister and Chancellor respectively, and headed a cabinet consisting of two other Labour members, four Conservatives and two Liberals. The bulk of the Labour Party went into opposition. Snowden produced an emergency budget which put income tax up *6d.* to *5s.*, and added *1d.* to the price of beer. He also cut the pay of those in the public service, including the forces. On 15 September sailors in the Home Fleet stationed at Invergordon mutinied and refused to take the ships to sea for exercises. 'Mutiny in the British Fleet' flashed across the telegraphs of the world. There was new speculation against sterling and great waves of money poured out of London. The National Government, formed to save the pound, could do no more. On 21 September Britain left the gold standard and devalued. The Governor of the Bank of England, Montagu Norman, was on a sea voyage recovering from a nervous breakdown when he received the cryptic telegram 'Old Lady goes off on Monday'. He is said, incredibly, to have thought it must refer to his mother's holiday plans. In the election which followed on 27 October the National Government was returned with an overwhelming 552 seats, 471 of them Conservative; the opposition, consisting of Labour rebels and Lloyd George Liberals, could only muster a mere 56.

The National Government could not save the pound. In fact a choice had been made between impossibly severe cuts in expenditure, wage reductions and higher taxes, and the gold standard. As Robert Skidelsky has written: 'Something had to break in the summer of 1931; and since it was not going to be the standard of life of the people, it had to be a monetary system which had ceased to serve their needs'. The extent of the sacrifice required to save the pound was beyond practical and political possibilities. And the new National Government was remarkably popular. A major reason for this lay in the word 'confidence'. The minority Labour government of 1929 was not merely politically weak, outnumbered in the Commons by 41 seats – its motives and competence too were suspect. With the change of 1931 the public felt it was in safer hands. The National Government was not blamed for going off gold because it was seen to have done everything it could to avoid it. It was felt, too, that there was little option when the gold standard had collapsed everywhere and the whole world was in monetary chaos. The Labour Party suffered from an unpopular association with monetary weakness, the collapse of 1931, and a pacifism which appeared increasingly dangerous as Europe became more militaristic and dictators revived the armed forces of Germany and Italy. The election of 1935 showed that people still wanted caution and conservatism, despite the continued high unemployment. The new House of Commons contained 387 Conservatives: the Labour opposition had revived to 158 and the opposition Liberals numbered 21. And Stanley Baldwin, who took over from MacDonald as Prime Minister in 1935, was the very epitome of prudence. An old Harrovian with a cabinet which contained six other old Harrovians, he was one of the first politicians to master the technique of radio; his voice was reassuring, his words calming, and his unruffled, pipe-smoking image conveyed the essence of careful circumspection.

The governments of the 1930s gained also from the better times after 1932, though their policies had little to do with the improvement. The truth was that Britain was less severely affected by the whirlwind of 1929–32 than many other countries, perhaps because the country was, already adjusted and inured to heavy unemployment, because there were some expanding industries and relatively prosperous areas in the country, and because it began to enjoy some elements of the boom it had missed in the 1920s, especially in housing and consumer durables. While in America Roosevelt's New Deal had failed to bring unemployment below 9m., and in Germany depression and unrest paved the way for Hitler, Britain was politically stable and, by comparison, economically comfortable.

* * * * * *

Social investigations made between the wars confirm the fact of material improvement. There were still poverty, malnutrition, overcrowding and slums on a massive scale. A survey of Bristol, by no means a heavily depressed city, made in 1937, showed as much as 10.7 per cent of working-class families to be living below the poverty line. A little earlier, in 1935–6, Seebohm Rowntree repeated his investigation of poverty in York, the city he had examined with minute thoroughness in 1899. He now used a more liberal minimum standard, one of 'human needs' instead of 'mere physical efficiency', and calculated that a family of a man, wife and three children needed an income, after paying rent, of 43*s*. 6*d*. a week to meet his new minimum. On this basis 31.1 per cent of the working-class population (17.7 per cent of the total numbers) were in poverty, with over 14 per cent in abject poverty, living on incomes of under 33*s*. 6*d*. a week. Nevertheless, there had been progress since 1899; for if his original, more stringent, definition were to be applied, in the interval of 37 years the proportion of those in want had fallen from 10 per cent of the city's population to just under 4 per cent.

The major cause of poverty, Rowntree found, remained the same: lowness of wages; though in 1935–6 unemployment had become a much more serious factor than at the end of the century, following very close on the heels of low wages. These two causes accounted for over 60 per cent of the poverty; old age contributed another 15 per cent, and the inadequate earnings of casual employment nearly 10 per cent. As in 1899 large families, those with 3 children or more, were most likely to be poor, and this evidence, with similar data from Bristol, was used to reinforce the case for the family allowances which were eventually instituted in 1945.

Poor diet and low nutritional standards remained as in the past a consequence, in part, of poverty, though there was impressive evidence that annual consumption of food per head had increased since before World War I. The investigations of Sir John Boyd Orr, published in 1936,

Proportion of the working-class population in primary poverty due to various causes in 1936 and 1899

Cause	1936	1899
Death of chief wage-earner	.61 per cent	2.42 per cent
Illness or old age of chief wage-earner	1.60 per cent	.79 per cent
Unemployment	3.04 per cent	.36 per cent
Irregularity of work	.40 per cent	.44 per cent
Largeness of family —i.e. more than 4 children	.54 per cent	3.43 per cent
In regular work but at low wages	.63 per cent	8.03 per cent
From all causes (Half scale)	6.82 per cent	15.46 per cent

Figure 7 A comparison of the causes of primary (involuntary) poverty in York at the time of Rowntree's investigations of 1899 and 1936. The main changes were the reduced significance of low wages, largeness of family, and death of chief wage-earner, and the new prominence of unemployment. (B. Seebohm Rowntree, *Poverty and Progress*, 1941)

indicated that a tenth of the country's population (containing a fifth of all the children) was very badly fed, and as much as half of the nation ill-fed. One of the effects of the poor diet of the working classes was to be seen in the stunted growth of so many of the children. The height and weight of all children had been rising for a long period before World War I, but there was still a very marked discrepancy between children of different social classes: public school boys aged fourteen, from Sir John Boyd Orr's figures, were on average 3.7 inches taller than boys of the same age at a council school.

Differences of social class were also marked by differences in housing. Again, the new survey by Rowntree showed that in York overcrowding had fallen by more than two-thirds since the beginning of the century, and the proportion of the working classes living in slum dwellings had fallen from 26 per cent to 11.7 per cent. In the later 1930s York, like other cities, was being extensively cleared of the worst slums, and by 1939 almost every home had its own water supply and its own WC, and a third of the homes had a bath.

Though there had been legislation before World War I concerning insanitary houses, little had been done. The war, however, produced two changes. One was the introduction of Rent Acts controlling the rents of working-class tenants. Originally this was to keep rents from soaring with the war-time inflation, but the policy was continued after the war, and indeed still persists at the present. Its main long-term consequences have been to discourage landlords from making improvements to the houses, and eventually to greatly reduce their number. The other change was a series of new Housing Acts, beginning with the Addison Act of 1919, intended to give more encouragement to local councils to build their own houses, and with other legislation, to get rid of slums and over-crowding.

74, **75** and **76** Three stages in the creation of a new London housing project, the East Hill estate, built on former open land. Note the builders' use of horses and carts, the traditional timber scaffolding, and the drearily institutional and overcrowded effect of the finished product. (Greater London Council)

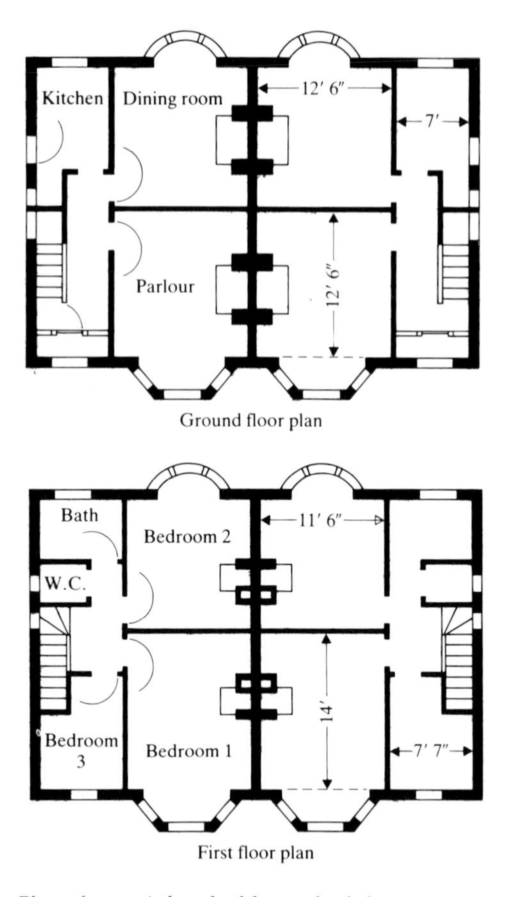

Figure 8 Plan of a semi-detached house built by a speculative builder for sale in York after World War I (B. Seebohm Rowntree, *Poverty and Progress*, 1941, p. 278)

Under these measures over 1m. council houses were built in the twenty years after 1919, while another 430,000 were built privately with the aid of a subsidy – over 1.5m. together. (It should be said that the very poor benefited little from the new council houses for although these were subsidized they commanded a rent – and its payment regularly – beyond what they could afford. Council

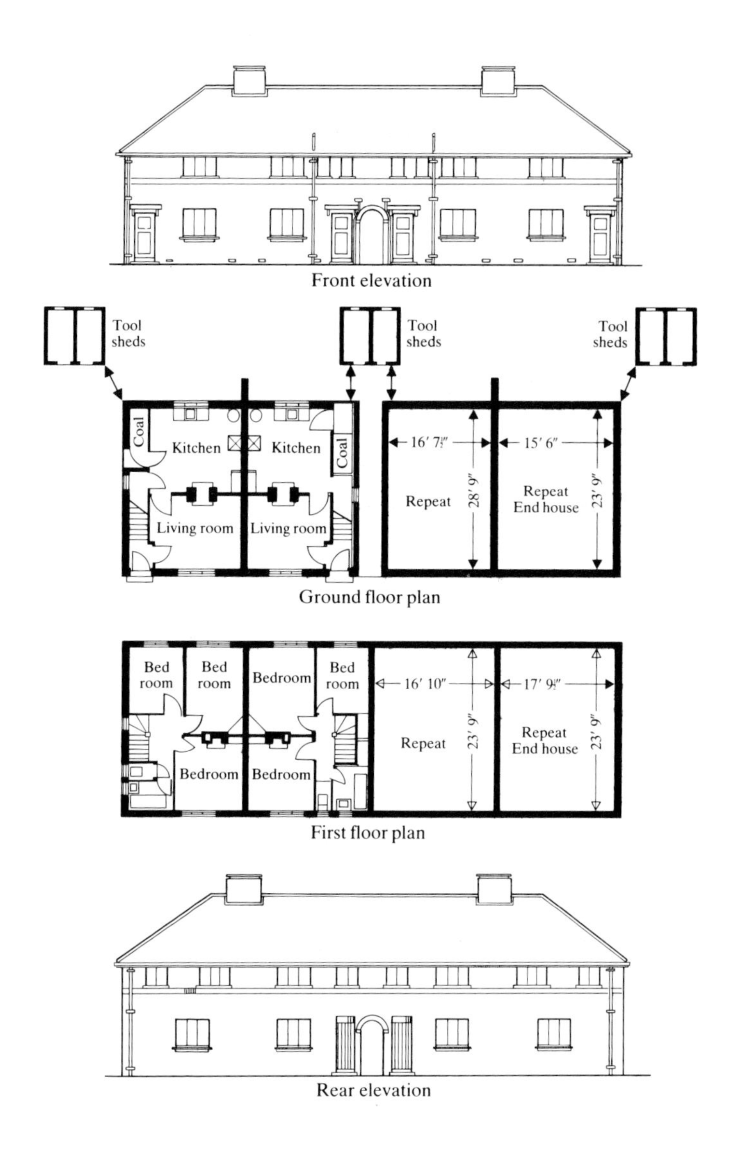

Figure 9 Typical plan and elevation of a non-parlour council house built in York after 1920 (B. Seebohm Rowntree, *Poverty and Progress*, 1941, p. 279)

houses, in fact, met the needs of the regularly employed working classes, somewhat superior in incomes to those of the very poor.) However, the figure for publicly financed housing was completely dwarfed by the nearly 2.5m. houses (having a rateable value of under £79, or £105 in London) that were built by private enterprise without subsidy.

Low interest rates, standardization of design, components and materials, and much use of semi-skilled labour, contributed to the housing boom which marked the middle and later 1930s. Monotonous stretches of identical terraced and semi-detached houses were quickly run up, the street names not infrequently those of the builders. Such houses provided much material for music-hall comedians: only the last house of a terrace was well built – it had to hold the others up. But, jerry-built or not, these houses helped greatly in reducing the long-standing housing shortage. In 1939 there was even, in statistical terms at least, a surplus of 585,000 houses over the total number of families. As a consequence there was something of a general post, with lower-middle-class and better-off working-class people moving into new suburban houses, and the less well-off taking up the older homes which had been vacated. Many families displaced by slum clearance were rehoused in council houses and tenements, giving rise to the celebrated cliché about keeping coal in the bath. And with the shrinking of families there were often rooms to spare. People moving to a new town could leave their bags at the station and take a walk round the neighbourhood, making a choice between the numerous houses displaying such signs as 'Rooms to Let', 'Apartment Vacant', 'Board Residence' or 'Bed and Breakfast'.

The easing of the housing shortage, and indeed the general advance in living standards, owed not a little to the trends in population. The birth rate fell drastically, so that in 1925 the proportion of women first married in that year who were destined to have 2 children or less was over two-thirds of the whole, compared with under a half in the years 1900–9. Similarly, the proportion having more than 4 children had more than halved, from over a quarter to a little over a tenth. The average size of family had been falling throughout the second half of the previous century: for those women married in the 1860s it had been over 6, and by 1900–9 was already down to 3.3. It was to fall further still, to only 2, by the end of the 1930s.

One element in the inter-war decline in births was the enormous loss of young men in the World War I, meaning that many women were unable to marry, or had first marriages lasting only a short period. (There were also effects of the loss on national physique, and on the supply of talent, since so many young men of promise had perished in the trenches and the casualty rate among junior officers was enormously high.) Other elements included the greater freedom of women to follow careers, wider knowledge of methods of contraception, and fashion. Large families simply became unfashionable, and especially where they were seen by parents as hampering material advancement. For many couples there was indeed a choice to be made between having a baby and having a baby Austin. And among the unskilled and semi-skilled, where unemployment was heaviest, the lack of a job, or uncertainty of keeping it, was a factor in delaying marriage and in limiting the size of the family.

Whatever the causes, smaller families had certain implications. When there was a smaller number to share a given income higher standards of comfort were possible, with more money to spare for both necessities and luxuries. Smaller families meant a reduction in overcrowded homes and a rise in housing standards; better diet and health care and so less pressure on medical resources – the death rate from tuberculosis was nearly halved; and less pressure on school accommodation. By 1938 nearly two-fifths of fourteen-year-olds were in full-time education, compared with under a tenth in 1902; and similarly for 4 per cent of seventeen-year-olds compared with 2 per cent. One has only to consider how much more limited slum clearance, secondary education, and improvements in living standards would have been if the country's population had continued to grow at the pre-1914 rate; that is, if nearly twice as many people had been added to the population in the inter-war years.

As it was, the increase in numbers did add to unemployment as the size of the labour force increased by some two-fifths. Another unfavourable trend was the rise in the proportion of people over retirement age. By 1931 this was more than half as large again as in 1901, reflecting an expectation of life which had lengthened from under 40 years in the mid-nineteenth century to nearly 59 years by 1930–2, 10 of these extra years having been added since 1901–10. The increased numbers of elderly persons put strain on family budgets and on housing and medical services. And old age, as Rowntree noted, was a significant factor in poverty.

* * * * * *

As we have seen, the main new development in the sources of poverty since 1899 was the much larger number of unemployed. In York unemployment was found in 1935–6 to account for 28.6 per cent of people below the poverty line, and in Bristol it was the largest single factor, accounting for over 32 per cent of the families in poverty. The problem arose largely because of the low levels of benefit payments. Whereas Rowntree estimated an income of at least 43*s*. 6*d*. a week after rent to be necessary to keep a family of man, wife and three children above the poverty line, the same family received during 1931–5 only 29*s*. 3*d*. in unemployment insurance benefit. This figure was even below the 30*s*. 7*d*., after rent, that was necessary to support a family on Rowntree's old 'physical efficiency' criterion of 1899. The same sum of 29*s*. 3*d*. was also paid in transitional payments – 'the dole' – after benefit rights were exhausted, and was subject to a means test. In 1936 a revised scale of payments gave this size of family about 36*s*., still well below Rowntree's 'human needs' figure. At that date the total unemployed stood at 1,749,000. (This was the figure of registered unemployed: many women and elderly men did not bother to register at the labour exchange, so the true figure of unemployed is higher.) Some 43 per cent of those registered as unemployed at this date were drawing unemployment insurance; 37 per cent were receiving the dole from the Unemployment Assistance Board, and most of the remainder were maintained by the local Public Assistance Committees, the heirs since 1929 of the old Poor Law Guardians.

The means test was hated for many reasons. Since it took account of all sources of income, including savings, pensions, rents, and lodgers, it penalized thrift and rewarded imprudence. Since it also counted in the incomes of employed sons or daughters living at home it threw part of the burden of supporting parents on to the young and encouraged them to leave home and marry. Moreover, as C. L. Mowat has written:

> The test was an encouragement to the tattle-tale and the informer, the writer of anonymous letters and the local blackmailer; to all sorts of unneighbourliness. It stimulated petty tyranny and insolence on the part of Labour Exchange clerks and managers; the weekly visit to the Exchange could bring the sudden, curt announcement by the clerk: 'They've knocked you off dole.'

At least the dole kept people from starving and from converting discontented mutterings into violent action. Sir Oswald Mosley's blackshirts stood little chance of bringing about a fascist revolution in apathetic Britain. Indeed, not a few, particularly the younger married men, were actually better off on the dole than if employed in many low-paid jobs, especially if the work were intermittent.

The unemployed sank into a pattern of daily life which rationalized unwonted leisure, curtailed outgoings and attempted to minimize boredom. At first, before the inevitable apathy set in, men tried to keep up appearances, wearing decent clothes, shaving regularly, and assuming an optimistic air. They scanned the papers at the public library for jobs, and were prepared to walk or cycle many miles if there was a rumour of vacancies at a distant works. Many of the older men soon realized they were never to work again, and in the most severely depressed districts there were thousands of miners, riveters, and foundry hands who had not worked for years. In 1936 nearly 53,000 had not had any work for over 5 years, and 205,000 more had no job for 2 years or more. Nearly a quarter of the total receiving unemployment pay had been out of work for at least a year. They hung about street corners in shabby half-dozens, their hands unusually white and soft, their shoulders bowed, and grey hopelessness in their faces.

Some of the younger men took it differently. They accepted joblessness as normal, as a way of life: some who had been unemployed since leaving school had never known about regular hours and the discipline of the factory bell. The more enterprising joined social clubs, attended rallies, played football or joined an adult education class. Others worked their allotments – allotments were in high demand in the depressed areas – kept poultry, bred rabbits or took up whippets and racing pigeons. Extra money might be earned as a bookie's runner, or by going round the houses distributing advertisements or collecting newspaper subscriptions. The wives took in lodgers, went out cleaning or did dressmaking at home. The whole family would scrabble over the coal tips for enough pieces to bring home in an old perambulator, and went out in the hedgerows collecting blackberries or helped farmers get in their apples, soft fruit and hops. In winter the men stayed late in bed, sauntered down to the club for a game of table tennis or billiards, and spent the evening at the cinema. The cinemas, often the newest and most imposing buildings in the town, did well: a half of the unemployed went to the pictures once a week, many twice a week. The women suffered most, confined to a comfortless home and trying to feed a family on a few shillings, patronizing the pawnshops and the stalls which sold second-hand clothing, worrying about how to keep up the payments on the furniture, making do with scraps and leftovers so that the children at least should have their bellies full.

There was resentment and some unrest, protest meetings and hunger marches. Rallies of the unemployed filled Hyde Park, and some dared even to invade the luxury of the nearby Ritz Hotel. Most famous of the protests was the Jarrow Crusade of 1936. It was Palmer's shipyard that had made Jarrow, beginning with floating batteries for the Crimean War and the making of the first armour plate in Britain. The population had grown ten-fold in seventy years to reach 35,000 in 1921. Then, in the depths of the slump, Palmer's yard was closed, its cranes and machinery dismantled. The town died: 69 per cent of its people were out of a job. In 1935 came Ellen Wilkinson – 'Red Ellen' – as Jarrow's Member of Parliament, and in the following October she led a march of 200 men to carry a petition to Westminster. They marched steadily, well-received in most of the places they passed, and on 1 November entered London wet through in a cloudburst, seeking refuge in a soup kitchen in Garrick Street. Next day their petition, bearing 12,000 names, was presented to the Commons as, in Ronald Blythe's words, 'bony, weather-reddened faces of the workless stared down like sparse carvings from the gallery'. In reply to a question Baldwin, the Prime Minister, enumerated the resolutions he had received on Jarrow's behalf, and then Runciman, the President of the Board of Trade, remarked that the unemployment situation in the town was somewhat improved. Demands to know why Admiralty orders had not been placed at Jarrow were disregarded, and then it was all over and time for tea. Three days later the marchers went home by special train, to find their dole had been reduced, because while they were away they had not been available for work, supposing any had been offered.

* * * * * *

77 and **78** Two photographs showing slum housing in Millwall, East London, about 1930. Open drains, broken paving and leaking roofs were merely the external signs of long years of neglect. Some such houses were swept away in the slum clearance schemes of the 1930s, but many others remained until World War II and after. (Island History Project)

The Britain of the 1930s wore a different face from that of today. In the depressed areas the rows of mean streets were marked by neglect, the houses unpainted, slates missing from roofs, broken windows stuffed with rags or brown paper. Youths kicked an old football about the street, children played hopscotch on the pavements and raced their barrows – fruit boxes on perambulator wheels. Men shovelled up horse dung from the cobbles for their allotments, combed through dustbins for something that might be saleable, picked up 'fag-ends' to accumulate enough tobacco to roll a cigarette. Even in the prosperous Midlands and South there were endless beggars. There were old men who had a regular pitch in the doorway of a public house, selling matches and shoelaces, and touching their caps for a penny. There were itinerant gangs of Welsh miners who sang lustily and were stared at as something of a novelty. There were tramps who knocked at houses to inquire if there might be any odd jobs or to see if a piece of bread or cup of tea could be spared. Coalmen's wagons, rag-and-bone men's carts, and knife grinders' hand-carts patrolled the streets, shouting their wares on the off-chance of a customer. Respectable, well-dressed men took demeaning jobs selling brushes, vacuum cleaners, or dusters from door to door, or even took orders for one particular grocery shop, the order to be delivered by a boy on a bicycle on the Friday or Saturday.

You did not need a great income to live relatively well, and outside the depressed areas the inhabitants of the 'other England' did just that. In 1937 over two-thirds of all working-class families had an average income of £3.15*s*. 10*d*., well above the level of 'human needs'; more than a tenth of them were very comfortably off on incomes averaging £5.17*s*.7*d*. Five pounds a week was a figure to envy, to be spoken of in bated breath – 'they say he's a £5-a-week man!' Moreover, with the unemployment pay and expanded social services there was a substantial transfer, via taxation, of income from rich to poor: some £200–£250m. in 1937, representing 5–6 per cent of the national income.

The families of old wealth, however, were under pressure. With agriculture in depression and farm rents long unremunerative, landed estates came under the hammer, many of the farms going to the existing occupiers. Higher death duties took their toll where young heirs had been lost in World War I, and there was a quick turnover of titles. Country houses were becoming too costly to maintain, and were let out for shooting, sold for colleges, nursing homes, offices or research establishments; in a few cases owners recruited revenue by opening to the public. An article published in *The Times* in 1922 was dramatically entitled 'England Changing Hands'. The return to agricultural protection and support of farm prices gave farmers a little aid, did nothing for landlords.

But there were still plenty of people with money, including the 322 millionaires of 1919, some of them no doubt the fabulous 'war profiteers' of endless jokes in *Punch,* munition-makers, government contractors of all sorts, and other *nouveaux riches*. They helped to constitute a social upper crust whose daily doings filled the pages of *The Tatler* and *Country Life,* and less respectfully, the columns of the popular press. They were the 'smart set', who patronized expensive London restaurants and gaming clubs, and danced into the small hours to the strains of Ambrose at the Café de Paris, Harry Roy at the Mayfair, or Carroll Gibbons at the Savoy. They rode in Hyde Park, followed the horses at Ascot and Goodwood, drove fast cars to alcoholic Brighton weekends, and wintered merrily at Antibes, Cannes or Monte Carlo. They provided much of the gaiety of the period, and also much of the scandal, contributing not a little to the more than 7,000 divorces of 1938 – over eight times as many as before 1914. They set the fashions – the short hair, short cylindrical dresses and silk stockings of the early 1920s, the more flattering modes and longer hems of the 1930s, while the menfolk moved into trilbies, double-breasted lounge suits of new, lighter materials, soft Van Heusen collars, Oxford bags and suede shoes.

The life-style set in Mayfair and Bond Street percolated down in diluted form to the local high-street shops and middle-class suburban homes. More and more people

79 Prostitutes plying their trade in Soho, 1930. Once a thoroughly respectable area of London – Dickens's Dr Manette in *Tale of Two Cities* lived 'in a quiet street-corner not far from Soho Square' – the district was later invaded by exotic restaurants, shops and clubs, and by the inter-war years had gained an unsavoury reputation. (National Museum of Labour History)

could afford cars, if only second-hand ones, and already by 1930 there were over 1m. private cars on the country's inadequate roads, over three times as many as in 1922; by 1939 the figure had doubled to 2m. Horrendous traffic jams were one of the penalties of the summer weekend rush to the sea, and in the later 1930s people turned out to gaze from the roadside at tailbacks that stretched as far as ten miles. For the great majority without cars there were the buses with their cheap fares, charabanc 'mystery trips' on a Saturday evening, and Sunday outings by excursion train, or for Londoners and inhabitants of the Medway towns by paddle steamers to Southend, Margate and Ramsgate.

Religion suffered with the end of Victorian earnestness, the relaxation of morals and the increased opportunities for Sunday leisure. Church attendances, on a declining plane for many years past, dipped yet further. Even in the villages, traditional strongholds of the Church of England, congregations came to consist very largely of the elderly

80 Motor charabanc outings were a new feature of inter-war summers: a group of men from the Great Eastern pub in British Street (now Harbinger Road) E14, pose for their photograph before an outing in 1920.

and the young, and parsons had to combat much indifference, even hostility. Apathy towards the institution of the church was, however, the major characteristic. As late as 1957 only 6 per cent of the population investigated by a Gallup poll admitted to being atheist, and 16 per cent agnostic. But of the 78 per cent who claimed to believe in God, only 27 per cent were zealous enough to attend a service. Over half of the believers claimed affiliation to the Church of England, but under 1 in 10 of these took the trouble to go to church. The parson himself had declined, in economic and social terms, along with Sunday observance, attempting to keep up appearances and to maintain a rambling Victorian rectory on a stipend which, for a large minority, was under £400 in 1939, and for some as low as £240.

In some ways, however, the manners of the age were improving, though it must be doubted how far the church's influence was responsible for the change. There was certainly a marked decline in drunkenness, accompanying a reduction in the number of public houses and a very large fall in the annual consumption of beer and spirits. The buses still carried signs prohibiting spitting, but this insanitary habit was disappearing and largely confined to elderly men. Smoking, on the other hand, was on the increase, except for a slight fall during the worst of the slump. The habit was spread by advertising and by imitation among the young, and here the cinema was influential – witness how much smoking was done by the characters in the films of the time. A major change was the growth of cigarette smoking among women, though it was still considered bad taste for a woman to be seen smoking in public. Betting, too, was flourishing, with the new greyhound racing adding to the opportunities for a flutter. Greyhound stadiums increased rapidly after 1926, and by 1932 there were 187 tracks patronized by many thousands. White City, West Ham, New Cross and Harringay became familiar venues, and horse racing (the tote was introduced in 1928), together with the

81 Greyhounds parade before a race at New Cross Stadium. By 1932 there were as many as 187 tracks, and greyhound racing joined horse racing to attract bets totalling hundreds of millions of pounds every year. (White City Stadium)

greyhounds as a very junior partner, were said to absorb some £240m. a year at the end of the 1920s. The following decade was the great age of the football pools, though they originated some years earlier. Between 5m. and 7m. people filled in their coupons weekly and 'invested' a total of £30m. a year with Littlewoods, Vernons or Shermans.

Yet there was a growth also of a more intellectual culture. The BBC, with its drama and talks, and with its daily broadcasts of concerts by its own wide range of orchestras, did much to raise the standards of the arts and introduced a whole generation to a world of classical and good light music that they might otherwise never have known. By 1939 nearly 75 per cent of the country's households had radio licences. Broadcasting also spread the dance music craze, with the regular tea-time performances of the BBC's own dance orchestra, first under Jack Payne and then Henry Hall, and with the broadcasts from London hotels every weeknight. Jack Hylton, Lew Stone, Roy Fox, Billy Cotton and their 'vocalists' became household names, and many thousands of couples went dancing every week at the local Palais to 'semi-pro' bands that did their best to imitate the styles emanating from the radio.

The sale of gramophone records expanded as the quality of reproduction advanced and they fell in price: the really cheap labels could be bought in Woolworths for 6*d*. The gramophone, indeed, impinged on the market for pianos, once the hallmark of working-class respectability. Gramophones were much cheaper, as well as much smaller and more portable. The piano industry hit back with new ideas for publicity, and it was a piano-playing competition launched by the *Daily Express* which brought the name of Cyril Smith out of obscurity to join other distinguished British pianists of the time, Myra Hess and Solomon. Books were as cheap as gramophone records when popular works appeared in cheap hardback editions at 2*s*. 6*d*. or 3*s*. 6*d*. Penguin paperbacks, priced at only 6*d*, first appeared on the bookstalls in 1935, originally as reprints of well-known novels, memoirs and detective stories, but with the Pelicans, two years later, came non-fiction works also, some of them specially written for the new format. Some of the new ventures into cheap large-scale publishing had a left-wing bias, as with Gollancz's Left Book Club, founded in 1936 and acquiring 50,000 members within a year.

For the great majority, however, the newspaper constituted their sole reading. Newspapers flourished, nourished by advertising and by catering for a wide range of tastes and interests, from the *Daily Mirror* and *Daily Sketch*

– originally aimed at women – to the somewhat more serious *Express, Mail* and *News Chronicle*, and the definitely more staid *Times* and *Telegraph*. People bought papers for the crosswords (first popular in 1924), for the cartoons and advertisements, sports commentaries, racing tips and fashions, as well as the news. Circulation was the great aim of the popular dailies: without it they lost advertising revenue and the ability to survive in an intensively competitive market. They fostered stunts, launched competitions with prizes for readers, and paid men to go from door to door seeking new subscribers in return for free gifts of books, sheet music and a variety of household items. It was said you could furnish a house for nothing if you changed paper frequently enough, but this was of course an exaggeration. Beaverbrook's *Express* in 1933 won the race for the first paper to achieve a circulation of 2m., its nearest rival being the Labour paper, the *Daily Herald*. The dailies and many of the popular Sundays, the *News of the World*, the *People, Sunday Graphic, Reynolds News*, thrived on the fascination of crime, especially murder, and there were some particularly horrifying ones, for example the Brighton Trunk Murders of 1934. The papers featured great figures of adventure, Sir Malcolm Campbell, who broke the speed record on land and water, and heroines like Amy Johnson, who in 1930 made a solo flight to Australia in twenty days, aided by the money and publicity of the *Daily Mail*. There was the perennial mystery of the Loch Ness Monster, and such tragedies as the loss of the submarine *Thetis*, which dived to the bottom on her sea-going trials and, though showing her stern above the surface, defied all attempts to save her. And there were intriguing scandals, such as that surrounding the Rector of Stiffkey, the Revd. Harold Francis Davidson, who for years, it appeared, had spent all and every weekday far from his parish, associating with London prostitutes. Late in 1931 his way of life suddenly became public knowledge, and very soon his congregation at Stiffkey threatened to exceed the total population of his

82 The radio, or 'wireless' as it was then termed, soon became widely popular and entered most homes during the inter-war years. It not only povided entertainment but also gave people a new sense of being in touch with events in the wider world. Here listening to an early crystal set, the 'cat's whisker' wireless, made by James McCartney (seated right) are Mr James and Mrs Emma McCartney in their home at 158 East Ferry Road, E14. The 'cat's whisker' had to be very finely adjusted to work properly, and the loudspeaker, when it arrived, represented a great improvement on the early headphone sets. (Island History Project)

little-known Norfolk parish, with special excursion buses coming from as far away as Bournemouth. The rector was defrocked but refused to sink shamefully out of sight. He took to the music-halls, and in the summer of 1937 made his final appearance in a lion's cage at Skegness Amusement Park, acting out, as Ronald Blythe writes, 'the classical Christian martyrdom to the full'.

The 1930s, particularly the later 1930s, was an age of diversions. Some of them were childish, as when grown men walked the streets playing with a yo-yo or bif-bat. It was a pre-television age and so families still played cards on winter evenings or the new craze of *Monopoly*, or went out to a local theatre, the music-hall, a dance or a whist drive. The cinema was still tremendously popular, with some 20m. people paying for seats every week in 1939. In a large town there was the choice of a dozen programmes, which usually changed twice a week. The 'picture house' took one out of a dreary, monotonous round of work, watching every penny and making do, of worrying about keeping one's job or about not having a job at all, into a world of romance and adventure, of exciting and strange locations, of smartly suave and elegant figures whose lavish life style might have been that of another planet. Little wonder then that romantically-minded girls avidly bought the film magazines and absorbed all the intimate details about the stars, Clark Gable and Ronald Colman, Greta Garbo and Claudette Colbert. And for the kids this was the age of western heroes, Tom Mix, Tim McCoy, Ken Maynard; and also of the great film comedians, Charlie Chaplin, Laurel and Hardy, Buster Keaton and Harold Lloyd, whose mythical antics also filled the pages of the comics, eagerly pored over before children graduated to the material in the *Girl's Own Paper* or *Wizard* or *Hotspur*.

In summer the long-established sports flourished, like cricket and tennis, and there were new crazes such as roller-skating, cycling and hiking. Serious cyclists and walkers covered long distances, and youth hostels were opened to cater for the demand for cheap overnight accommodation – by 1939 about 300 of them, with over 10,000 beds. Seaside holidays were more popular than ever in the scorching summers of the late 1930s, particularly for day-trippers: the cost of a boarding house, at over £2 a week per person at the height of the season, was beyond the means of large working-class families. However, more people were becoming newly entitled to holidays with pay, the numbers rising rapidly at the end of the 1930s to 11m., and the new holiday camps, developed by enterprising figures such as Billy Butlin, drew vast crowds to the chalets at Skegness, Pwllheli, Ayr, Lowestoft and Clacton. By the end of the decade there were over 100 commercial camps accommodating half a million people.

Millions more took some other kind of holiday each year, as during the rest of the year they could afford to buy more of the foodstuffs whose consumption was closely linked to income – meat, butter, fruit, milk and eggs. And there were scores of cheap items in the shops, as well as services, which helped to make life a little more convenient and pleasant: electric fires, irons and kettles, radios and gramophone records, books, newspapers and magazines, ice cream and confectionery; tea shops and milk bars, laundries, dry cleaners and hairdressers. To the great majority of the people, the near 90 per cent who had jobs, and the smaller but substantial proportion who earned enough to live comfortably, this, and not unemployment, poverty, distress, and despair, was the reality of the time.

* * * * * *

Thus Britain in the transition of the 1920s and 1930s. The decline in the relative position of the British economy can be readily illustrated in a number of ways. Most telling, perhaps, was the decline in Britain's share in world trade in manufactures: this had been over 37 per cent in 1883, fell, but was still over 25 per cent in 1913, and was to fall further in the next two decades (as it was also to do subsequently). By 1937, at 19.1 per cent, it stood at only a little over a half of the share obtained fifty-five years earlier. In terms of total world industrial production Britain held first place in 1870 and third in 1913, and was then no longer the 'workshop of the world'. With the rise of the new industrial giants, the United States and Germany, such a decline was inevitable. Indeed, as has been pointed out, what is the more remarkable is that Britain, a small country with only limited resources, managed to achieve for a span a position of industrial supremacy during the first half of the nineteenth century.

Economic historians have spent many years and much ink in debating the turning point at which Britain's pace of growth began to falter and decline. There is much disagreement, but certainly from about the 1870s Britain lost her technological leadership in a number of important industries, though plausible reasons have been put forward to explain and justify this lag. What was really worrying about Britain's progress, however, was its relatively slow start in the rising industries of the future, such as electricity supply and engineering, motor vehicles, machine tools and fine chemicals, which failed to develop fast enough either to secure a large place in export markets or to make good the inevitable decline of the old staple trades of coal, steel, shipbuilding and textiles. World War I may have served to hinder the process of catching up, as some authorities have argued, but both old and new industries showed a certain lack of innovation and a sluggishness in adopting the new techniques developed abroad. There was a general lack of investment in new plant, and the rate of increase in British labour productivity fell away in the later nineteenth century, and by the Edwardian period was nil, or even slightly negative.

Many learned dissertations, replete with more or less doubtful statistics, have been advanced to explain Britain's industrial decline. The growth of her markets, both overseas and at home, was inadequate as the basis for a satisfactory rate of growth; the level of investment was too low to provide the new equipment needed by industry, and too much of the available capital was sent abroad; the cheapness of industrial labour discouraged innovation, and British industry suffered the penalty of an early start, meaning that high costs were involved in the rebuilding of plants on a larger scale. All these propositions have been argued and counter-argued in detail. In the end, it seems likely that at bottom there was a fatal weakness in the attitudes and social values of British industrialists. Many of them were the third generation of proprietors of family businesses and, it has been said, were spending more time in becoming gentlemen than in innovating in the business. They were cautious, attached to familiar forms of production, and fearful of risks that might jeopardize their control of the business. Few, if any, had technical training. They were amateurs, proud of their amateurishness, and contemptuous of the man who had 'studied', the trained specialist.

The picture is over-emphasized, of course. At all periods there were some entrepreneurs of extraordinary ability, many of moderate achievements, and a large number of failures. But it does seem that from the later nineteenth century the rapid pace of change and growing technological complexity of industry found British industrialists unprepared and unwilling to change rapidly enough. The education system deserves some share of blame. As has already been mentioned, at the level of the public schools and secondary schools, and of the old universities, there was emphasis on the liberal education, especially on classics and to a lesser extent other literary subjects, and a woeful neglect of applied science. Technical schools and colleges, as we have noted, were late in appearing and long looked down upon, and although the new universities in London and the provinces turned out a substantial quota of chemists and engineers, industry provided few openings for them. Industrialists neglected research and put little value on recruiting trained scientists. The engineer or chemist had a lowly status, esteemed much below the solicitor or civil servant. Higher education did much to widen the catchment area for top people in business and the professions, though as a whole it was backward – compare the 13,000 university students of 1913, working in small and under-provided institutions, with the 60,000 of the large German universities, learning from first-class staff and training in splendidly equipped laboratories.

There was a failure in British industry to marry scientific knowledge and the trained people that there were with the workaday world of production. At some point about the end of the nineteenth century fundamental changes should have been made to keep Britain industrially competitive. Changes were made, but tardily and on too small a scale. How significant in this was the attitude to business of the British middle and upper classes? For long the more successful men of business had bought country houses and become thoroughly gentrified, eagerly adopting the way of life of the landowning class. The moderately successful could not afford to follow suit but still liked to move into country villas or superior suburbs and distance themselves from their place of work. The business became less an all-absorbing passion, more a rather humdrum source of income, while the family's real interests, and the re-investment of their profits, lay elsewhere. Partly because much business remained in family hands and small-scale, a large proportion of the young talent of the period was diverted into the professions, the armed services, and the Civil Service and colonial service. The established professional man deliberately kept aloof from mere 'money grubbing', and spurned those who vulgarly struggled for custom in the competitive world and had to talk prices and profit margins every day of their lives.

But aristocrats, professional men and men of business were at one in ensuring that their scions were educated in the common mould of the liberal education. The leaders of the future from both public schools and grammar schools, learned to look down on industry and were taught to associate technology with the unsavoury world of muck and brass. Even the great engineers and scientists, like Brunel, T. H. Huxley and Lyon Playfair, sent their sons to public schools to go through the classical mill: given the current attitudes of the upper classes there was little alternative. The English way of life became associated with the idealized country life, not with foundries, factories and shipyards. Even English radicalism had a potent backward-looking strain, a yearning for a lost golden age of 'well-fed peasants, contented, if illiterate, craftsmen, and compassionate profit-sharing landowners'. Tory tastes often went (and still go) with radical opinions. The deep conservatism of British society at large was reflected in and encouraged by a socialist movement that looked for gradual amelioration rather than revolution, trade unions that clung tenaciously to a bitter past of hostility and distrust, and blindly opposed the technology of the future, politicians who admired the traditional ordered society, and businessmen who above all craved security and a quiet life rather than the hazardous instability of risk-taking. Thus it was a Britain which accepted, indeed expected, amateurishness, crass negligence and bland procrastination as normal in all walks of life from the highest to the lowest, which admired national habits of tea breaks and 'muddling through', and which tolerated – perforce – the corollary of a declining economic strength, a slowness of improvement, and a standard of living on its way to becoming among the lowest in all western Europe.

Further Reading

In making a small selection from the vast literature available rather more preference has been given to books which are both readable and likely to be accessible in public libraries, and rather less to highly specialized works or those whose merits lie principally in the advanced nature of the material or novelty of interpretation.

A good general introduction is provided by François Bédarida, *A Social History of England 1851–1975* (Methuen, 1979). Some of the best historical studies of this country have been written by French scholars, perhaps because they are better able to stand back and take a detached view, and this book, with its comprehensive and lively treatment, is no exception. The same may be said of François Crouzet's thorough survey of *The Victorian Economy* (Methuen, 1982) which guides the reader on to many more specialized discussions.

Older works of a general introductory kind include G. D. H. Cole and Raymond Postgate, *The Common People 1746–1938* (Methuen, 1945) and two short volumes in the Oxford University Press Home University Library series, J. D. Chambers, *The Workshop of the World: British Economic History from 1820 to 1880* (1961) and R. S. Sayers, *A History of Economic Change in England 1880–1939* (1967). On a larger scale are S. G. Checkland, *The Rise of Industrial Society in England 1815–1885* (Longman, 1960) and Sidney Pollard's highly detailed text, *The Development of the British Economy 1914–1980* (Arnold, 1983).

For comprehensive and systematic treatments of the political history of the period reference must be made to the relevant volumes in the great Oxford History of England series: E. L. Woodward, *The Age of Reform 1815–1870* (Clarendon Press, 1938); R. C. K. Ensor, *England 1870–1914* (1936); and A. J. P. Taylor, *English History 1914–45* (1965). P. Adelman's brief study may be consulted on *The Rise of the Labour Party 1880–1945* (Longman, 1972), and for the politics of the inter-war years the fine and most interesting study by Charles Loch Mowat, *Britain between the Wars 1918–1940* (Methuen, 1955) is indispensable.

Turning to some of the topics featured in the chapters of the present book, the growth of the towns and their problems may perhaps be best approached through local studies such as those by H. J. Dyos, *Victorian Suburb: a study of the growth of Camberwell* (Leicester University Press, 1961), Roy Church, *Economic and Social Change in a Midland Town: Victorian Nottingham 1815–1900* (Cass, 1966) and Sir Francis Hill, *Victorian Lincoln* (Cambridge University Press, 1974). John Burnett's *A Social History of Housing 1815–1970* (Methuen, 1978) is an up-to-date treatment of this topic. S. E. Finer's fascinating *Life and Times of Sir Edwin Chadwick* (Methuen, 1952) deals at length with the early years of the New Poor Law and public health reform, while Chadwick's own report of 1842, *The Sanitary Condition of the Working Population of Great Britain* was republished in 1965 by the University of Edinburgh Press with an introduction by the late Michael Flinn.

There are many books on the major industries of the nineteenth century, and they are discussed also in the standard economic histories mentioned above. Of particular interest among the recent specialized works are Duncan Bythell's study of the surviving hand trades, *The Sweated Trades: Outwork in Nineteenth Century Britain* (Batsford, 1978) and Cyril Erlich's *The Piano: a History* (Dent, 1976), while invaluable for reference on the technical developments in nineteenth-century industry is T. K. Derry and Trevor I. Williams, *A Short History of Technology* (Clarendon Press, 1960).

The varied character of the labour force is dealt with most interestingly by John Burnett's collection of memoirs, *Useful Toil: Autobiographies of Working People from the 1820s to the 1920s* (Methuen, 1974), while John Lovell provides a concise and up-to-date history of *British Trade Unions 1875–1933* (Macmillan, 1977).

The revolution wrought by railways is well treated by Philip S. Bagwell in his *The Transport Revolution from 1770* (Batsford, 1974); the railway navvies by Terry Coleman in a Pelican with that title published in 1968. Much of the most recent work on shipping has come from the pen of Francis E. Hyde in, for example, his *Cunard and the North Atlantic 1840–1973* (Macmillan, 1975) and *Far Eastern Trade 1860–1914* (Black, 1973).

The most recent and comprehensive survey of rural life and farming is published in G. E. Mingay (Ed.), *The Victorian Countryside* (Routledge & Kegan Paul, 1981). Recent specialized studies include J. Obelkevich, *Religion and Rural Society in South Lindsey 1825–1875* (Clarendon Press, 1976) and Susanna Wade Martins, *A Great Estate at Work: The Holkham Estate and its Inhabitants in the Nineteenth Century* (Cambridge University Press, 1980). Some older authors are well worth seeking out for their contemporary views, notably Richard Jefferies, *Hodge and his Masters* (1880), George Sturt (pen-name George Bourne), *Change in the Village* (1912), and *Memoir of a Surrey Labourer* (1907), and Rider Haggard's *Rural England* (1902), a tour of the depressed countryside at the turn of the century.

Historians have examined the subject of poverty mainly from the administrative viewpoint of the Poor Law, which however touched only part of the problem. For an analysis of the extent, nature and causes of poverty one has to consult the investigations carried out by Seebohm Rowntree in *Poverty: A Study of Town Life* (1901) and subsequently in the 1930s, *Poverty and Progress: A Second Survey of York* (1941). Contemporary with Rowntree's second study, and providing interesting contrasts is H. Tout's *The Standard of Living in Bristol* (1938).

Even more of the seamier side of urban life is revealed in great detail by Henry Mayhew in *London Labour and the London Poor* (1851), which Kellow Chesney drew upon for his well-known study of *The Victorian Underworld* (Temple Smith, 1970). An interesting account of the life and origins of the 'fallen women' who frequented the less reputable districts of all large towns is provided by Frances Finnegan, *Poverty and Prostitution: A Study of Victorian Prostitutes in York* (Cambridge University Press, 1979).

On the improvements in living standards which marked the inter-war years the relevant chapters in Charles Loch Mowat's *Britain between the Wars*, mentioned above, are invaluable. For the major reforms which were gathering pace at that time, Derek Fraser's *Evolution of the British Welfare State* (Macmillan, 1973) should be consulted, while a much older study, Ray Strachey, *The Cause* (Bell, 1928) is a substantial treatment of the various aspects of the women's movement. There are, finally, many good histories of education: S. J. Curtis, *History of Education in Great Britain* (University Tutorial Press, 1953) is one of the most comprehensive.

Index